T0198728

CLAIMING YOUR MIND,
CLAIMING YOUR SOVEREIGNTY

A JOURNEY OF HEALING AND TRANSFORMATION

Anne Elizabeth Ph.D.

BALBOA.PRESS
A DIVISION OF HAY HOUSE

Balboa Press books may be ordered through booksellers or by contacting:

Balboa Press
A Division of Hay House
1663 Liberty Drive
Bloomington, IN 47403
www.balboapress.com
844-682-1282

Because of the dynamic nature of the Internet, any web addresses or links contained in this book may have changed since publication and may no longer be valid. The views expressed in this work are solely those of the author and do not necessarily reflect the views of the publisher, and the publisher hereby disclaims any responsibility for them.

The author of this book does not dispense medical advice or prescribe the use of any technique as a form of treatment for physical, emotional, or medical problems without the advice of a physician, either directly or indirectly. The intent of the author is only to offer information of a general nature to help you in your quest for emotional and spiritual well-being. In the event you use any of the information in this book for yourself, which is your constitutional right, the author and the publisher assume no responsibility for your actions.

Any people depicted in stock imagery provided by Getty Images are models, and such images are being used for illustrative purposes only. Certain stock imagery © Getty Images.

Print information available on the last page.

ISBN: 979-8-7652-4022-9 (sc)
ISBN: 979-8-7652-4023-6 (hc)
ISBN: 979-8-7652-4024-3 (e)

Library of Congress Control Number: 2023904683

Balboa Press rev. date: 03/17/2023

Dedication

So many people to thank for their support and wisdom: teachers, mentors, authors, and friends. I acknowledge my mother Emma Louise Richards Bausch and father Henry Melchior Muhlenberg Richards, my parents, who gave me a steppingstone on which to stand to begin life's journey. I also want to mention the unseen forces of the "spiritual" world that played a tremendous role in directing and guiding me in myriad ways. I want to thank my Future Self, for providing access to the portals for healing spiritual dimensions.

A heartfelt thanks to my editors Hannah Sheinkman, Marnie Mueller, and George Centanni for their line editing and insights which helped me to focus the presentation of this material more clearly. And to those at Balboa press who helped with the production of this book and its audio version. I am deeply grateful to all for your patience and perseverance in this endeavor.

Contents

Part 4 Anthroposophy

Part 5 Spiritual Encounters

Part 6 Relationship to Nature and Stars

Part 7 Overcoming Mind Programs

Epilogue: Coming Full Circle

Dear Reader,

I ask the question whose thoughts am I thinking? Are they mine or do they belong to my parents or mentors that I have engaged through life? I am searching for a sense of my own mind, my thoughts, and their origins. I want to sort out that which truly belongs to me and that which I have incorporated which no longer fits with who I feel myself to be.

Even though people have died, they live in our memory: those who have had a positive effect and those who have not. Obviously, those that we have loved or been close to tend to be imprinted positively and indelibly in our hearts. Those who have hurt or abused us live in our memory in a negative way and can eat at our souls, much as a parasite would eat its host.

When we think of shared moments either pleasant or not, these thoughts live inside us, and with time these memories can morph and shift focus, either to include more positive or more negative reflection. Sometimes someone else's account adds more information which enlarges one's perspective or reveals a more positive side of a person. Of course, the reverse can happen as well, and a more negative or even sinister aspect can surface. This can contribute to the experience of someone, disappearing from your life in gradual or sudden way. Or it can contribute to the experience of one's unexpected delight at a new and unexpected connection which seems to grow out of the blue.

Do we ever really know anyone else's mind deeply, especially our own mind? I think not. This is true for me and my consciousness, but also that of my parents who raised me and with whom I have relied for introduction to and explanation about the world we live in. Even though we have lived for a time together, this does not mean I know what they really think or feel. Now, since they are gone, I can only guess and surmise what they thought and why. Moreover, they did not know what I thought or how I felt. This memoir is an opportunity to inform them about what I thought and felt and how these feelings and thoughts changed throughout time.

So much of life is about this struggle to unmask hidden meanings, thoughts, and experiences that occur internally as well as externally in the world. Even when we think we have found meaning, this meaning evaporates or morphs into something else over time. We thought we knew the whole picture, but it turns out we only knew a portion of the truth. We knew it for the time being but who we became through experience and travelling brings out a new set of variables, and ultimately a new sense of self.

My quest is to find my own mind, to heal my mind and consciousness, by separating it from the mind of my parents, friends, teachers, or other mentors who had an impact on my life. New information from many different sources, brings about a recapitulation of the pieces of a puzzle which results in a different perspective and ultimately a different lens with which to view the world and oneself. After many nights and days of stirring the primordial stew, I returned to the original idea and knew it from a different perspective. This was the case when I determined that I needed to find a way to communicate with my parents and loved ones through letters, even though they are dead.

I had been writing letters for years using old onion skin backing with carbon paper on an old corona typewriter and keeping copies in my notebooks. Most of the originals were sent. Over time it was great to look back on these copies and remember thoughts and associations with people who were no longer in my life but who had meant something to me at the time. I thought that writing this memoir in letter format was a way to share with others especially my parents who I was and who I have become: a way to become intimate with myself even in their absence.

Intimacy did not seem possible while my parents were alive, for many reasons. The walls of their own beliefs, the ones they were raised with, coupled with their own transgenerational abusive patterns from their families of origin created a fog through which truth became distorted and ultimately lost, or put on hold until such a time when it was possible to communicate with clarity. But this truer knowing did not occur to me while they were alive.

Nevertheless, I have arrived at the letter format as an informal and viable tool to know myself and others through an intimate way of communicating. This differs from the truncated messaging we have now become accustomed to through e-mail, messaging and other cyber tools which have come into vogue and have largely replaced the written letter. I want to bring the letter back to the front burner as a way of communicating, sharing, and rejoining with others: those who are still alive like friends, teachers, and others with whom I have shared ideas and perspectives. They too can be addressed through these letters which I am writing years after the original contact, but contact which still holds importance because of their original impact upon my thinking and my life.

Now I take this opportunity to share with them because I am dissatisfied with the lack of deeper connection to my parents and friends no longer on this earth and do not want to forgo the chance to make this attempt. Of course, I have no guarantee that those who are dead will be able to receive what I am saying since they inhabit the spirit world and have for some time now. However, I am hopeful that I will reach their spirits and the readers who read these letters and who may choose to write their opinions or share their feelings with me or with their own family member. These letters are for me as well as for them, a vehicle to express my truth as I have come to know it through the centrifuge of memory, cleansed, and sharpened by the vicissitudes of life and finally coming to rest in my heart as a token of gratitude and love for the opportunity to live that my ancestors gave me. And my inquiry is also for the reader who may be asking the same question or who is inspired to sort out concerns about finding your own voice, discovering your sovereignty, as you uncover the family beliefs and obstacles which may no longer serve you.

Introduction

Dear Reader,

Some 45 years ago I was hired to teach 3rd grade in an elementary school outside of Denton Texas while I was enrolled in a Counseling Ph.D. program. I was one of four teachers specializing in a variety of subjects: mine was Reading and Language Arts while Doug specialized in social studies and was a gifted artist and musician. I asked him to draft an artistic memento for me which I could hang on my wall, which he did. The thought was: *We Live to Become the Oneness.*

In viewing that thought I imagined my memoir title would be *We Live to Become the Oneness.* That message is an endpoint, but in this memoir the initial thrust has become the exploration of my mind and ego consciousness, its origins, and its implications for establishing sovereignty. My journey is not unlike going to the Carlsbad Caverns of New Mexico, which I did some years ago. Amazingly these caverns are carved by sulfuric acid, not water, and extend for miles underground, much of it yet unexplored. There are no streams or rivers flowing through these caves which were originally mined for bat guano. The great variety of formations in the caves mirror the formations of consciousness which have continued to grow in the consciousness of my mind. I call it the space in between because it describes the sacred place where my thoughts and feelings merge to form my awareness of the conscious and unconscious world.

I know that my perspectives are subjective and have been sculpted through memory and a variety of life experiences I have had over the years. They are not intended to be seen as incontrovertible historical fact. Nor could they be, since they have been preserved through changing lenses of each stage of my life and continue to morph as my consciousness grows and expands. I am reminded of the Uncertainty Principle which I believe is active here.

In 1927 Heisenberg announced the Uncertainty Principle for which he received a Nobel Laureate award. This principle states among other things, that the outcome of whatever is being observed will be affected by the observer. Therefore, if two different people are observing an experiment, there is a good chance that what each observes will be different from each other.

This memoir is affected not only by my observations which have an impact on what is seen, but also my memory which is colored by many filters which are shaped by my character, my history, and the social and political events of the time. Therefore, while I attempted to be true to the memories of critical events in my life, there is a margin of shift brought on by my own individual personality and the imprint of time on my memory.

The first thrust of this memoir is the exploration of the origins of my conscious thinking, which originated and was impressed upon me by my parent's own indoctrinations, their own comprehension of their family beliefs and constraints and the social events of the times.

The *second thrust* is the thread of the development of ego consciousness, soul, and spiritual growth through my life. Yet, I came to arrive at my conclusions from my experience with my world and to claim these thoughts as my own. I have chosen to use the teachings of Rudolf Steiner as a primary lens through to view spiritual development processes. Steiner describes the evolution of soul consciousness[1]:

The sentient soul and ego-consciousness penetrated one another first in human development in northern Europe. What happened as the result of ego-consciousness establishing itself in the sentient soul of European peoples before Christ entered human development and before they had assimilated what developed in Asia?

The result was that a human soul force developed in the sentient soul which was only able to develop because the sentient soul, which

---

[1] Steiner, Rudolf. The Christ Impulse and the Development of Ego-Consciousness, Rudolf Steiner Press, 2014, 109-110

was still completely virginal and uninfluenced by other cultures, had been permeated by ego feeling. That soul force became conscience: the penetration of ego-feeling with sentient soul.

Conscience speaks like an urge and yet it is not an urge. Those philosophers who describe it as an urge are far off the mark. It speaks with the same magnificence with which the consciousness soul itself speaks when it appears; but it speaks at the same time with more elementary, with more original forces.

The *third thrust* of this memoir is my encounter with Christ and the beings from the interdimensional or supersensible worlds as Steiner calls it. This spirit-led journey has taken me to the depths of my Lower Self and to the heights of my Higher Self, even my Future Self. I have gone through the dismemberment of my soul which was part of the experience of the Dark Night of the Soul and have come out to claim my truth in the halls of my own consciousness. My story is an attempt to honor the human journey as a divine journey through which the soul evolves and ultimately experiences itself, its sovereignty, and its higher self through the impact of Christ and the resurrection.

So, we see how on earth love appears in the East and conscience here in the West. They are two things which belong together: how Christ appears in the East, how conscience awakens in the West to accept Christ as conscience.[2]

We are heading toward a new Christ event in that the soul is becoming capable of perceiving Christ in a certain etheric clairvoyance and experiencing anew the Damascene event within itself. [3]

I think I have learned that experience with others creates an internal connection which is cemented through memories that are shared. And my relationship to these memories, the essential vibration of our resonance is what I relate to. Each time I connect with a person that memory changes: each feeling, and experience builds and creates the

---

[2] Ibid, Steiner, 110.
[3] Ibid, Steiner, 111.

fabric of our relationship together. Memories are made of these bits and snatches, pieces of a moment in a person's life that we shared. In a way life relies on these bits and pieces and make it almost impossible to really know a person fully because those bits and pieces are always changing and connecting to other bits and pieces which, in turn, change the landscape of what is recognized as that person.

This is true I think of myself. I know bits and pieces but they also changing and morphing depending on a complex of feelings and experiences which seem to come from nowhere or everywhere. That shaping and reshaping goes on inside me without my conscious direction but as a response to the voices that are telepathically communicated to me, through my Higher Self or through the struggle my Higher Self has as it transforms and transmutes the Lower Self, ultimately exposing my Future Self, FS. Sometimes the battle seems over, and the conflict put to rest, only to find out that sometime later the battle rises again, and the same struggle must again be overcome or transmuted, but at a new level of understanding.

Indeed, I have found in writing my memoir that while I thought I knew myself, the self that I experienced yesterday or last month, or six months ago is not the self that I feel I am today. That self may well shift again tomorrow or in the next little while, and new aspects may come to the fore. This is the beauty of living, watching the internal ever- changing internal landscape which seems to have a momentum of its own. Like a daisy struggling for purchase from under a rock, one day It blossoms into a lovely white flower.

The writing of this memoir is like a flower that needs sun and water to live. So wonderous and painful a journey, to experience the emotional history of past events and relive one's life in bits and pieces, to find the gems and the nodules from which beauty, and the struggle for truth are displayed on the page as reflections of the heart's discoveries. Significant memories I have extracted from the past are presented as I remember them, using the lens of my growing and maturing ego consciousness which often drew a context different from the original one I remembered. In so doing whatever seemed harsh and unforgiveable gave way to understanding, to an enlarged perspective which included the projection of my parent's internal life and their struggles. I now celebrate and transform a world of hurt and loneliness that I experienced as a child, and I can forgive myself for not seeing the larger picture until now and for holding resentment and anger for so long. I am free to let go of any negative traces I have continued to harbor internally and to open my heart and arms to my own sovereignty as well as freedom and redemption for all my ancestors. This is the freedom my soul and sovereignty has been wanting and is now experiencing. Gratitude for my life and for the lives of others. All my love their way. And all my love to the readers who are journeying with me through the episodes of my ego consciousness and spiritual evolution.

Whose Mind Is Thinking Now?

Dear Reader,

Have you ever wondered to what extent your mind has been shaped by forces outside yourself? Have you ever questioned the beliefs and thoughts you learned from your parents or family members because they did not quite fit with what you thought? Or perhaps they continued to tell you were wrong to think differently from them? Have you ever wondered about how much media or religious groups have shaped what you think about the world? Certainly, we have all had our thoughts shaped or reformed in many ways by the members of family that have raised us and by friends as well. Since my mind was strongly imbedded with the thoughts of my parents, when I went to college away from home, I had a huge awakening, where I began to question whether the thoughts, I was having were truly my own or had been shaped and planted by my parents, and even generations before them. What they believed had been carried through many decades, even centuries and had been sculpted by environmental events, the wars and health concerns.

In an episode of Star Trek, the Next Generation, Patrick Stewart as Captain Piccard of the USS Enterprise is captured by a sociopathic leader who tries to take over his mind. Piccard is bare-chested, handcuffed with arms tied overhead. He is questioned and tortured repeatedly about how many lights he sees behind his tormentor. Even with manipulation and more torturous pain, he continued to say what he sees which was five lights. His tormentor wants the captain to betray own mind, to avoid more punishment. If he had, his tormentor would know he had captured Piccard's mind. But the Captain holds out and is rescued. Even after his rescue Piccard would cry out in moments of stress, five lights, five lights, just to reaffirm his connection to his own mind. That link with his mind had been severely challenged but had not been broken. Even so Piccard is shaken and needs to reassure himself that he still has his own mind intact.

Linking and memory. These are some of the essential components that form mind and facilitate its functioning. But what do we mean by mind? What does it involve? Many definitions have evolved over time. I like to think of mind as a force field of consciousness incorporating a sense of self and of the world around. Actions initiated by the mind are based on memory, which involve the ability to link associations, to reason, to have perceptions of the world and people in the world, to imagine, to generate ideas which connect to language, images and sensations, the sense of being able to develop a moral compass (knowing right from wrong), connecting feeling and desires with actions through one's will. All this complexity makes up what we call the functioning of the mind and consciousness.

I did not feel I had my own mind for many years. I have spent a lifetime trying to know my mind and still don't know it completely. Perhaps it is not possible to do so. Not having a sense of my own mind left me in a very empty and lonely space. It became critical for me to discover my mind because I was lost, trying to navigate the world with no clue about where I was going, or needed to go, or how to get there like being afloat on a dark ocean, with words, demands, harassment from my parents at home and from the exterior world. Opportunities flew before I could consider taking action, but I was never sure if a certain outcome was what I really wanted.

As an adult I came to see my mind as a conglomeration of thoughts and opinions from both parents and wonder where my own thoughts and feelings had gone. My father loved to bombard us with his diatribes on history and economics, grandstanding for whatever audience he could capture. My mother was an even stronger force for me to contend with. For me, she was on a pedestal and directly or indirectly controlled where I went, who I associated with, how I dressed, and even what I read. She discounted what few inclinations I could manage to articulate as not good enough. It was obvious that I was indoctrinated to believe that she knew best what I needed, that she knew me better than I knew myself. I was raised to become a mirror image of how she perceived herself. To get along and because I wanted to please her, I tried very hard to reflect her image back to her......and luckily and perhaps with intention failed to do so.

I first had to discover that I had my own mind. Then slowly it was possible to dive, deep into the cave of my unknowing to explore what might be hidden there. To rely on this inner journey rather than the thoughts and ideas from family and friends in the exterior world, represented a huge leap into the unknown. The struggle to find my mind has been long and arduous. Not until I realized that I had to go inside myself, to the unknown territory, through the breath, through meditation, through the deep, deep silence of inner calm, did I begin to realize that I might have a connection to something large, directing and informing me about life. Was this God or was this mind or was it beyond both?

Having a mind and awareness of your consciousness means you have an interior or inner world that is yours to explore which includes your thoughts, your feelings, and your ability to act according to your will. In the beginning and for many years, I was left alone to explore my thoughts. There was no one available to share my mind with me, as parents were not available or blind to the need to do so. There were no living relatives or adult persons nearby that I could come to trust that might help me know and probe my own mind. Thinking and feeling were both dismissed because I was taught to depend on the decisions and perspectives of both my parents...they would make the decisions that were "right" for me. I learned to ignore or hide my feelings and thoughts as dangerous because they challenged me to choose between their opinions and my own weak voice. If I dared follow my own voice, this left me with feeling disloyal and disrespectful of my parents. Silence and obedience seem like the least resistant pathway to take and the only way to survive.

MIND SHAPING IS INTERGENERATIONAL

Noteworthy in the study of "normal" mind shaping is the fact that it is intergenerational. That is the shaping of the minds of our parents started generations before with grandparents we may have heard about but never met. Environment, financial affluence or the lack of it, health concerns and wars all have taken their turn in shaping the lives of our forebearers. How each generation chose to respond to these external forces affected the ways in which they handled themselves and dealt with family members. Those influences can start out being good and helpful and turn to negative effects depending on numerous factors which tend to work together behind the scenes as it were. Perhaps driven unconsciously these factors can have both positive and detrimental impacts on those who are influenced by them. What we did with those effects and the choices we made, helped to construct our personalities, create a lifestyle which we can call our own, and influence and shape the next generation.

Mind shaping is not only intergenerational but unconsciously beliefs are passed down through the generations as familiar knowledge because it was the code of being and thinking of our parents or grandparents, the signature pattern which identified the family. It could have been very right for the time in which those ancestors were living or very distorted, debauched, even twisted into something quite negative because of environmental circumstances. Nevertheless, these beliefs and thoughts tend to persist through the ages, often unchallenged, accepted on faith, and adherence to these beliefs was expected.

These beliefs are not installed through the conscious or deliberate deprivation of food, or traumatic interruptions of sleep, or extreme isolation, or drugs or extreme torture as they are when enacted by government or military operations as in MKUltra. This mind shaping is of an everyday variety with less extreme forms of assault and deprivation which happen unwittingly most of the time and which are interspersed with kindnesses and with opportunities for having contact with more positive experiences or more loving connections. These more positive moments may not last in time, but the impact of positive interludes contrasts starkly with the darkness and pain of ongoing negative influences. These positive memories become a beacon of light and give hope and a bit of peace in a world of seeming dark unending madness. Positive memories reinforce hope that darkness can change.

Mind shaping is to a certain extent inevitable. The problem is that when outmoded beliefs are passed down, the resulting lack of correspondence between what parents think, and what you think and feel becomes dissonant, irritating, disorienting and can even create a division within the family. Following the family beliefs can result in a loose of connection within yourself and your own thoughts. This is what I felt for so long and what to some extent drove me to seek therapy as an adult.

INTERGENERATIONAL TRAUMA

While doing research, I uncovered an article by Lloyd deMause of a speech entitled "The Childhood Origins of the Holocaust" delivered September 28, 2005, in Austria at Klagenfurt University. DeMause outlines major social and emotional contributing factors in the environment which made it possible for the Holocaust to exist at that time in Germany. DeMause points to the elements of child rearing in the Austrian and German cultures.

Since my mother came from Austrian background and my father from German background, these elements were embedded in the child rearing practices that they experienced in their growing up years and subsequently were passed down to me.

The German and Austrian populations were raised by their parents and those before them to be authoritarian. Perhaps this was "justified" by the need for survival of the family, and ultimately the culture and nation. Or perhaps it was convenient for parents to scapegoat their own children on whom they depended for work on the farm or in factories later. Children were seen by older generations of parents as "useless eaters," [4] DeMause, 2005. This is a phrase that has been used even today by Henry Kissinger, referring to certain populations in America.

Girls were considered of lesser value than boys and these girls were sometimes put to death in their infancy, [5] deMause. Fear was used as a primary motivating factor to gain obedience and compliance with what parents wanted or needed. Lack of compliance led to a child being punished, shunned, or even abandoned. Children were seen as filthy and dirty,

A nation-wide ritual was common which involved giving enemas to purify and cleanse the child. Enemas were designed in various lengths to fit the larger and smaller child. And there were enema facilities established in the community to assist parents when travelling with their child.

Often, if a child was neglectful or failed to comply with parent's directives, beatings were common. It is said that Adolf Hitler was beaten unmercifully by his own father. Children were seen as appendages of their parents and were not encouraged to be independent, at least not as young children. If any attempts were made, children were discouraged and punished for attempting to be more independent. If the child wanted something for him or herself, that the parent did not have, or had not had themselves when growing up, or could not afford, the child was told he or she was being selfish. This was punished by dismissal or abandonment so that the child's sense of integration and worthiness was severely compromised. This left the young child in a very fragile condition, with the sense of being an unworthy or bad person.

This feeling was intolerable and could be projected unconsciously to another person or group (race) outside the family domain, who then became labelled as bad. This could and did happen to any who were considered to be undesirable: Jews, Romani, Gay or Lesbian individuals. In short, these people were seen as a threat to those who "prided themselves" as being "good" or compliant with authority

---

[4] deMause, Lloyd, the Childhood Origins of the Holocaust, speech, Klagenfort University, Austria, September 28, 2005, 10.
[5] Ibid, deMause, 8.

figures ruling the Motherland. Those who complied feared what the non-compliant groups represented: materialism, degeneration, socialism, dancing and sexual license, [6]deMause. These seeds of restriction, repression and punishment led to war because people were entrained by what deMause calls the amygdalen psychotic core in the brain.[7]deMause. The fear of punishment and lack of protection, of separation from the authority of the Motherland, and of ultimate abandonment, even annihilation of one's family, society, and person all played a role in setting the stage for the Holocaust to come in the 1940's.

These fears became beliefs which did not die with the end of the war but were passed on to children of the survivors and their children. The child rearing practices of their parents crossed the generational lines almost without question as one generation begot the next. Over time social and political changes began to influence the younger generation to see their world and options as different from those of their parents. Through education, children of both genders were able to advance themselves in society through positions of prominence and power. The introduction of psychoanalysis, beginning in the early 20th century with Freud and others, which included the study of consciousness, began to reshape the way in which society could attain new perspectives of their lives and choices. Even so remnants of authoritarian child rearing practices still linger to this day. Bullet points include but do not comprise an exhaustive list:

- motivation using fear (punishment)
- integrating the sense of helplessness
- growth panic (fear of exploring, trying new ideas, making mistakes, learning)
- being seen as selfish
- fragility or disintegration of a sense of self
- mother being depressed, overworked, angry
- fear of being cut off from the motherland
- lack of good or nurturing touch, being held/comforted

---

[6] deMause, Ibid, 13.
[7] deMause, Ibid 18.

- fear of freedom, choice
- fear of questioning authority
- fear of being abandoned/ being alone
- fear of being shunned, cut off from parental love
- fear of being hated, despised
- fear of being dirty, needing to be purified
- fearing worthless, of no account

The beliefs with which both of my parents were raised were unwittingly projected onto me during my growing up years. I know now that my parents learned these ideas through their own parents, who must have grown up in similar circumstances. For example, I know that my paternal grandmother repeatedly questioned my father and his two sisters about whether they had had a bowel movement that day.

Both sets of grandparents experienced WW1 in one way or another and my parents experienced the depression, breadlines, and the effects of WW11. This intergenerational programing was deep and is woven through the fabric of the lives of many generations. As it came to me in the 20th century, I was raised within the parameters of certain basic tenants:

[8]deMause.

1. I was a "bad" person, which resulted in self-loathing because I was unsuccessful in pleasing either of my parents although I tried.
2. I was a "useless eater" because I could not give them what they needed and thought it was my job to do so.
3. I was deeply resentful because I saw that other parents talked to their children, did not treat their children as extensions of themselves, and asked them what their children wanted or how they felt.
4. I was selfish because I wanted some things just for me. But I knew or felt I did not have the right to ask for them. This was

---

[8] deMause, Ibid, 2005, 11.

true even in kindergarten. I remember I needed to ask for a pair of scissors to finish cutting out my project, but I was too ashamed and frightened to ask for what I needed. I saw others asking for the same scissors and could not understand why I had such difficulty asking. I had pain and anxiety over why I could not ask for what I needed.

5. I wanted freedom and independence which I got in small doses, (my father taught me how to ride a bicycle, to drive a car to play ping pong and to play the piano.) But I had to wait until I went off to college to learn about myself and to grow. I had to work through my feelings especially my guilt about leaving my parents behind, about not satisfying them, and ultimately about "abandoning" them, sacrificing them so that I could grow.

6. Eventually, I explored my own feelings through therapy and learned how important it was to connect with my feelings and thoughts. I eventually chose to become a psychologist which my father could not understand and felt I had betrayed him when I told him my choice. "All psychologists are quacks," he said.

7. I was taught to live a minimalistic life, to enjoy having little or no money, and to be satisfied with that. When I had a chance to travel to India with a college class, and first love, I asked my father to appeal to the Chamber of Commerce to supply one half the cost of the trip, which I think was around $900 or less. My father refused to approach the Chamber and to give me any money. Travel to India was a frivolous idea in his eyes. Sadly, I did not go.

8. A second opportunity to travel to India, a spiritual place of power and mystical wisdom, occurred during a time when I was a financially poor student, living on student loans and yet wanting to travel to India. I prepared to go by getting the required shots only to learn that the loan I needed to finance the trip did not come through. Again, I was denied the trip to India because of lack of money.

9. I did undergo some enemas as a child for constipation. This only lasted for a short time. After a month or so, my parents'

interest in giving enemas waned and stopped. For this I was deeply grateful.

10. Children should be seen and not heard. It was important to be silent, and invisible so as not to cause parents any trouble. Children should have no special needs and learn to satisfy or make do with what was available without asking for help.

The outcome of transgenerational trauma was seen in the way the child was raised and the trauma that I endured. My parents did not allow me to make choices, to share feelings, which meant I was hampered in learning who I was growing up. My mother may not have been given help by her husband and then became depressed, overworked, and angry for shouldering the entire burden of raising children in her husband's absence while he was at war in the Pacific theater, WW 11.

While I was only a baby, I was allowed to cry, to scream without intervention. My mother was instructed by Dr. Spock's book, the authority on baby care at the time, not to "give in" to the child's screams to avoid being controlled by your child. Touch and soothing were kept to a minimum to keep me in a needy and dependent position so that my mother could always retain the upper hand, be in control.

Breast feeding the baby was not seen as proper. In 19th century German culture, breast feeding was seen as "swinish" and filthy. Women who did this were looked down upon. Needless to say, my mother did not breast feed me and I doubt very much whether her mother breast fed her as well.

I was left to play by myself, while my mother attended to household chores. There was little interaction and little talking with me until I grew much older. The exception for me is that my mother read me bedtime stories when I was very small. This was the singular most positive and memorable time I had with my mother as a child, made sweeter by the fact that I had her full attention for a time.

Up until the time I could contribute to the household by setting or clearing the table or sweeping the floor, I felt like a "useless eater." Talking to me about how the I felt or what I might want was not at all within the scope of what was allowable or appropriate. I had to prove that I had a right to be alive by working in some way to contribute to the well-being of the family. This could be accomplished through small chores, or when a teenager, to earn money babysitting or as a soda clerk at the local college canteen. Any job which would get me out of the house and earning a money for my own independence was a welcome breath of fresh air.

Still, I had lot of anxiety about making decisions of a personal nature when I was a young adult. During my freshman year in college, I was to travel to NYC to sing with the Rutgers University Choir, Eugene Ormandy conducting. I wanted to purchase a special blouse for the social events that would be happening that weekend. But when I entered the department store in downtown New Brunswick to shop for this blouse, I had a panic attack, had to hold on to the display case, became dizzy. I was overwhelmed by all the many racks of blouses and had no sense of what I wanted or needed to purchase. I went outside of the store for a time just to catch my breath. Then I returned telling myself I only need to find one blouse, my size which I liked. Finally, after another hour of anxiety and lip biting, I found a blue and green print blouse which I liked. It took time and wrestling with my overwhelming anxiety before my rational mind prevailed. With pure grit I returned to the task of choosing the blouse that I wanted. And it took some time to recover from my panic.

The fear of losing the love of my caregiver, my mother, because I did not find a way to please her was very strong. When I did not please her, which was the usual case, I was "bad". I was terrified of her abandoning me for trying to do things which did not confirm to the mirror image that she was looking for. I needed to grow beyond her parameters she had drawn for me. But I was paralyzed. Some psychoanalysts call this growth panic and psychologists call it abandonment depression. I felt unworthy of my mother's love if I resisted her restraints. To avoid the sense of abandonment I felt I had to comply, had to sacrifice, or put on hold aspects of myself which needed to grow, to explore and to journey beyond the confines of the family expectations.

deMause states that when the mother feels alone and unsupported, she may need her child as an extension of herself in order to lessen her own despair, deMause[9]. Indeed, because I had no voice, or none that

---

[9] deMause, 2005.

anyone listened to, I did become a shadow of my mother, followed her voice, her direction, clung to it because I had none of my own. I did my best to meld my personality with hers, even though we were natured very differently. I felt I had to subjugate my thinking to hers so I would reflect her thoughts. This made it difficult to know my boundaries: where she ended, and where I began. This was especially true since I was very empathic and impressionable, a saving grace but also a detriment. I often swam in the ocean of this boundaryless merger looking for a life raft to cling to. My only escape was to seek shelter alone wherever I could find it.

Thoughts are Entities

Dear Reader,

To say that thoughts and words are entities seems counterintuitive. And yet thoughts or words have power and form. Entities are defined by an amalgamation of frequencies which can both be seen and unseen depending on the nature of the energy present. Entities have a coagulating force which influences the onlooker or the person who may have entities attached to them or housed within them. In cases where photography is used, sometimes entities or the shadow of entities can be seen and witnessed as having a physical form. Entities can harbor both beneficial and malevolent intentions which may not be known even if we are able to converse with them. Only their actions will support or verify their indicated intentions or purposes.

In the early 20th century, people were caught up in spiritism, had seances and witnessed manifestations of weird happenings, voices, materializations of matter in some form or another. These sessions were attempts to commune with the dead. It seems that most of these manifestations came from the astral realm, and it was unclear whether the presence of these was beneficial or harmful. However, this kind of evoking was unstable at best because the origins of these manifestations was unclear and unpredictable. As psychiatry and psychology became more and more acceptable in the 21st Century, these manifestations were deemed spurious and even dangerous. The scientific study of the brain and of psychic manifestations was considered more predictable and grounded in a reality that most people found acceptable.

Energies come in many forms, some of them seen and some unseen. For example, we see the results of the wind, the blowing of leaves, the ripple or cascade of waves on bodies of water, even the flying dust in the air. But no one has ever seen the wind. Yet we name it as something that exists and the effects in nature are the proof of this.

The same is true of thoughts and words. Thoughts made up of words are entities. They have a force, and effect, both positive and negative but we do not see the thought itself. In fact, thoughts are manifestations of energy coming from the consciousness of the body, just as feelings are generated and housed in the body. All unseen, but felt in one way or another, thoughts can be spoken or unspoken.

Sometimes the most powerful thoughts are unspoken thoughts: they have a force or power which can be debilitating, injurious, or on the other hand, to be enhancing, uplifting, and positively supporting.

Three major themes shadowed my life and impacted the choices I made and didn't make.

During my childhood years a major thought that impacted what I did and said:

I feel unloved and unlovable.

This extended into adulthood and was overlapped with a second theme which is:

I am not worthy of love.

This began in childhood and carried me into the time of the Dark Night of the Soul and beyond.

The third theme which was concurrent with the last two and extended into the present is

I am not enough.

I was not enough to make my parents, especially my mother happy. I had failed to fulfill something inside her. Only after years of therapy did I realize that this was not my responsibility and was really her responsibility to create her own happiness. But I took it as my own until she married for the second time. When that happened, I breathed a sigh of relief as I felt the burden of making her happy lifted from my shoulders. These three themes were the building blocks of my emotional consciousness that I had to change into their opposites.

They were obstacles on the path of my growth and therefore in my best interest to transform.

The power of these thoughts, which were unseen but felt deeply, was unwittingly transmitted to the unsuspecting and the innocent parts of me and to many others that I worked with in therapy. These three themes were over-riding notions for the majority of clients I worked with as a psychologist.

As a young adult, I offer an example of learning to love myself by claiming my voice. I decided to leave a graduate program in Art History, after one semester, and move to NYC to get my head straight. I had been depressed since the breakup with my first lover and needed to find a way to know myself and to love myself. Fortunately, my Art History mentor, himself in therapy, suggested that I seek psychoanalysis in New York. With ninety dollars in my pocket, no friends, and no job, I headed to New York, because I was determined to find a life. It was do or die.

I knew I needed the help from the Divine as I could but could not do this on my own. At first, I struggled to survive by looking for roommate ads in newspapers and offering to be a temporary roommate, pay a minimal amount of money per night until a permanent roommate was found. I took babysitting jobs over the dinner hours, and would carefully raid the customer's refrigerator, choose a piece of cheese from an open package or piece of lunch meat from the bottom of a pile.

Later, after I secured a position as a social worker, I typed for other analysts in the Sullivan White Psychoanalytic Community and earned money for therapy. My analyst connected me with one of his patients who was looking for a roommate so that I had a place to stay at least for a time. That roommate became a close friend whom I could trust and who supported me along my path as I did her.

During this time, I received a letter from my mother calling me "an ungrateful wretch" because I was making a life without her in NYC and had not returned to her home as she wished.

(This is the Ahrimanic voice wanting to control and to subjugate my desires to conform with her desires. (See Part 5 on Ahriman). When my analyst learned about my mother's letters, he told me to burn them. I was afraid even to do that, so I threw the letters into the garbage where I knew they would be destroyed. Someone else had to destroy them because I could not do it at that time. After I did not respond to her letter, my mother wrote to me again and announced that she had made an appointment for me to request entrance into the Ph.D. program in English at the University she had graduated from. This would have meant a return to her. I was to mirror her path, follow in her footsteps because she knew what was best for me. I kept thinking that she had insulted me by thinking for me, that she could make this arrangement without first consulting with me. She did not trust my ability to think for myself. Frankly, I had doubts about my ability as well since, she had made most decisions for me up until that point. But still I wanted the opportunity to make my own decisions about my life.

With my analyst holding my hand to steady me because I was trembling with terror, I wrote a note to my mother, saying simply that I was not interested and to please cancel this arrangement. I went to the post box to drop off the letter, and ran from the box, as if a bomb would go off as soon as the letter reached the bottom of the box. Of course, that did not happen, but it felt like I had delivered WMD (Weapons of Mass Destruction) to her. Perhaps she would never speak to me again, and perhaps that would be good. But no. In another week I received another letter with her *insisting* that I keep this appointment, complete with time, day, and place where the appointment was to be held. I was trembling when I read this. I had to brace myself for another confrontation, telling her *no* again. With my hands trembling, and with my analyst's support, I wrote to her again saying that I would *not* be keeping this appointment and that she needed to cancel it so that she would not look foolish. Again, I posted the letter, with a little less fear, but a little more anger rising in me. Surely, she would get the message now and finally take my word seriously. But no, again, a week later, she wrote a strong letter saying that if I did not comply that she would be shamed and humiliated and it would be my fault. Does this sound familiar?

This time I was angry. How dare she put me through the torment of having to confront her once again. It was like looking at the head of the Medusa: I feared she might turn me to stone. But I had to write this again and I did with my analyst saying you need to respond. Yes, I needed to put this immobilizing, stinging control and rage back on her. It was not mine. So, I wrote the response to her using one word. *NO*. That was all I wrote. No argument, no defense. Just *NO*. And I mailed it.

Time went on and I did not hear from her for quite a while. I don't think we spoke or wrote letters to each other for at least for eight or nine years. But when she and my father divorced, she asked me to intervene on her behalf, to ask my father to return to her. I refused to do this because it was not my battle to fight. Furthermore, I knew that my father had waited a long time to finalize his decision to leave her and had finally sprung free as I had begun to do. In fact, I was supportive of his departure, although I did not tell that to my mother, at least not directly. He was determined to leave her orb of influence just as I had done.

Years passed, my mother remarried and happily so. I returned to PA where she lived with my Ph.D. in hand and started a clinical practice. When I was awarded my Ph.D., my mother flew to Texas for the graduation ceremony and celebrated my achievement with me. I remember how she carefully adjusted my robe and scarf for the procession. That moment frightened me because I could not believe it and at the same time I was proud that I had gained her respect. I had stood my ground and I knew she was proud of me. It was an end and a beginning…. of a new a different relationship for us.

Those three major themes were being transformed and distilled in my heart and mind:

1. I am loved and loveable.
2. I am worthy of personal love.
   (At the same time, I feel dwarfed and unworthy of the gifts given by Christ but that does not diminish my sense of being a loveable person.)
3. I am enough (to receive love and to be loved by someone else, and also by the Divine).

The Space In-Between:
the luminous force

Dear Reader,

I mentioned the importance of the internal space. This is the space in between, the one that is inhabited by your consciousness and your connection to the spiritual realm. It is the world you can locate as you begin to quiet your mind, to empty it through re-focus on your breath.

The internal world is filled with nothing and everything. It holds a space without dimension or time. It is a product or a projection of consciousness in which images, thoughts, feelings, and dreams. When this space develops between people, the thoughts, feelings, memories, and interpretations of actions that have emerged between people live in this space. They define the nature of the relationship which can shift and change with the exchange of energies between people. Interestingly, what people relate to is the ingredients and elements that they hold in their interior space, recollections of the person or situation that they are acquainted with. They think they know a person or a place because they hold in their memory fragment elements of a person. Does this mean they really know someone? This is questionable at best.

The same can be said for one's relationships to one's own interior mind. Those elements that have been erected as the building blocks or foundations of consciousness, that define who we are, or who we believe ourselves to be, are the products of our own constructions, which may or may not be built on true, partially true, or even false premises. The self that I hold internally may be only partially seen by others and may shift as the elements of my consciousness incorporate new insights and perceptions about myself or others. At times I may not recognize myself, may even deny having done something that others may have seen. Or I may have thought about something I never actually expressed in so many words, but others felt what I was thinking through the resonant exchange (nonverbal) between us.

I say this because I think our primary relationships with ourselves and with others exists within the consciousness space held between us and only partially within our knowing. If we can assume that this is true, then the consciousness space is a co- construction between people, energies, ideas which are unseen, intangible but which exist, nonetheless.

This is particularly true of what I define as luminous or plasma space, which is the space around the experience of something far beyond the self. I call it luminous because it is filled with energy, usually light but also sound, which is not detected by our eyes or ears, but which is felt strongly by the internal consciousness. It is a space where spirit or the supersensible world lives. It is the energy that fills us, and which has created us.

This luminous space exists around us and is the plasma that exists around us. When working with clients, either as a psychologist or later as a polarity practitioner, to enter that luminous space that exists between me and a friend or between me and my client by resting in the emptiness of not knowing, by being open to the sensations or images that came into my consciousness, and by then addressing those images or thoughts by storing them in my internal space. There they remain for a time while the field of luminous inquiry is opened, and the client's energetic system sends signals to me. In this situation the luminous space of the practitioner and the client meet and overlap in that empty receiving space where they can join, merge, and comingle transferring information through vibration which could then be alchemized in the treatment process.

This luminous space is another name for the Divine, God, or plasma force, which exists everywhere, and even inside the self. Through the experience of subliminal energy, energy which enlightens consciousness, or feeds the soul, a sense of a relationship develops.

Nurturing this subliminal space evolves and develops so that the presence of a Force much greater than the self evolves. In this space it is possible to access other dimensions of energy. For the most part, we live in the third and fourth dimensions but other beings from other dimensions and beyond may appear like Ascended Masters or Angels, or Enlightened Beings. You can access this luminous space because you as a human being are multidimensional which means you are able to access different dimensions of existence at different times. Or you may access portals beyond this dimension into other worlds of luminous space. The more you can hold the higher frequencies in your consciousness, the more you will have access to different experiences of dimensionality and the more you can grow in your knowledge and understanding of the layers and frequencies that this complex world and other worlds, parallel worlds.

Entering this luminous space is also entering the world of your Future Self. The effect of the intermingling of the energetic fields of the client and the practitioner, is so powerful that the client can feel changes occurring before the partitioner employs any direct work on the client. Holding space is the key because in that energy moves. It is as if we could watch and even to some extent "direct" the movement of the electrons and protons in their orbits by simply observing with an open mind and heart. The atoms of energy follow our awareness and can promote healing, can facilitate the renewal or rebalancing of energies in the client. It is through the assemblage of internal forces and taking the time to hold the space open without insertion of personal thoughts or feelings, just holding the space open without intervention that allows positive energy for healing to move freely.

The power of this consciousness space which holds the luminous is intelligent and immeasurable. Because it has no dimensionality, no boundaries as such, it can go anywhere and do anything. This energy is totally free to morph to travel to any place and to assist in the healing process if there is openness for it.

It is unfortunate that during this day and age, understanding the importance of taking time to cultivate this luminous space is lacking. So much distraction, interference and promotion of activities and material goods which acts as a detour from getting acquainted with the interior self. Because of so many societal demands, the need for time to experience silence in luminous space is totally eclipsed. Opportunity is lost and so is connection to that luminous self which needs nurturance and attention to be experienced and utilized, to grow as an integral and necessary aspect of being human-divine.

At this moment in history when humanity is being challenged, to the point of its very existence, one important tool is commitment to allowing and entering this luminous space through conscious breathing. It is the one place where the truth of who you are, and who you are becoming exists. It is the space which individual internal messages which emerge and can be trusted because these messages or instincts do not lie. This internal space holds the most trustworthy mentor, God, or the force that encompasses unconditional love and acceptance for each human being. You do not have to be religious, but you do have to be conscious in that space to show you are ready to have the experience, to know the Divine, a force greater than yourself, a force of intelligent mind which directs the energy of our universe, in yourself, and which supports constructive action and energy. This force is probably the only force that man can merge with which will overcome the many attacks and assaults on human beings at this time. This connection within the luminous space is the one safety zone, which man can rely on, and which exists no matter what. (See Appendix A)

Origins of Thinking: an Analytical Perspective

Dear Reader,

While exploring the origins of thought from a psychoanalytic point of view, I looked at two aspects: initial thinking is linking as related to the caregiver/ child process and the use of linking as a way of processing thought.

ON THE ORIGINS OF THOUGHT

On reflection, it is not abnormal or unusual to wonder about where your thoughts came from. As children we were indoctrinated by family habits, rituals, and ethics to think about the world in ways that our parents thought depending on messages from their parents. In my case, my mother followed her father who was an intellectual, raised by the Jesuits in Czechoslovakia. She would often hear him in the early morning reciting Biblical verses in "socco voce," soft voice. Since he was fluent in several languages, she often heard him speaking German. But her family was raised Catholic so that the Bible was not read to the rest of the family as far as I knew.

On the other hand, my father came from a staunch Lutheran family where the Bible was the rule. Biblical verses were often quoted, and the verses were used as a sledgehammer to control a family member's thinking on a multitude of life activities. I did not see this but am told that my father was punished if he did not speak in coherence with the teachings of the Bible. His mother was swift and unforgiving in her treatment of him. Since my parents were deeply shaped by European ideas of what a child should be, the adage that children should be seen and not heard was a guideline in our household. As a result, whatever I might have thought or felt about a variety of topics was squelched before it had a chance to be thought, known, or spoken to myself or anyone else.

For a long time, I wondered who was thinking? Was it my father or my mother or some combination of their parents' thought inside of me? This led to my investigation into the roots of my thinking from a psychoanalytic point of view. I discovered the work of Wilfred Bion, schooled in the British Psychoanalytical theories who spoke at length about thinking which origins he called linking. He was an original thinker in the school of psychoanalysis. He contributed to theories of projective identification, splitting, unconscious phantasy, and countertransference.

Bion worked with Melanie Klein's theories of infant phantasy and developed his own theory of thinking. He was deeply influenced by the psychoanalytic work of his teacher and analyst Melanie Klein. However, his theories extended beyond Klein's projective identification. In her analysis of children, Klein viewed the fear of death as central to the child's feeling of anxiety. Bion 's theories on thinking concerned the destruction of linking which goes on with the mother and infant through either denial, dismissive attitudes or attacks by the mother on the internal aspects of the child. The nature of the attack can be a person's mental thoughts or images, feelings, or sensations. Bion was interested in what allowed people to think, even to think unthought thoughts[10] (WR Bion, 1994) He called the things that cannot be thought, Beta elements or raw sensory impressions, which have no organization and do not seem to have meaning attached to them[11]. (Britton, 1992). Bion went on to develop a mathematical language to explain the levels of thinking possible. He claims, "Thinking is a

---

[10] Bion, Wilfred, Learning from Experience, Jason Aronson, 1994, chapter 3.
[11] Britton, Ronald, Clinical Lectures on Klein and Bion, editor, Robin Anderson The Oedipus Situation and the Depressive Position, Rutledge Publishing, New York, 1992.

development forced upon the psyche by the pressure of thoughts, and not the other way around."[12] Bion, 1994.

The beta elements are the ingredients that are used to develop thinking in the mind. A young baby having beta elements can tolerate the deluge of sensations from the world at large by having another mind which can think for him or her, like the mind of the mother or caregiver. The child's experience is metabolized by the mother whose thinking becomes the container for the child's experiences. The child relies on the mother's alpha function[13] (Ibid, Bion, 1994) to assimilate these beta elements and place them in an organization and context until the child can learn to assimilate these elements into him or herself. The mother is important in her ability to transform these elements, and thus to begin the thinking process for the child. She holds them until the child can learn to create and build his or her own alpha functioning. Thus, the mother models for the child the capacity to think and to take in raw sensory experiences, add meaning to these beta elements and project them back to the child who can begin to incorporate them as new thoughts. The child's consciousness is contained within the mother, and rests in the container (the mother) until the child learns to think for him or herself (Joseph 1987). Bion calls this mother child interaction *the thinking couple*, container--contained.

What happens in this process is intricately connected with what is projected between the mother and baby. Again, the term projective identification comes into play as the baby projects his undigested beta bits to the mother. She digests them and feeds them back using her alpha function, her thinking function. Bion[14], Second thoughts:

Attacks on linking origins in what Melanie Klein calls the paranoid schizoid phase. This period is dominated by part-object relationship.

I could imagine that my mother said to herself, "I don't know what is wrong with this child or how to calm her". F Bion, Second thoughts[15]

---

[12] Ibid, Bion, 1994.

[13] Ibid, Bion, 1994

[14] Bion, W.R., Second Thoughts, Selected Papers on Psycho-analysis, William Heinemann Medical books, Ltd., 1967, 101.

[15] Bion, Ibid, 104.

My desire was to know what the child wanted, that the mother should treat the infant's cry as more than a demand for her presence. From the infant's point of view, the mother should take the child into her and thus experienced the fear that the child felt. It was the feeling of fear that the child could not contain. He or she (the child) strove to split it off together with the part of the personality in which it lay and project it into the mother. An understanding mother can experience the feeling of dread, that this baby was striving to begin to understand by projective identification into the mother or caregiver and be rewarded with the mother's digested understanding which gives the child a balanced outlook. In one example, Bion told of a patient who had to deal with a mother who could not tolerate experiencing such feelings and reacted either by denying them ingress or alternately by becoming a prey to the anxiety which resulted from introjection of the child's feelings. The latter reaction must I think have been rare: denial was dominant. Bion[16] Second thoughts,

For example, when the Patient (baby) strove to rid himself of fears of death which were felt to be too powerful for his personality to contain, he split off his fears and projected them into me as practitioner or (the mother or analyst), the idea apparently being that if they were allowed to repose there long enough, they would undergo modification by my psyche and "could then safely be re-introjected." Bion[17], Second Thoughts

Denial of the use of this mechanism (projective identification) either by the refusal of the mother to serve as a repository of the infant's feelings or by the hatred and envy of the patient (baby) who cannot allow the mother to exercise this function, leads to destruction of the link between the infant and the breast (part object) and consequently to a severe disorder of the impulse to learn to hold thoughts on which all learning depends.

But when the mother misses, dismisses, or denies these beta bits of the baby, the baby can feel that he or she is bad, or his or her parts are indigestible. As the mother deflects or rejects these bits, the baby feels this rejection personally and his bits become negative

---

[16] Bion, Ibid, 103
[17] Bion, Ibid, 106

information defining who he or she is, or what he or she thinks, "I must be bad, not loveable, a piece of dirt." These dirty beta bits become part of the baby's self- image and identity. In this case, I felt unworthy to be loved and cared for by my mother.

Later in life I began to find my own voice, my own thoughts, my own words, my own perspective because what I was experiencing did not fit with who I felt myself to be. A missing link, a missing resonance grew through the years until I realized that I was caught in a matrix of parental thought, attributions, and feelings in which I was cocooned from birth. Through the process of my own psychoanalytic therapy, I became intensely aware of how these thought energies affected me. I felt the restrictions of the boundaries of those energies and questioned who I was at my core. This lack of linking began in childhood and continued until I realized I could break through using my own images and words which I came to own and honor.

(See Appendix E for further discussion).

Developing Ego Consciousness

Dear Reader,

In the beginning when I was very young, I listened to my mother's voice as she read bedtime stories. Then I came to discover there were voices within me. Some echoed my parents' voices and others were very different. These voices within, which I encountered, you may have encountered as well. They were mystifying and confusing. As a young child, I awoke in a world I did not understand and did not know where I fit in. In time I began to wonder whose voices were speaking and which voices should I follow?

Does this sound familiar? Or is it painfully close to some sense of reality that you may have toyed with or allowed your mind to stand close to this reality, hoping that it was not true, or was not you? That is where my story begins. Being brought into a world without a purpose or roadmap of where to go, what to do, or how to participate in life was bewildering to say the least. It begins where I, as a young girl, try to pick up clues from my mother to help me understand what I was feeling and what I was supposed to focus on.

It began with bedtime stories about the fantasy world I was to know, a fantasy world which had little to do with the reality of everyday life. It was easy to slide into the story and live that story out in daily living. It was comforting to have a friend who came alive in a story and who accepted me, the young girl, and who was willing and able to enact whatever stories came to mind. Below, I write a personal letter to my mother, as if she were alive and could read this letter. I share this with you the reader as I write to my mother.

Anne Elizabeth Ph.D.

Dear Mother

In the beginning there was you and me, the *pippsissawa* and the *skeezicks*. These creatures came out of the James Thurber, The Thirteen Clocks,[18] which you read to me, our bedtime ritual. I pictured the *pippsissawa* as a penguin- like figure with a traveler's hat with a brim and a twinkle in his red eye. I guess it was a male character. The *pippsissawa* liked to skip and hide in various places and jump out to scare me. He was grey in color and wore a little shirt and pants which tended to blend in with his grey color. He was fun and silly. Every time I remembered him, laughing I saw his nose get bright red.

Then there was the *skeezicks*, a rather serious piece of work. Tall, slender with a rather critical gaze if I ever saw it and I am not sure I did. But I felt a look that went right through me. He carried a sword or a knife. When the duke in the story spoke of slitting someone from the *guggle* to the *szatch*, I pictured the *skeezicks* with the sword in hand ready to launch his attack on the duke. His thin shadow would ripple against the wall like the shimmer of breeze on a small lake with his sword or knife raised high in the air ready to slice the *skeezicks* or me, but it never did.

Who can say why these names, these sounds stayed with me? Was it the rhythm, *Pippsissawa,* "wa, wa, wa"? That was seven syllables which I loved to sing. Or was it the sound of the "S" which also resonated in the name *skeezicks*? That "icks" sound was like the slice of the knife. It had definition and direction and I felt strong when I said it. That sound empowered me when I said it.[19]

Mother, you must have loved Thurber's word play as much as I did, although I did not recognize it at the time. Only after these many years, as the memory of this story continues to engage my consciousness do I recognize that these sounds were like friends, whose memory stayed inside and tickled my fantasy all these years.

The title of the book, the *Thirteen Clocks*, was another catch phrase which arrested my attention. Why thirteen, not twelve or twenty? The choice of the number of clocks was never explained, nor should it have

---

[18] Thurber, James, The Thirteen Clocks, Simon and Schuster, New York, 1950.
[19] Ibid, Thurber

been. Thirteen clock remains a tantalizing mystery, especially since I try to picture thirteen clocks and have a hard time doing that. Were they grandmother or the larger grandfather clocks? Were they small alarm clocks? Were the on the mantel above fireplace or beside a bed? And why were they guarded? And how was the duke able to slay time?

Another resonance for me was frozen time. The duke had frozen all the clocks at ten minutes to five. I did not wonder that this could happen because it seemed to me that time was frozen for me as well. I seemed always to be waiting for events to happen, whether it was a holiday like Christmas or a birthday, or a babysitter to care for me while my mother was at school. Time seemed heavy and endless. I was in a space which I had to endure, to hold my breath until finally something had arrived, and I could let go, perhaps and be glad something had happened or disappointed that whatever happened did not meet my expectations. Take deep breaths and take in what was occurring in the present moment. Search for the pleasure, the freedom I so desired. Often, I felt frozen, cold, and unyielding. Perhaps a possible excitement or pleasure was just around the corner. I was always waiting, waiting, waiting to see. For me, it was not a foreign idea that the duke had stopped time. I thought I was not the only one experience frozen time. The duke must have experienced frozen time as well.

The question was always, "Why 13 clocks?".

All these questions started as a child and came to my conscious mind when I reread the story as an adult. That is when I tried to make sense of the rhymes and riddles which fortunately continued to be unsolved. It was fun to play with them as I knew them, to continue to wonder if I would ever make sense of them, and to allow the sounds to sprawl across my mind in a never to change way. This was a comfort to me as I knew I could bring them out to play as they would always be waiting for me.

For me, mother, our most precious moment was of you telling the story of the two turtles. This was a short story which consisted of you placing a hand on each of my hands and introducing a turtle on each hand. Each turtle would go up my arms to my shoulders, followed by a hug and the comment that this is where the turtles like to meet each other, right at the nape of my neck. Perhaps it was the quiet slow movement of the turtles that made me comfortable as it was slow and unthreatening at the same time. It was the dearest moment of my early childhood as I knew you had found a way to enter my space in a tender and playful way, a way that reflected your love for me.

My family of fantasy figures enlarged when you began to read me *Uncle Wiggily's Story Book*[20]. Uncle Wiggily was a huge caretaking rabbit, maybe a hare, with long ears which emerged on the screen of my heart memory along with Miss Fuzzy Wuzzy, his muskrat lady housekeeper. They were both so kind to others, so caring. I remember Uncle Wiggily making sure that all his animal friends had food or shelter as needed. And of course, Nurse Jane Fuzzy Wuzzy was available for whatever Uncle Wiggily needed for his friends. Neither of these were like people to me, even friends, even safer than friends, that would come to wish me sweet dreams and to secure themselves in my memory so that I did not feel so alone.

As it turned out, I had only one playmate in the apartment building we lived in, a boy named Michael, my age, who was not a safe person to play with. Because his father had been injured during the War, he was mostly powerless to carry out any disciplinarian measures. This left the burden of care up to his mother, who had a hard time controlling Michael. His play was rough, wild at times, even unbounded. I remember being glad for the times when our play was soft and quiet, but this was rare. In contrast, one day Michael put a rope around my neck and tried to treat me as his horse, saying, "Giddy up," and pulling on the reins. As he did so I began to choke and cough. Apparently, you heard me struggling and came running in from the other room. You saw the dire situation I was in and immediately told Michael to let go of the rope as you released the tension around my neck. Even Michael's mother stood by quietly scolding him with a look of helpless despair on her face.

When you took the rope off, there was a circular brush burn from the taut rubbing of the rope that Michael had been pulling. You were very distraught about the neck burns and shook your head. Since I could not see the burn marks and barely felt them, that was not a

---

20 Garis, Howard R., Uncle Wiggily's Story Book, Platt and Monk, New York, 1949.

concern for me. What was a concern were the moments when I was having trouble breathing, catching my breath, choking. I supposed it was possible that Michael could have strangled me. In the end, I feared him and was hesitant to play with him again Needless to say my play dates with Michael were numbered after the horseplay incident.

I welcomed the story book playmates, now expanded in my memory as these characters seemed safe and did not harm me. Although I never realized until this moment, I am thankful for the peace and security I felt with my imaginary friends that you brought to my internal playground through the reading of these stories. And I am so grateful to you, mother for reading these stories to me. Although I did not say it at the time, this meant the world to me because it allowed me to begin forming my ego conscious world.

Developing Ego Consciousness from Scratch

Dear Reader,

My *ego consciousness* had to be developed from *scratch*. I needed to learn to ask for what I needed. I needed to figure out what I needed and then ask for help. But I did not feel I had the right to ask. This meant that my ego development was greatly hampered as was my ability to know the world and to know myself. As a young child I feel I need to tell you that I did not have the right to have my needs granted. It took many years of therapy to feel entitled and guilt free enough to ask for what I wanted without apology or guilt. The first scene I remember is in a pre-school situation where I felt lost and separate from all the other children.

The memory of this scene was triggered by a black and white photo I found in an album my mother kept of me as a young child. In the photo, I about five and in a playground in NYC atop a building many stories high with a huge wire fence around it. There was a sandbox on this roof which was the area designed for children to play outside. It was very cold that day and so we all wore coats, hats, and mittens against the wind. I was sitting on the edge of the sandbox looking at the other children, feeling very separate from them, just watching. It was a winter day I believe, and I think I was feeling chilled and ready to return to the warmth inside the building. I had a very faraway look as if I was thinking of something in another world, daydreaming, or not having a clue about how to play in the sand box with the others.

Inside that same building, I remember sitting around a table doing an art project. Each child had paper, glue and one pair of scissors for each table. I am not sure what we were creating but I remember that another child was using the scissors which I needed. However, I did not feel I had the right to ask for those scissors because that child might be annoyed by my asking. I continued to sit there watching and doing nothing because *I did not feel I had the right to ask for what I needed.*

That was a block, an obstacle that I had to work to overcome. In so many words I did not feel I had the right to ask because it would disrupt someone else's needs. I know it sounds crazy but that was where my ego development was stuck at the time—unentitled and suppressed by guilt and fear of being an imposition on others.

That sense of being an imposition was a very all-pervasive feeling that I had with the other children in school and at home. I was truly terrified to ask for anything which might be seen as asking for something which would cause my parents stress or discomfort. I know, it seems strange to be concerned about that at such a young age, but the fear of asking was so strong, because of the sense of disapproval when I did ask, that I learned not to ask. This reluctance stayed with me throughout most of my teen years until I went to college and lived away from home, where I was freer to ask. At school I found I was forced to ask for what I needed because otherwise I would miss opportunities to learn what I needed to know. This hindered my progress in school so when I saw others asking questions and getting the information they needed, I knew I had to learn to do this.

Feeling guilty about having needs which might "impose" on others to get what I needed was a major impetus for engaging in therapy. I needed to neutralize the fear of being an imposition and become comfortable with asking for what I needed. Therapy happened after I graduated from college and was living on my own in NYC. It was a long slog to finally come to the realization that asking and receiving what I needed was important and necessary for my growth and the discovery of who I was as a person and learning how to address my needs and alternatives in the world.

The Naming of the Essence of Things

Dear Reader,

I want to tell you about the trouble I had as a child with language, with words, with the naming of things. Because I thought in images, as many young children do, I had to translate from image to word. This was not easy as the image had to be unpacked layer by layer. To convey the true essence of the feeling behind the image was difficult and frustrating because the right word to convey that kernel of truth was not immediately apparent. The search for the right word or words often continued over time until something appeared within me, the word or phrase that best mirrored the truth I experienced. These words related to my internal and external speech, which was emerging in various ways through my schooling and childhood experiences. Even so I find that my speech was still hesitant and uncertain and so I often refrained from speaking until I was surer of my voice.

But when an experience occurred and I wanted to talk about it with someone and did not have the words that I could trust to communicate what I saw or felt, I was totally frustrated and often opted to remain silent. It took many years of wrestling with myself, giving in to speaking words which I felt were partially true, but not fully accurate, to describe what I wanted to communicate. This was a way of joining with others even if the joining was only partial.

Out of frustration and loneliness, I condescended to speak in terms that I knew others would understand but were not necessarily what I really wanted to communicate. In the autumn of 1950 when I was eight years old, I had a break-through. I chanced to hear the words of

Robert Louis Stephenson, in the poem My Shadow that my mother read to me.

> I have a little shadow that goes in and out with me,
> And what can be the use of him is more than I can see.
> He is very, very like me from the heels up to the head;
> And I see him jump before me, when I jump into
>   my bed.
> The funniest thing about his is the way he likes to
>   grow—
> Not at all like proper children, which is always very
>   slow;
> For he sometimes shoots up taller like an India-rubber
>   ball,
> And he sometimes gets so little that there's none of
>   him at all.
> He hasn't got a notion of how children ought to play,
> And can only make a fool of me in every sort of way.
> He stays so close beside me, he's a coward, you can see;
> I'd think shame to stick to nursie as the shadow sticks
>   to me!
> One morning, very early, before the sun was up,
> I rose and found the shining dew on every buttercup;
> But my lazy little shadow, like an arrant sleepy-head,
> Had stayed at home behind me and was fast asleep
>   in bed.

I did not know what some of the words meant, like arrant for instance, but I had a connection with having a shadow that followed me around. Hearing this poem affirmed the fact that others had shadows that lived with them as well. In some way, this poem legitimized my experience with having a shadow, which was like a silent companion that I could talk with but never did. It felt too scary to think I could talk with something unseen, even though at a younger age I had a telepathic conversation with the lion who also approached me from behind. (See Part 5 for the story of the lion).

As I grew, I hoped for a connection with someone, a friend or playmate, I could talk with who could relate to my struggle with saying what I saw and how I felt. The words of that poem mirrored my experience closely and helped me to feel hopeful that I would meet someone with whom I could communicate, and we would understand each other.

My mother continued to read to me and chose Alice in Wonderland by Lewis Carroll as a story that I continued to love, even to this day. What I loved most at that time was conversation that I heard between people. I listened to how they spoke to each other, the tone, and the sound of words. Often, I would bypass listening for meaning and just listen to tone and facial expression. If my mother was trying to tell me something, she would see a distant look on my face and say, "What did I just say?" I would stutter and say, "I don't remember," and she would repeat herself in an irritated voice. What was important to me were the sounds that were coming together. I was in awe that these sounds connected to form words which had meaning. The very fact that people could communicate in words and that these words were taken seriously, had meaning, and could be understood was eye-opening for me.

This is probably one reason I loved the poem by Lewis Carroll called A Whiting and a Snail because it is a conversation between a fish called a Whiting and a snail. They are communicating and they hear each other.

> 'Will you walk a little faster?' said a whiting to a snail.
> 'There's a porpoise close behind us, and he's treading
> on my tail.
> See how eagerly the lobsters and the turtles all
> advance!
> They are waiting on the shingle—will you come and
> join the dance?
> Will you, won't you, will you, won't you, will you join
> the dance?
> Will you, won't you, will you, won't you, will you join
> the dance?

You can really have no notion how delightful it will be
When they take us up and throw us, with the lobsters,
out to sea!"
But the snail replied, 'Too far, too far!' and gave a look
askance—
Said he thanked the whiting kindly, but he would not
join the dance
Would not, could not, would not, could not, would not
join the dance.
Would not, could not, would not, could not, could not
join the dance.

'What matters it how far we go?' his scaly friend replied.
'There is another shore, you know, upon the other side.
The further off from England the nearer is to France—
Then turn not pale, beloved snail, but come and join
the dance.
Will you, won't you, will you, won't you, will you join
the dance.
Will you, won't you, will you, won't you, won't you join
the dance.

I loved the fact that the fish is asking the snail to walk faster, to join the dance which the snail refused to do. I loved the repetitions of *will you, won't you*. It suggests the snail's decision- making process is honored and giving time to the snail to conclude.

The fish mentions the other shore nearer to France and again invites the snail to come and join the dance. We don't know what the snail decides to do so I am left to guess. I loved not knowing which helped me join with the snail who is taking time to decide.

What is great about this for me is that the words of the snail are taken seriously when he says no, he would not join the dance. The snail is beckoned to dance a second time. Although he might have wanted to say yes, to dance, the snail was afraid to do so because to cross the ocean seemed *too far to go*, for a snail that is. It is the conversation that the fish gives the snail a choice and even though the whiting presses, the snail still is given a choice. The voice of the snail is taken seriously by the fish and the snail has an opportunity to decide what he wants to do. This reflects the power of words and the voice, the power of being able to make up your mind, to say no, if you don't feel safe. That was a power I was discovering as a young child and did not feel I had. Even though words were confusing and often did not convey the meaning that seemed expressed in other ways, still there were times when one could communicate, could declare, or decline an opportunity and one could be taken seriously. This conversation was a portal to understanding the power of language, the meaning of words, and of being able to make decisions which I felt allowed me to be self-protective.

Many years after my first love abandoned me when I was 20, I was curious about what had happened to him and did a search to locate him. He had changed his career path from one of being an entomologist working with insects and birds to a child psychologist. We had a brief letter exchange in which I shared with him one of my favorite poems, *Hope is the thing with Feathers* by Emily Dickinson, 1891. It turned out to be one of his favorite poems as well.

> "Hope" is the thing with feathers—
> That perches in the soul—
> And sings the tune without the words—
> And never stops—at all—
>
> And sweetest—in the Gale—is heard—
> And sore must be the storm—
> That could abash the little Bird
> That kept so many warm—
>
> I've heard it in the chillest land—
> And on the strangest Sea—
> Yet—never—in Extremity,
> It asked a crumb—of me.

Perhaps it was the theme of hope, that we could see each other again, or the use of the bird symbolism because he loved birds and travelled the world noting the birds that he saw and heard. Or perhaps it was the *tune without words*, the *tune that never stops* and to my way of thinking never lies, is always true to itself that appealed to me. In any case although I did meet my first lover one more time, I found that he no longer held sway over me. But this poem that we shared was imbedded in my heart as the jewel that would nourish me without flaw or abandonment. My take-away was permanently embedded in my heart and could sustain me for as long as I needed it to, even now.

A memory of making my own choice for the first time

Dear Mother,

I want to talk about what happened in the shadow of Mother Goose at the Rumsey Playground, Central Park, we frequented in New York when I was a small child. I don't know if you remember this incident, but for me this was a game changer because it reminded me of how alone and unprotected, I felt. I had made a decision to do something without your permission and it had turned out badly. It wasn't just the fact that I had been violated in some fundamental way by a splinter, but that I did not feel you were able to empathize with the terror I felt in being assaulted in this way. This was especially true because I was reaching beyond my normal boundaries by going to an area where I had to figure out what I could do or not do on my own. The experience taught me that even things which look like fun can be dangerous and that I had no one to steer me away from pitfalls which I was bound to encounter. On the other hand, I wanted to experience the world on my own terms and come to my own conclusions without being hampered by what your opinion or viewpoint might be. I took a chance and was invaded by a splinter.

You did not know that I had taken a chance to investigate on my own and that I felt punished because I had taken matters into my own hands and gotten injured. You saw this as a mistake because I had not asked for permission to travel beyond your sight. Perhaps the incident made you feel helpless and aggravated because I had been injured on your watch, and you were responsible. At the same

40

time, I recognized your energies were divided between me and your school responsibilities…and your determination to make something of yourself. So, you too got punished in a way for trying to do what you needed to do for yourself because you tried to divide your energies between your work and me and it did not work in that moment.

Here is my version of what happened that day in Central Park at the Mother Goose Playground. Note: The Statute of Mother Goose was designed by Frederick George Richard Roth and erected in 1938. It is composed of granite and is 8 feet 8 inches, by 4 foot, 6 inches, by 5 feet high. Mother Goose rides a goose and is dressed in flying cape with a witches' hat. In bas relief at her feet are Humpty Dumpty, Old King Cole, Little Jack Horner, Mother Hubbard and Mary and her Little Lamb. The state resides at the entrance to Rumsey Playground in Central Park, New York City, New York.

A day which should have been fun turned out to be traumatic and indelible in my memory. It began at the Mother Goose Playground in Central Park, NYC. Again, I was about four or five years old. As I recall this memory, it feels like a dream. I will speak about it in the present as if it is happening now.

The brick entrance walkway of the park has low brick risers, so it is fairly easy for short legs to find their way up without help. At the entrance was a large granite statue of Mother Goose with Disney Characters at her feet. Her cape is unfurled and so large that it blots out the sky if you stand next to her. I stand in her shadow, her witch's hat is perched on her head, and she is resting on a flying goose. Reins are in her hands, and she has a smile on her face. I am not sure if she is welcoming or warning me off, but she is always there when I come to this park. She is large, very large and made of stone. Mother Goose symbolizes my sense of who you my mother are for me at this time, a huge impenetrable figure made of stone, a witch's hat on your head which indicated some form of power and magic over me. Just like the Walt Disney figures following along at your feet. I was one of those figures just wanting to be part of your life in some small way.

Ahead was a canopy of green leaves on trees shadowing the playground area, the jungle gym, seesaws, and swings. Sun mottles the leaves and grass and I am fascinated by the shadows they create.

You encourage me to hurry along. I know you are eager to sit and study as soon as you can. Preoccupied by your studies, you choose a seat where you can view me and still concentrate on your schoolwork.

I am eager to move to the swings which I find eventually and begin to pump myself into thin air. Such freedom and delight. The air is balmy and clear, and it feels so cool and lovely on my skin. It is spring and the birds know it because they are singing in the sunshine, celebrating the warmth of the sun and the new daffodils, yellow and proud along the walk. There are other children around, but I don't know them. Some have parents to push their swings. Others are just hanging around waiting for a vacant swing to use.

After some time, my legs grow tired, and I decide to try the jungle gym. You have told me to be careful on these bars, but I like hanging upside down on the jungle gym bars. So up I go swinging by my legs, I want to call to you, but know you cannot hear me because you are absorbed in your work. I hang upside down, watching the world from this view. I wonder about the ants and other small creatures below. What must they think of seeing me like this, my eyes watching them from way up here, a good distance from them? And I wonder what they do. Do they watch me as well? And do they wonder why I am hanging upside down from a bar watching them? It is funny and weird, but I enjoy thinking about them. I am hanging until I begin to feel lightheaded. Then I get down slowly. My legs are feeling wobbly like I have been a sailor on the seas and just getting my land legs back.

I head for the seesaw area where five or six wooden ones are vacant. It is beyond your scope of vision, but I do not care. I want to travel beyond your sight, on my own. No one is using the seesaws now, so I lay on one of them in the sun. It feels warm and comforting, like being held, wrapped in warmth. Only the breeze cools me and just enough to feel really good. I decide to push myself up and down against the warm wood, like a dog rolling grass and feeling the texture of the grass against skin. But suddenly I feel a pain in my stomach. I am stunned by this and look down. There is a huge splinter of wood sticking out of my stomach, about four or five inches, straight on. I am terrified and in shock. I am breathing rapidly now because I am so scared. What have I done? I have broken two rules, one being out of sight and the other not asking permission to do something alone. I think you will be upset as you will have to take care of me in this situation.

I walk slowly so as not to jar this splinter and find you in the park. It takes some time because I have wandered quite a distance away from you. Finally, I see your face which is snarled into constriction, worry and other feelings that I cannot identify, I know you are not pleased and that also frightens me. I ask you to pull this splinter out. I feel that I have been pierced, violated in some deep way. It has gone to the very essence of who I am. I am injured in a way that I cannot explain. I know that I want this splinter out now.

However, alarmed and annoyed you are, you do not want to touch it. Instead, you decide to take me to the doctor, and you tell me that the doctor will take it out. Now I am in more terror. What kind of pain will this be and who is the strange doctor that will touch this part of me? I do not know, and I am too terrified to ask.

We walk out of the park, past Mother Goose, with her cloak still unfurled, her witch's hat still attached and still riding the goose. We take the low risers one by one but the terraces seem so much longer now. I am quietly crying and stepping as quickly as I can without disturbing or moving this huge splinter sticking out of my gut. Now the warmth, the sunshine and flying in the air have vanished. And something else has disappeared which will only be named in time to come. I am feeling punished for breaking the rules, for trying something on my own and very alone.

Finally, you hail a cab and tells the driver our doctor's address. The cab hurtles down 5th Avenue toward the doctor's office. I am holding my breath because I feel the splinter digging in every time, I take a deep breath. You look out the window as the cab slows and comes to a stop at East 57th Street. We get out and walk to the office building just around the corner. I am trying to tread lightly as I don't want the splinter to go in any further.

After a long elevator ride, or what seems long, we reach the Dr's office. He is not expecting us so when we ring the bell, he opens the door with his coat on as he is on his way out. But he sees the look on my face and ushers me into the inner office. He takes off his overcoat and slips on his white medical coat and motions for me to come over to his long examination table where I sit in a chair next to the table. He smiles and reassures me that this hurt will be taken care of very soon. He pulls out a metal tool from his drawer which looks very big and scary. He informs me about what he is going to do in a gentle and soft way. "I will slowly turn the splinter with this tool and as I turn, I will gently pull the splinter out toward me." By this time, I am shaking with fear. I look over at you and you are sitting in a chair against the wall, watching the doctor. You seem concerned and are gazing intently at the doctor's movements. Slowly, he attaches his tool to the splinter and begins to turn and pull it toward him. I can feel it move inside my stomach and it scares me. I feel tense and look away...perhaps not seeing it will make it go faster. The doctor continues to twist and pull for several more minutes until finally the entire splinter is out. He smiles and pats me on the shoulder. "You have been very brave, and we got the entire splinter out. Nothing broke off. Isn't that good?" I knew it was but was still too much in shock to even look at the spot where it had punctured my stomach. He carefully puts red medicine on the spot and a band aid to keep the wound from being infected. He smiled at you, and you smile back at him. You thank him and say, "We should not keep you any longer." The doctor was very kind and spoke softly to you, "I am glad I was still here so I could be of service." You again thank him, and we travel down the elevator to the street, hail another cab and go home. Once home, you head to the kitchen and start dinner. I head for my safety place, under the dining room table which is covered by a long white tablecloth. There I sit and try to relax. Carefully, I touch the bandaged spot where the splinter had been. It feels a little sore but not terrible. I know the doctor had done a good job as he has gotten all the splinter out. He and I had done this together while you watched. I can hear you in the kitchen putting a pot on the stove. I wonder how you are feeling toward me and wonder if you would punish me for breaking the rules, going out of sight. Or would you overlook it because I am injured. I wait to see. I am trying to remember whether we talk about how I feel, but I don't think anything was said.

That was the first time I had ventured into unknown territory in the park and felt assaulted and unprotected from danger. What a contrast between feeling so free on the swing and the impaled on the seesaw.

I felt alone, and vulnerable without reassurance or comfort from my parents.

I can see now that this was alarming to you because you might have felt you "should have seen this coming and prevented it." But in the end, the trauma was not so much the physical injury but the fact we could not talk about what happened. I did not think you understood the depth of my emotional injury, how much I felt violated. The doctor seemed to be more empathic, supportive and encouraging, saying I had been brave to endure this injury and his removal of the splinter. You seemed relieved for doing what you could not or did not feel comfortable doing. I think we both were injured during that event: I did not get the support from you that I needed, and you also felt the guilt and inadequacy of not know how to respond to me while meeting your school responsibilities.

I think we were both struggling and both feeling bewildered and confused about what actions and conversations were needed at the time, to give support to each other and to fill in the emotional gaps in your upbringing which were projected onto me. We needed help and did not get it at that time. I cannot hold you responsible for what you did not know or the conversations you were incapable of engaging in. So, I am offering my gratitude that we each were faced with a learning experience which for me led to a great deal of internal work to purify and expunge the negative image of being a bad person, being ashamed to have needs. I realized that I had travelled beyond your eyesight, beyond the boundaries you were comfortable with. This initially led to resentment because my first decision to explore had resulted in an injury. Only later I came to understand your side of the picture, that you were concerned and did not feel capable of soothing my pain. And I no longer fault myself for going beyond the boundaries because sometimes you are allowed to make mistakes. I hope this letter frees you from any residual feelings you might have by not being able to help me. Please know that I know you did the best you could and I learned what I needed to know. I send all my love your way.

Your loving daughter, Anne Elizabeth

In Search of a Place

Dear Reader,

Through my many life experiences, I became aware of a strong desire to find place and community. I was searching for a new family or community to belong to, belonging being the operative word, accord to Maslow's criteria for the growth of a healthy person.

I kept wanting to be a part of a group, of spiritually like-minded people. The church communities I had belonged to had not met that need. The self-help Acumen community in New York had met that need for a short time as had the macrobiotic community in Brookline Mass. where I ate in silence during the four months I spent there. I hungered for the feeling of working in concert with a group, of praying together in silence, of creating gardens, and meals together, of living together with the same desire for connection with Spirit. But did not find the feel there either. To gain more information, I had several past life regressions to learn about where these longings originated.

I learned that I had many past lifetimes living as a nun in a variety of stone sanctuaries. As a nun, my life was defined by prayer and religious rituals that were enacted according to the liturgical calendar. I listened for the sound of the bells which announced the next events to be fulfilled. There were no clocks or sirens to alert us to the next tasks. Only the church bells or sometimes following the footsteps of other nuns who seemed to know when the next ritual was to occur. We worked together, often in silence, and moved together ready to help each other, to follow in each other's footsteps, wordlessly. We knew what we were doing was to promote the word of God, to manifest his excellence in our lives and in the lives of others.

During my lifetime now, I felt lost without the rituals of the church, lost without having the structure of my day already defined by the tasks ahead of me which I did not do alone but in the company of those I lived with. In each physical home that I lived in, and there were at least four different ones, I hungered for place, a place that felt like mine. In each home, I had a room which was my bedroom which was assigned to me as my place to sleep. I did not decorate it as many teenagers do with posters of favorite bands, or popular sports icons, or even travel posters of places visited or wished for. These bedrooms felt temporary, as if I was a lodger only there for a short time. They were not mine but only lent to me for as long as I remained in the household. Altogether there were four rooms in our apartment in New York City. The three of us shared one shared bedroom with one double bed and a single bed resting against one wall, my bed. I do not remember the bedrooms I had in several other homes except one in Jenkintown when I was eleven. That bedroom had flamingo-pink wallpaper with flowers in ornate vases. I remember counting the flamingos when I was sick in bed, listening to the *Shadow* on the radio and waiting alone for my mother to return from her position as a schoolteacher in the nearby town.

They we moved into the Dean's house in Allentown Pennsylvania when my father took the position of Dean of Faculty. This was a large six-bedroom home on a main street in the west end of Allentown, Pa. My father had taken this administrative position at his alma mater which afforded us occupancy of the Dean's House where I sought my place within the choice of three bedrooms that were available. I wandered from room to room trying to decide which of the three I felt most comfortable in. I never settled on one but kept roaming the house seeking a place that felt like mine.

This mansion invited hospitality with the right occupants with a wraparound covered porch which extended beyond the living room and an uncovered porch stretching across the length of the home in the rear. Summer breezes could waft off the covered porch through the opened French doors in the living room and often did. The living room was long, perhaps 30 feet, but only about 15 foot wide with a fireplace which was never used. Things would have been so different if my parents had been able to take the time to light the fire in the fireplace. Then we might have come together as a family and been able to sit in the living room and talk about our day, what happened and what did not happen, a scene that would have been a delicious moment to remember. But that never occurred.

On the second floor the master bedroom was about 20 x 20 and the other three bedrooms were about 15x 20. Two of the bedrooms had a shared bathroom in between the rooms. One bedroom, adjacent to the master bedroom had a large, covered porch about 10/10 where I could hang out undetected by anyone. It was private, lonely and I could sit on the brick wall there listening to the birds and no one would know. I preferred the bedroom at the back side of the house because traffic was not so easily heard back there. However, I never actually moved into that room because it did not feel private enough. The large windows were open to the sky and at night the headlights from the cars danced their panorama of shadows across the walls in a ghostly shadow play, like uninvited visitors. Were they friendly or not? Often my parents would attend social events outside the home and leave me by myself in this huge house which would creek and groan. Ghostly figures would emerge from the closet or under the bed. I would cocoon myself under the covers, clutching the sheets, heart beating rapidly, and in a state of panic until I heard the front door open and their voices. Only then could I relax and allow myself to feel safe enough to fall asleep.

Although the house was huge and I could hide in this house, the downside was the house felt empty, cold, distant, and uninhabited much of the time. I might well have been in a museum, with the rooms, empty of warmth, offering little comfort. I was living in the labyrinth of walls and halls walking and waiting for something, a welcoming voice, or a release from the tension of all the walls that grew higher and higher.

On my sixteenth birthday my mother organized a party for me with some of my high school girlfriends. The weather was perfect, sunny with a slight breeze and not too hot as August days tend to be. The party would be held outside on the large, covered patio next to the living room French doors. I heard my mother ask my father to take photos of us as we were eating and talking. My father refused saying he had no time for taking photos and had other plans. So, he disappeared. My mother stood silent, with grimaced face. I was both in a state of shock and relieved as the tension that was always there when he was present had disappeared. I had enough anxiety about knowing and not knowing what to say to my girlfriends without his presence choking my mind and driving my psyche into the ground. As it usually did.

In the summer, the pool just below the property and across the road, was filled with laughing boisterous teenagers. I could hear their voices along with the 1950's music that played every afternoon by the pool. The words to Elvis' song Love Me Tender came through loud and clear as I sat on the patio or walked across the field. When I was with other girls, I seldom joined in the conversation because I never knew what to say. Nothing inside me to give me a clue about what I was thinking or feeling. It was easier to be quiet and laugh when they were laughing. I did not believe that what I had to offer was wanted or received. My feelings were sequestered inside leaving me, hollow and frozen.

Just like the fleeting shadow that pass too quickly to be identified. I was a teen entertaining shadow: my shadows, their shadows, all those presences that were lingering from generations before that had not been addressed, incorporated, or acknowledged. These shadows, especially the shadows from my parent's past were long and recalcitrant. My father's shadow was of an angry, unfulfilled musician, who was beleaguered by a dominant selfish wife yet unfulfilled. At that moment he was attempting to fulfill the role of teacher and administrator at his alma mater, a place he had been battered and mistreated when he attended as a student.

Even though we slept and ate in the same house, the house felt like a boarding home. Supper time was obligatory since we all had to eat at some time. But even in a boarding house, people would tend to chit chat about social or political events, even about the weather. At least it would have some semblance of social contact. Not so in my family. We were confined to our roles which were fixed and unbending. We were eating so we could continue fulfilling our obligations in the world. We were not living together in any way.

At dinner times I would see my mother with apron covering her work clothes, as she struggled to mash the potatoes with a hand masher. She was in a hurry to get dinner on the table. With pursed lips she would push the masher into the cooked potatoes and add some milk for consistency. I would set the table waiting for my father's footsteps in the hallway. That footstep brought tension into the household. Hearing them, I wanted to be invisible so that I did not have to speak because I had no idea what to say to my parents who were virtual strangers to me. I was a stranger in a strange land.

We did not meet in the large dining room complete with a mahogany dining room table, a hutch which housed very fragile and cherish white china with delicate blue flowers. That would have been too much work and taken too much time from other activities which both of my parents felt obligated to address. Instead, we ate at the table in the middle of the large kitchen which faced the street. The house might have accommodated many joyful times with so much lightness of air and sunlight filtered in through those windows. But in our house, this was not the case. Whatever was going on in the minds of my parents was unspoken. The tension that was created by their unacknowledged thoughts and feelings were thick, heavy. We lived in the shadows of these thoughts as they floated around us and constricted every muscle and bone of our body. My throat was strained into silence. I watched my mother, consumed with meeting the expectations and demands of her high school teaching position, of succeeding to find a respectable place in society. I watched my father, learning how to meet the expectations of an administrator and meeting the political needs he faced as Dean of Faculty. He was living in the shadows of his ancestors who had founded the institution he now headed and giving service to the church as a deacon, writing a 500-page history of the Lutheran Synod. All those expectations were like a chain around his neck and body. And I felt chained as well, working to earn the best grades possible, to get into the best college possible, so that I could escape the environment that I lived in and move out.

We were all waiting for something: my mother and I watched behind glass walls and waited to see if there was a space for us and my father waited to see if he could master the politics of administration in his position. The three of us lived together in this house which tried to be a home for six years but through no fault of its own, it never succeeded in being a place of comfort for any of us, especially me. During the time we lived there, our shadows took their most intense and unforgettable forms, the unspoken parts of ourselves. They proliferated behind closed doors and remained separate and distinctly insulated from each other so that when we met, we were strangers struggling for a connection which was not there. We did not know how to communicate and had not shared our feelings so that we were clueless about who we were and why we were together as a family. But because we lived together, we pretended, acted like a family for the sake of our individual goals, and for a place in the world. We acted out the expected roles but inside we were imprisoned in the detritus of our frozen souls.

In search of community.

Dear Reader,

To trace the trajectory of my "I" Consciousness, my ego, please follow with me as I explore my thoughts about community and the evolution of my "I" consciousness or Higher Ego and spiritual growth as it evolved through my connections to community.

Reading Simply Lasting, Writers on Jane Kenyon[21], I am struck with Jane's struggles about finding place. She found it difficult to feel at home in the world, my struggle as well. She felt dislocated and unsettled and tried to overcome that feeling through her writing. This reflected my own struggle with finding place. But my pain is traced to the numerous past lives I have encountered as a nun, sequestered in monasteries, rising to the early morning bells summoning me and the community of nuns I lived with to mass and meditation at least three times a day. And to the fact that I feel lost without living in the community of other flesh and blood persons, feel lost with accomplishing tasks in my garden, or cooking and eating alone, and that I have had to discipline myself to food shop, prepare meals, pay bills on time, and take care of a variety of household issues. I have learned to do this successfully more as a defense against stress and as a way of avoiding the penalties that accompany derelict duty. Unfortunately, at times this discipline has outstripped my energy and overtaken my more delicate need for creating mind space to write or play music, a balancing act I have been working with for some

---

[21] Peseroff, Joyce, ed, Simply Lasting, Writers on Jane Kenyon, Graywolf Press, 2005.

time. Only recently have I begun to give more attention to creating a writing space and to surrendering the compulsive need to keep the vicissitudes of ordinary tasks in first place.

Through life, I have hunted for community, which I had as a member of the church, through acumen, macrobiotics, and through various church affiliations. These attempts have all come to naught. (See Part 4 on Lucifer).

I have tried to come to community through writing groups and have been moderately successful, through connecting with other poets. A recent attempt was successful for a time and then was blown apart by the paranoid reaction of a group member to an innocent laugh on my part, at an incongruous phrase used by this writer in our small group. Although I was repentant and apologized in writing and speech I was never forgiven, and the group fell apart.

All this time I have satisfied my need to share my perceptions, my truth through my written memoir which has been the most rewarding endeavor so far. I have chosen to use the format of a personal letter through the memoir as a way of inviting an intimacy between the writer and reader. I continue to seek writing groups which may fulfill my need and desire for intimacy with a writing companion or two with whom to share my work.

In the meantime, writing my perceptions, my spiritual journey, and exploring my relationship to nature, to the birds and trees, to the water of the beautiful small lake or pond as some call it has greatly nurtured my soul. I have become my own best friend and have learned to honor and trust that friendship. This includes a growing awareness and relationship to my Higher Self, my spiritual center, which has sustained me and continues to inform me about my world and relationship to it. I have become kinder to myself and treated others with more caring and concern. My social relationships have been more tender and at the same time more circumspect. I am greeted with a wave and a smile by my neighbors and feel welcomed in most places I travel.

What is paramount to me is that I write and grow in spiritual consciousness. That is what I live to do, to write and to seek truth in living. I write in part to illuminate the mystery of my life, my spiritual evolution, and now with my memoir to share the journey with the reader in hopes that they too can join with me in the mutual sharing of the energy of our thoughts, feelings, and insights about living itself. That we can reflect and mirror the amazing bits and pieces of our lives so that our celebration of life can be enriched, deepened, and shared. I write to know and acknowledge Spirit that lives within me and directs me.

Given my past lives as a nun, it was no surprise that I was drawn to the physical sanctuary of the church where I eventually became a member of the Episcopalian Church because I loved the ritual of the casting of incense, the communion of the bread and wine as the body and blood of Christ and the Anglican liturgy. And I hoped to find a community of kindred spirits there. I was a cog in the administration of procedures which supported the church: I was a member of the committee which screened candidates to enter training to become priests. I attended meetings, dealing with people who were more interested in finding a place in the church rather than in sharing the sense of passion for Christ that I felt.

Nevertheless, I felt the spirit of Christ within me unfulfilled because I was not comfortable sharing with those who did not seem to experience a divine connection on the same level as I did. Over a ten -year period, I was active with the Anglican women of the Church and with Creation Spirituality and still could not get past a glass wall I felt and saw. It kept me at a distance from an intimacy and closeness which I strongly desired, but which seemed to elude me no matter what I tried.

At about this time I was invited to attend a talk on the use of crystals in healing at a local college near my home. Randall Baer, the presenter, kept referencing the book, The Keys of Enoch authored by James Hurtak, Ph.D., Ph.D. I was intrigued, purchased the book, and began to read. In my opinion this book is an intergalactic bible which Dr. Hurtak had received through a long and complicated download in 1973 and which contained information about the sciences seen through a spiritual lens. This book was fully layered with complex material in physics, genetics, mathematics, biology, astronomy, and other sciences. A spiritual portal, the reading of this book left me feeling that this was a book written in code, much like the traditional Bible, and the Keys included Hebrew fire letters for each of the 64 codes in the book. But it was difficult to understand because of its complexity so I began to attend workshops and classes with Dr. Hurtak and to delve into various archeological remnants that Dr.Hurtak and his wife Dr. Desiree Hurtak visited and studied. I felt that suddenly I had graduated from high school represented by the traditional church into a "spiritual Ph.D. program" that Dr. Hurtak offered. I also felt that I no longer belonged in the traditional church because I had access to a larger understanding of a spiritual world through the work with Dr. Hurtak. Since I was no longer drawn to attending church, I put my efforts into the study of The Keys of Enoch, combined with study of the traditional Bible which fed me spiritually and socially. I realized that in this lifetime, I could not return to a monastery setting, although I had thought about it over the years, because I had to develop an individual ego, an "I" and a higher self that would sustain me through the next epoch.

For a time, the work with Dr. Hurtak continued to feel deeply fulfilling. It was exciting to attend conferences in various sacred geographic positions in the USA and to hear about other studies that related to spiritual evolution on our planet from other parts of the world. This continued for about ten years or more until I began to feel a change in the direction of the work, a pressure to comply with chanting the 72 names of God in a fervent and overly zealous manner. This made me uncomfortable. But the more important facet was that I felt this study had become patriarchal, more like a religion, which had de-emphasized the feminine or female aspect of the sacred, and its connection to the Divine.

During this time, I also studied Buddhism based on the Bon traditions, because I wanted to learn more about healing with sound. Our studies included sound healing using bowls and gongs. I was very interested in using sound as a healing tool and expanded my studies: I worked with the Globe Institute of California to integrate sound healing knowledge, to master the use of gongs and metal bowls I studied with Mitch Nor, and to work with tuning forks as a healing tool I studied with John Beaulieu ND.

Learning about the Bon religion appealed to me greatly because it was based on the feminine archetype, the earth as mother. I traveled to Tibet with Tom Kenyon where we toned with the monks in monasteries, met with the nuns and delivered mittens, scarves, pencils, and art supplies to the orphans of Tibet. For some time, I benefited greatly from meditation practices and felt the Buddhist had discovered a way to navigate life beyond death, through the Bardo. At the same time, I learned that long ago, the Bon Religion, which was a shamanic thread, had merged with the patriarchal structure of Buddhism and had become a Bon- Buddhist philosophy. With this integration, the female archetype was de-emphasized. After time, I started to feel uncomfortable with the lack of equality for women in this lifestyle. Also, I did not feel a deep connection, or resonance with the lamas, perhaps in part because of the language barrier. I chose to leave to devote more energy to the Hurtak work, until I let both Buddhism and the Keys of Enoch work fall to the back burner because *my "I" consciousness* was growing and asking for something which I was not getting from these studies.

During a period of dormancy, I began to study qi gong and the Tao through a local master, Michael Winn, Healing Tao, USA. I found his exercises and philosophy very profound, especially the teachings of the Wandering Tao. I felt the body movement connected to the Qi Gong work healing and helpful to calming the mind as well as instilling the body with harmonious, beneficial energy. I still practice qi gong to maintain a balance of physical and non-physical energy, qui.

Still searching for a philosophy and a spiritual community of like-minded individuals which held the feminine archetype as central to the connection with the earth, I chanced to see information on the Sophia Grail Circle workshop (based on Rudolf Steiner's philosophy) and through that workshop connected with the anthroposophical group in my area. This group has at its center the feminine archetype in the form of Sophia which is directly connected with the Christ Impulse energy. Moreover, this feminine archetype, Sophia, was part and parcel of connection with the earth and reverence for nature. This was an added and necessary plus for me: it felt like the teachings had captured the essential aspects of what needed to be addressed spiritually and explored on my spiritual journey.

I found the work of Rudolf Steiner and the mediations lead to the supersensible world, the world of Christ and other beings connected to the spiritual world. His work also incorporated a body movement called Eurythmy, similar to Qi Gong but with different intentions. Nevertheless, I found both to be a beautiful expression of connection and healing with divine forces enacted through the physical body. Additionally, I was able to connect with group members on a deep intimate level both philosophically and spiritually. At last, I felt a sense of intellectual and spiritual kinship with those who were earnestly pursuing the *internal I AM* and the evolution *of ego consciousness,* which was stressed in the Spiritual Science of Rudolf Steiner. It seemed to me that a spiritual path had been cultivated through the Spiritual Science that was opened to all, without dogma, and within the context of occult knowledge of the cosmic world. Steiner presented a way for humanity to pursue the spiritual path while keeping Christ and Sophia, who represents connection to the earth, at the center of the teachings. (See Appendix B for more).

My Mother: her adult history

Dear Reader,

Separating from my mother, the major force in my life, was the path I needed to take to establish my own sovereignty and to claim my own mind and voice. Here is a sketch of her adult history that shows her journey into a position of prominence.

This woman, whom I call my mother, had many aspects to her, most of which were unknown to me as a child. As an adult I was able to connect the dots to give you an overview of her life, her accomplishments, and the ways in which she overcame many obstacles including the loss of her father and poverty, spurred on by depression and later WWII. She was a first generation American with her family coming from Austria. One of seven children, she lived in a small home in the country with her five living siblings, a brother and three sisters. She believed in the value of education because it was a path which would allow her to escape poverty and anonymity.

At the age of 19 or 20, my mother left home and the Catholic Church when she moved to New York having married my father. At that time, my parents joined St. Bartholomew's Episcopal Church where they attended social events. As transplants from Pennsylvania and without nearby connection to family for both mother and father, in New York City, they reached out to the community by joining St. Bart's Episcopal Church, although religion was not their primary concern. What my mother was most concerned about was her free schooling at Hunter College where she worked very hard to gain her degree and graduated Cum Laude.

It seemed from all appearances that she was mainly interested in being valued as a productive member of society, as a person of stature and authority in the community. Much later she joined the Presbyterian Church where it was politically correct to become an active member because membership connected you with other members of the community who were powerful and important. Likewise, membership in the local country club offered the same advantages, which she pursued. My father, however, was unwilling to actively engage in most of the country club activities or to accompany her in doing the same. My mother was left to pick and choose those activities which did not require a husband to be present.

My mother was skeptical of anything that did not further her goal which was establishing a secure position where she could be admired and respected as a member of the community.

Spiritual issues were not top priorities for her, and she did not spend anytime nurturing religious beliefs. Her main objective was to be respected and held in high regard in the community.

I recall one occasion where one of her associates took issue with something she said or did. I did not know the particulars and I am not sure she did, but she was horrified and aghast that someone would brush her aside and ignore her. This was deeply offensive to her, especially since she had no way of remediating the situation which apparently continued for some time. I know she avoided this individual whenever she could and felt very constricted in social situations when this individual was present. Mostly she was annoyed that this individual was interfering with the image she was trying to present and maintain in the community. Perhaps too my mother feared that there was negative gossip about her from this woman. My mother had no faith that this would be resolved in any constructive way and simply endured, trying to ignore the situation.

My mother created walls behind which many of her personal feelings and doubts lived. I did not hear about those because she felt uncomfortable sharing those. Instead, she built an image based on her need to be admired and be seen in a positive light. She did not want to be publicly vulnerable, to show her sad or more sensitive feelings, or even her anger in any social context. Her shadow side was reserved for those at home, my father and myself. We got the brunt of her frustration, disillusionment, her rage at those aspects of life which impeded her progress toward establishing a loveable and acceptable image.

After they divorced, my father called her *selfish*. I don't think she was so much selfish as she was self-absorbed and driven by the need to look good, to be admired account and were. Being both controlling and abandoning meant that anyone who lived with her and did not fulfill her needs was in danger of being ignored or belittled. She looked for love and admiration and if she felt loved or admired, she could view you with loving fire in her eyes. But if she didn't like you or you had diminished her in some way, she could just as easily throw you under the bus. You were now dirt, worthless. The walls she created were built on her need to be loved and be seen in a positive light. She did not want to be publicly vulnerable, to show her sad or more sensitive feelings, or even her anger in any social context.

Sometimes a person or event would occur outside the home that would make her feel loved and the walls would dissolve. Sometimes an unpredictable event would occur which would overshadow her feelings of being unloved and the walls would disappear for the most part. Most of the time, the only thing that could be done was to wait it out, endure the cold atmosphere that permeated the home, and wait anxiously looking for an opening, or a chance to shift the scene to something new which would overshadow the tense situation. It was difficult to know if you were in favor or out of favor. There was always a shadow, an ambiguity, a need to watch carefully lest you step on a land mine and have your calm shattered in an unforeseen and unexpected moment, when she turned her back on you. Since these were unexpected moments of losing a sense connection or affection you had, being hypervigilant was a way of life. Never secure and never safe, I felt glad when I felt a sense of acceptance. At the same time, I knew I had to take in as much as possible in that moment because I could not count on it being long- lived.

Regarding her religious or spiritual life, near the end of her days, she admitted to me that she was agnostic or skeptical about whether there was a God or not. Although she came from a family whose appearance and rituals were Catholic, she did not claim or honor the beliefs that accompanied church going, the confession, church attendance or the prescriptive dietary recommendations like eating fish on Friday for example. Nor did she encourage me to attend but did not stop me when I decided to join the Catholic Church and receive a Holy Communion.

That is, in part, where my spiritual life began while she remained a social Presbyterian, attending the church that her friends and those who were seen as "pillars of the community" attended.

She was an intellectual and scholar, listed in the Director of American Scholars and the Who's Who of American Women. Her interest in history led to her to writing several published articles for the Journal of Baltic Studies, historical accounts for the history of Swain School, Allentown, PA and a Chapter in Allentown 1762-1987, a 225-Year History, Lehigh County Historical Society, 1987. In this last publication, my mother described Allentown's growth and development between the years 1945-1952, following the Second World War.

The Luciferian forces had pushed her beyond her meager upbringings and poverty and helped her to land a position with authority and respect in her community. She was a model for the enterprising and independent woman as she had become someone well known and acknowledged for her contributions to the educational and literary community. She was more comfortable being outside the home than in it. Her capacity to be vulnerable and to be nurturing to her family was limited and inconsistent so that I could not depend on empathic support from her. It simply was not there. But what financial support I did get, helped to launch me on my own journey toward establishing a position of professional authority through which I could contribute to the community and support myself.

TRIP TO MOTHER'S HOMETOWN: HER FAMILY HISTORY

When Emma, my mother was about seventy, we visited Bridgeville, her birthplace, just outside of Pittsburgh, she directed me to drive to a small street high up on a hill. The home was a bungalow perhaps 20-30 feet. It looked like one story, but it might have been two. It was quite small. She explained to me this home was where she and her three sisters and one brother were raised. I was astonished as to how seven people could live in such a small dwelling, probably no privacy as all the girls had to share a room. Not sure at all where Tony, the only living male sibling lived. The first born was a boy who died shortly after birth. A second boy Vincent was born after my mother's birth, but he died shortly thereafter, leaving the five siblings, one boy and three girls. Emma sat in the car wistfully eyeing this home, a frown on her face. She didn't say it but her look, both sad and amazed by this smallness of this house. I imagine that she remembered seeing it through child eyes. Now through adult eyes, her home was reduced in size, eclipsed to doll house size from her early memory.

During that trip we visited Helen, Emma's mother's grave, situated in a small church graveyard a few miles away from her childhood home. I think her father's grave was there as well, but I am not sure at this point. I know that she mentioned that her father was an orphan raised by the Jesuit priests. Her father Paul was gifted with language, so when Paul and Helen first immigrated from Austria to New York City, her father, knowing at least five languages, worked as a translator for the Cunard line. Apparently, he surrendered this job in New York City, to move to the Pittsburgh area so that his wife, Helen could be close to her sisters who had settled there. Helen and her sisters had married men who farmed but Paul was not comfortable with the farming life and eventually resorted to drinking as a way of escaping the pain of being jobless and dislocated. Nevertheless, my mother remembers her father in the mornings reading the Bible in German. She remembers his soft voice, and the way his voice softened the air at the beginning of each day. Perhaps she also remembered his pain but did not speak about it. If she had, she might have realized that she was returning to the city that brought him employment and a meaning to his life. Perhaps inadvertently she hoped for the same chance for herself that he once had.

From photos of her growing up years, I know that she loved to dance and was in a ballet costume complete with long flowing wings and a gossamer skirt, her face turned to one side with a wistful smile. She said that her older sister, Ethyl took care of her and would save money to buy her a special outfit. Perhaps being Ethyl's favorite was a problem for the other two sisters, Polly and Bertha, who were apparently very competitive with each other. Emma heard them arguing quite often and said her mother had pitted one against the other, so much so that Emma could not stand the drama. Instead, she retreated into the world of literature and became the one who excelled in school. She substituted the worlds she read about for the world she needed to escape.

Emma did not speak about her sisters very much, if all. She did imply that her childhood ended just two months before she was to graduate from high school when her father passed away. She did not know the circumstances of his death other than he had a boil on his neck which did not heal and he had diabetes. She was not sure if he was being treated for it. In any case, the look of wistful longing in her eyes said it all. He had been her voice of calm and peace in a difficult family and now he was gone. As she mentioned his passing, her eyes teared and the surrounding air breathed of sorrow and loss.

I looked at her, wanted to squeeze her hand. But it was not safe to do that because I did not know if she would accept it for find it an intrusion. An armor of impenetrable pride surrounded my mother. I would have liked to question her about her living conditions with three sisters and a brother, would have liked to know where she found a safe place to read or if she found safety in a local library close by. But to pierce the veneer of her pride never seemed possible. Her armor was held tight by her shame, by her need to be loved, which she doubted would happen if the chinks in her armor showed. This steel covering protected her tender side, which was not visible. Only a sense of pressure and self-protection suggested an immense well of feeling behind this exterior cover. Oh, how I longed to tear the veneer away, but I was afraid of what I might find. What If I was looking into a chasm filled with deep longing and grief over the death of her father? I was not sure I could bear to witness her dissolving into tears. She needed to present herself as a strong role model, someone who was worthy of admiration, not someone who was vulnerable and not in control. I needed that from her as well to avoid my own precious tears which might fall unnoticed on the ground she walked on. Through time my tears were held in suspension until I found a safe person who could hold them with me. That was a long time in coming into my life. I did not have the courage to see my mother 's brokenness and I did not have the courage to share my vulnerability with her. It did not feel safe.

Now I ask myself what If I had challenged her? What If I had been able to challenge that veneer of protection, of gently creating a place of safety where she could release the old grief over the loss of her beloved father, over the loss of connections to her family, over the loss of deep connection to her own daughter? I might see myself saying, "I know you still feel sad about what happened to Paul your father. I know you want to feel loved, and I know that you won't think you will be, if you are vulnerable and not maintaining a "strong" image." "No," that would never go over, I thought. That might raise her amour even more. But maybe I could say I too have tears and I would like to be able to share them with you. I too feel abandoned and unwanted as perhaps you may have felt with your family. I too need to be loved and held. Let me hold you, dear mother, and let us be real with each other in this moment. I know she was carrying the shame of abandoning her family which stopped me from confronting her guarded and inaccessible self. I was carrying the pieces of her she had planted in me and ironically this had become my unwitting albatross.

BUT BACK TO MY MOTHER'S TRIALS:

The depression came just after the stock market crash in 1929. Work was difficult to find and whatever wages were earned went to support the family. With her father dead and her mother, a homemaker, still speaking German or Czech, it was up to the children to support the family. It was very unclear as to who worked and who did not. But finally, Emma got a job with Dun and Bradstreet where she met Henry, my father, when she was 19 or 20. He pursued her until she finally gave in and decided to marry him. It took a long time for her to give in because she had liked, perhaps even loved, another man in her Bridgeville circle. But he had no ambition and worked at the steel mill, and he could not provide a life beyond poverty, but my father could. Marriage to my father was her exit plan, to live in New York City, and to have the opportunity for education beyond high school. This was the city where her father had flourished and found meaning through his work, a city where she too hoped to find a meaningful life.

And in fact, she was the only one in her family to earn a college degree and she graduated with a BA. And after 10 years or so, she went on to earn a master's degree and finally a Ph.D. degree while working as high school teacher, she had achieved her intellectual goals, but she was emotionally unfulfilled in her relationship to my father. Although they supported each other's intellectual supports, emotionally they were miles apart.

Her determination to lift herself from poverty and to extract herself from the drama of small-town life where lifestyles were limited was an unrelenting motivation. She was willing to sacrifice her connections to her birth family to pursue an intellectual life she could not have had in Bridgeville. In that sense, she followed in her father's footsteps, returning to New York City which once gave him employment and purpose in life. I think she hoped to do the same.

While she wrote letters and sent money and sometimes night gowns and slippers to her mother, her contacts with her sisters were minimal. As I was growing up, she would take me to visit my cousins, aunts, and uncles in Bridgeville for two weeks during the summer but she did not stay to visit with them and would return after two weeks to retrieve me, only to leave again until the next year. I guess she loved them and or felt guilty about abandoning the family. But I know she needed to find a life for herself in a city where she could get an education, use her mind, and fulfill her desires.

In the process, she sacrificed any close connections I might have had with my maternal grandmother and cousins as my relationships with them and short-lived. My maternal grandmother spoke little English, and communication was difficult or nonexistent. My maternal grandfather had been dead for many years. Summer times with my aunts, uncles, and cousins were brief, lasting for two weeks over several summers through my childhood and ending as I became a teenager. At that point, and my parents were more involved with their work and the community and so traveling across the state was not part of their plan.

When my mother was 40, she had a second child, my brother who was seventeen years younger than me, and raised during a time my parents had achieved financial security. He was just a baby when I entered college. My mother doted on him, even "owned" him, needed him emotionally, and did not allow me to spend one-on-one time with him. I did not feel she was open to negotiating time with him and so I decided to wait for some future moment and to concentrate on establishing independence in NYC.

When my brother was in grade school, Emma enrolled at Lehigh University to earn a Ph.D. in English. She was teaching high school English at the same high school I attended as a teenager. She spent long hours putting the yearbook, the Canary, together as well as teaching English classes and completed her course work at Lehigh University for her Ph.D. degree. This occurred while my brother who was in elementary school. For after school care for my brother, my mother enlisted two elderly sisters, Helen, and Louise, who lived nearby. These wise and wonderful Scottish old maids were also teachers, Helen in elementary school and Louise an English teacher, like my mother, working at the same high school. My father was otherwise working as a professor and not available for after-school childcare. For me to survive emotionally, I realized I could not return to PA and the biological family. To establish my voice and sovereignty, I had to move away from the family. I decided to move back to NYC, my birthplace, where I could engage in therapy, could maintain some separation from my biological family and could grow, and learn to live unrestricted by old patterns from my growing up years.

With time, my mother achieved her goal of having a respected position in a community.

In the end, she was a model of academic success because of her position in the academic world.

But the price she paid emotionally was estrangement from her sisters, her brother, and her mother. Her reluctance to swallow her pride, even with my father and I, created a chasm, a distance which left a vacuum, an absence of emotional closeness or vulnerability. If I could ask her today if she made the right choice, even with this sacrifice, I think she would say that she had. But she might also add, if she had been more vulnerable, she regretted creating a void in the family, for my father, my brother, and me which was never bridged and which she regretted. Ultimately when my brother reached his eighteenth year, my father left, and they divorced.

My mother's lack of emotional involvement in my life, meant that we both missed out on a more intimate connection. Painfully, I realized I had been raised by a mother who did not know me, and coincidentally I did not really know her either, even though we lived together for the first eighteen years of my life.

When I was thirty-eight, my mother, age 60, remarried and spent the next seventeen years travelling the world with her new physician husband. She felt loved, appreciated, and supported most of the time and her security allowed her to love and respect me when I received my Ph.D. She outlived her second husband by 20 years and achieved professional recognition and a successful marriage during that time. Of this she can be proud. She modelled independence and intellectual accomplishment, having a respected position as a teacher at the university and in the community. She was admired, loved, and respected and sometimes feared by those closest to her.

My Father and Ancestral Grandfather

Dear Reader,

You may be wondering about my other half of the family dynamic, my father.

My father's background will explain so much of why he treated me the way he did, and what he himself had to endure as a child and as a young adult going to college, first time away from home on his own.

My father, the only boy of three children, was expected to become a pastor and was sent, you guessed it, Muhlenberg College, his namesake, with that plan in mind. However, in his childhood he had learned to play the organ and piano under the stern and punitive guidance of his dominating mother and so spent much of his "free" time, practicing, and playing for various churches and social groups. While in college, he was offered a music scholarship at an Ohio University. He approached his parents about it who said they would cut off his funds if he pursued this desire. They expected him to be a pastor and lead the people to the church as part of the Lutheran heritage. Secretly, he wanted to learn to be a musical conductor of orchestral works. But that dream fell by the wayside as he feared the lack of money and support from his family.

Once he was able to escape to college, he could begin to have a degree of freedom from his mother's incessant programming and begin to open his mind to other avenues, which he did. As it turned out, he stayed at Muhlenberg College but did not end up being a pastor. Instead, he graduated with a degree in economics and history. I don't know if his parents cut him off at that point, but I know money continued to be tight. No surprise, there because issues with money which went along with being poor and relying on heaven for your riches had been instilled in him. It was sinful to want more and so for many years he lived on the edge financially, making just enough to keep family together, to finance his advanced educational degree in Economics and ultimately to become an Economics professor. It is no surprise too that he ended his academic career at Muhlenberg College as head of the Economics Department, the very same college established by your ancestors which ultimately became your alma mater.

Here is the real kicker---his parents, in particular his mother was obsessed with the words of the Bible which they quoted endlessly to him. It was not possible to have ordinary conversation as the only words that could be tolerated where scriptural repetitions. All else was deemed nonessential or even a distraction from the "truth" of the written Biblical word. My father was choked, beaten down by these phrases, repeated, night and day. I am sure he could not wait to get away from this "religious brainwashing" (my term) that his mother had been spewing at him since he was very young.

His father, Charles, did not stand up for him or for himself. I heard the story that his mother convinced Charles, a homeopathic doctor trained at Hahnemann, to give up his practice. His mother thought Charles was too passive and introverted and she did not think he could handle the social and business end of running a clinical practice. She pressured him to quit his profession and work for a factory as an accountant, a job he hated. He was to come home for lunch every day and return to work, bring home the paycheck and keep his mouth shut…. which he did. It may be no surprise to learn, he allowed his wife to wear him down. Between hating the job and trying to escape his wife, he became almost speechless. He was of slight build, a shadow of himself and had relinquished his personal power and thus did little to support you against the admonishing tirades of his wife. My father and his father were out-numbered by his two sisters, and out-voiced by his mother. Everyone in the family was outgunned by Laura his mother who directed all affairs, like a military captain who must be obeyed, or else verbal and perhaps physical abuse would ensue.

Understandably, my father rejected the religious indoctrination and as far as I knew never had developed a positive or supportive relationship with God. He did become a pillar of the Lutheran Church and gave lectures on the history of the Lutheran Church in America to local churches in the area, but he did not fulfill the traditional legacy of becoming a minister. How could my father feel anything but contempt because when he had been so bludgeoned by religiosity. His mother poisoned the path on which he might have trod. Still, he remained supportive of the church in another way.

Throughout life, he carried a resentment of the restrictive and punitive measures that he was subjected to by his mother and in fact he told my brother how much he hated his own mother. He continued to keep himself locked into a default position, teaching economics, and performing on organ in a variety of churches as a kind of hobby. His family's ideas about money lingered on and he did not see any need for giving himself or me the freedom to explore musical or other options which would require financial investment of varying amounts.

A self-fulfilling prophecy: he never had enough money and money was always tight especially in our family. When we moved from West Oak Lane, PA to Jenkintown, PA so my father could finish his Ph.D. at New York University, I had only one red plaid pleated wool skirt and one white nylon blouse in my wardrobe which I wore to school daily and continued to do so until the early fall when we moved again. Even though we lost money on the Jenkintown home because we sold our home after only nine months, my father received an offer to be Dean at Muhlenberg College in Allentown, PA which he accepted. (Perhaps it was to finally show the College that he was worthy of respect and position on his own terms). I know that he mentioned while he was a student at Muhlenberg College, he received a lot of teasing about being named after the patriarch of the Lutheran Church in America, Henry Melchior Muhlenberg, and about being very short and slight of figure. Unlike the young boy, Rocky, in the Bogdanovic, 1985 movie, *Mask*, who also had a lot of teasing about his physical appearance but found a way to neutralize it, my father had no idea how to deal with this. His resentment of having to study a subject, not music, was overlayed with your resentment about being teased about your "unfortunate" name which seemed deep and never- ending.

We moved to Allentown, PA so my father could fulfill his new role as Dean of Faculty, a political and social position he was ill prepared to assume. In my opinion, he had neither the social or political skills to comfortably fulfill this role and ended up resigning after seven years because of the distress and betrayal he felt by the administration. But he stayed at Muhlenberg and remained a professor and head of the Economics Dept probably for financial reasons until his retirement in 1979.

During this time, he continued to act out the old patterns and beliefs he had been raised with the notion that children should be seen and not heard. This idea lived on the edge of expectation along with never taking risks which might bring more leisure and more enjoyment, but which might cost something financially. The sense that religion was a social structure for the community and had little to do with faith or relationship to God dominated our household along with the sense that it was improper to speak about feelings. The overall belief that individuals had to pay the price interminably for living under the confines of what their parents or ancestors had culled for them, without rescue, dominated us. This was like an octopus, comprised of a delimiting and restrictive belief system, which limited permission to explore potentials, take risks to grow beyond what was envisioned as a possible future. This repressive force was overlaid with guilt and shame which continued to gnaw at my father and was projected on to me as well. He never really gained freedom from those restraints, and he tried to make my mother and me live within these restrictive boundaries, which to some extent we did just to survive in the household.

As an adult, my mother told me that when we lived in NYC and I was seven years old, she had wanted to order a child's coat which had a little fur collar, but my father refused to agree to that purchase because it was too extravagant and unnecessary. In my mind, I can hear your bitter angry voice say, "She doesn't need that." Mother capitulated to keep peace in the family, but she resented doing so and never forgave him for his lack of generosity toward me, for his stringent and even punitive attitude toward spending money beyond the bare necessities for me. His vision and sense of what was possible was curtailed by the bare bones constrictions of his family which believed that anything more than the essentials was sinful and unholy.

This intergenerational programming of the mind was not challenged at that time, but were seeded in my mother, and in me as my father's daughter. I admit that as far as I can remember, I was not physically or sexually abused by my father, but neither was I held, or loved or told I was precious to him. The emotional and mental constructions and constrictions that my father continued to live by, remained in my head and were deafening to say the least. As an adult of 33 years old, and without a career at that time my father asked me in a derogatory tone, "When are you going to grow up?" This was more of a reprimand than a question. I had no clue as I was lost and still searching for my identity and for the freedom to find myself without being dogged by failure and humiliation. These fears grew from the ways in which my father demeaned me, talked to me as if I didn't know anything and that he knew everything that was important. My father did not think I had anything important to say so he did not take the time to listen or ask what was on my mind. He had little or no respect for me. I think my father tried to impress others with his diatribes on economic issues and his authoritarian posturing.

My father represented the Ahrimanic forces for me, a reflection of how he had been raised. He insisted on following the rules, on being content with doing what was tried and true. For example, he was asked to be an economic consultant in Laos, which would have required a temporary relocation of the family for a period. He refused to consider or give this opportunity much thought. He ended up being right to make the decision he did because war and social upheaval erupted about the time we would have gone. Still, the fact that he would not consider this possibility exemplified his reluctance to think outside the box, or to expand into new territories.

His relationship with me was fraught with authoritarian pronouncements about what I needed to do or not do. He had his own schedule of events which he did not like to alter in any way. For example, when I needed to have a ride to and from my waitressing job at Howard Johnson's restaurant, which was about ten minutes from our home, he would come to pick me up, somewhat wordless, and driving fast to get home and finish whatever he was doing. I had interrupted his schedule and he showed his displeasure by withdrawing.

The tone of his language was rough, demanding, and unforgiving. He would say, "Sit down and eat now." Or "You forget to get the napkins, get them now." Or "Why can't you look where you are going?" I don't believe I ever heard him say," I love you" or "You look pretty today." He did not claim me as his little girl, rather I felt like an imposition in his life, something that robbed him of silence that he required to think or that took him away from a task which he preferred to do rather than to be with me. I did not feel wanted or needed in his life.

I felt like a nuisance, an imposition to him and someone he would rather not have to deal with.

When choosing a college, I did manage to state what I wanted, and my father somehow listened. When I was preparing to choose a college, I was told we only had money to choose a college on the tuition exchange list, a list afforded to him because he was Dean of Faculty and a faculty member of Muhlenberg College. The list earmarked several colleges that were willing to waive tuition in exchange for allowing the relative of a faculty member to attend the schools on the list. Three colleges stood out as possible candidates: Wittenberg and Ohio Wesleyan, both in Ohio, and Douglass College, on the Rutgers campus in New Jersey. My father and I travelled to both Ohio schools as my father wanted me to choose an Ohio school, (and relive the schooling he had failed to pursue many years before). While visiting, I was able to speak with some of the female students at both Ohio schools and was disgusted and let down to find the women, focused on boys, clothes, dates, and the next party. I learned that the Ohio schools had sororities that dominated the social life at each of those schools. Although that was not the number one deciding factor, it was a definite black mark against the Ohio schools to my way of thinking. The focus on dating and parties reminded me of my high school years which I mostly disliked, because of the cliques and the superficiality of seeking a date or a husband. We were only eighteen with our lives ahead of us. Where was the interest in learning and thinking? I wanted to learn and explore the world and college was a way to begin to do that. Obviously not primarily for them.

But then we visited Douglass College, and I was impressed with the women who seemed much more intelligent and open to possibilities. They were interested in ideas and culture as well as dating, but seemed less cliquish and more open to talking about any number of issues, including the state of the world. Wow. I also noted that Douglass College had no sororities, which I preferred as I thought they were artificial clubs drawing women together based on popularity and false comradery rather than shared mutual interests about the world at large or personal growth. Since Douglass College was in New Jersey and thus a stone's throw from NYC, my hometown, I knew that travel to various cultural events was possible. And I yearned for contact with the cultural experience that I knew was possible in New York.

These three factors, the intelligence and open mindedness, the proximity to New York, and the lack of sororities made my decision easy. Douglass College was my first choice. I told my father about my decision. He reluctantly complied and allowed me to attend Douglass, although he thought I had made an error in judgement. Although I felt I made the right decision regarding the college to attend and still do, I resented the fact that my possibilities were limited by the college exchange list by which I had to draw my possible choices. Again, it was about being restricted by money to a limited number of college choices at a time when both father and mother were fully employed and could afford to consider broader options.

In fact, originally when I reached eighteen my father said he was finished supporting me. So perhaps the College Tuition Exchange program was a concession that my father could live with because in fact it cost my parents very little money to send me to college. He could justify supporting me in college because it was a small expense. Fortunately, my mother felt differently, but that is another story.

Much later in life, I chose to enroll in a doctoral program to become a psychologist. After I paid my way through school with some financial help from my mother, received my degree, and established a clinical practice in Allentown, PA my father said to me, "You can do what you want, now that you earn six figures." Again, my father's resentment about money, or not having enough money dripped like red poison in the air between us. I knew that I had broken with tradition, had begun to learn the importance of communication, had put myself through years of therapy, had learned the importance of having and sharing feelings as well as thoughts and as a result had established a career which I loved, and which allowed me to be financially independent. I had taken a risk (many risks) and they had paid off.

Fortunately, I did not have the outpouring of religiosity which my paternal grandparents used as a weapon, a battering ram against my father, a battering iron which crushed and wounded my father, beat him down, disempowered him so he could not see beyond the choices which were limited and circumscribed. This meant that I was free to engage in some religious practices like getting a Holy Communion at age seven which he permitted, and which allowed me the chance to take a path which brought me the knowledge and connection through religion and later through spirituality. I was free to explore a spiritual presence, within myself which I have come to honor and rely on. I appreciate that space and that untinged avenue that was left open to me.

Happily, his influence was laced with moments which embodied Luciferian forces which helped me to become independent. I experienced these traces as moments of freedom in teaching me to ride a bicycle, to drive a car, and moments of beauty as I learned to play the piano. However, even though my father and I both loved music, he was not a forgiving piano teacher for me or I daresay anyone else. He was stern and had no clue about how to teach an eleven-year-old how to play the piano. With so much tension around practicing and my fear of criticism from my father, I quit the piano after about six or eight months.

The positive take-away from this was I learned to read music, but the negative take-away was that I was terrified to play for anyone else for fear of criticism. This extended to my adult years as I decided to learn to resume my connection with music, rather than the piano, I chose to play the harp. But I had to neutralize the fear of playing for an audience so that I could play for others and enjoy doing so.

SPIRITUAL LINEAGE: MY ANCESTRAL GRANDFATHER
HENRY MELCHIOR MUHLENBERG

From Hanover Germany, my father's ancestors came to the United States in about 1742 as part of a calling to begin the Lutheran Church in North America. My ancestral grandfather Henry Melchior Muhlenberg born 1711, had three sons. One became the First Speaker of the First House of Representatives, Frederick A. Conrad Muhlenberg, elected April 1789. There was a tradition that the sons of the early ancestors become Lutheran pastors and the head of a church. My father was also expected to do the same but, in the end, became a professor. Another ancestor, Peter Muhlenberg, did start a church in the mid 1700's, but his history which occurs at the beginning of the Revolutionary War, is rather dramatic as was already mentioned. Subsequently becomes Peter Muhlenberg becomes a Brigadier General in the Continental Army which is instrumental in bringing victory to the colonies in their effort to win sovereignty from England. Muhlenberg College, in Allentown PA was established in his name Peter M. Muhlenberg, with his statute, he in military uniform riding his horse, rifle at his side, on the campus lawn at the college.

The harp was one of the six musical instruments my great grandfather played. In addition to our spiritual connection, playing the harp made me feel even more connected to my ancestral grandfather.

I have been in search of a spiritual connection in my biological family and found none. That is until I came across this ancestral paternal grandfather. I don't how many *greats* it would take to indicate how many generations ago this ancestral great grandfather lived, but it is quite a few.

This was a connection which both surprised and delighted me, especially since I had no encountered anyone who was either religious or spiritual in my immediate or extended family. On my father's side of the family, religion was used as a bludgeoning weapon, so my father kept religion at arms-length. My mother's family went through the motions of following the Catholic rituals: communion, confession, and church going but I did not hear anything about spiritual passion or commitment which is why I wish to talk about my paternal grandfather named Henry Melchior Muhlenberg. Through several books and papers depicting his life, I learned about his passion for Christ and how this passion led him to move from Germany, to begin the Lutheran Church in an America, still wild and untamed in the 1700's.

It began over 300 years ago but I didn't know it. At the same time "it" skipped many generations and came to rest within me, much to my surprise. It certainly was not present or demonstrated in any way with my mother who was an acknowledged agnostic from a Catholic family or from my father who was born into a Lutheran family and whose great grandfather many generations ago had organized the Lutheran Church in America in the mid 1700's before the Revolutionary War.

The "it" is the experience of having been imbued and healed by the presence of Christ in my life. Or as Rudolph Steiner, the originator of anthroposophy would say, the Christ Impulse. This impulse which is a part of each human life, who embraces God no matter what religion or denomination, is marked by an openness of heart which embraces Divinity or Lifeforce as the central living force directing a person from within. My parents never acknowledged being led by their own Christ impulse. I don't think either parent was aware of such an impulse. In fact, in my father's case, the Lutheran religion and in particular the Biblical verses and teachings had been weaponized and used as a cudgel to beat anyone who attempted to speak on any terms that were not seen as religious, especially him. Conversation between my father and his parents was limited to quotes from the Bible led by his mother, who was like the sergeant at arms directing the flow of conversation and blocking any non-religious thoughts with condemnation and judgement. Although my father continued to speak to Lutheran congregations in various churches, it was mainly to speak about the history of the Lutheran Church in America and to promote the Lutheran Synod, the administrative body of the Lutheran Church, he spoke out of loyalty to his lineage, not out of love for it.

Several ancestors after this grandfather, Henry Melchior Muhlenberg, born 1711, were named Henry Melchior Muhlenberg and my father was one of them. This name, Henry Melchior Muhlenberg, became an albatross around my father's neck because of the yoke of expectation that came with it. He was supposed to become a minister as the sons of HMM's ancestors had become. He was expected to attend Muhlenberg College, named after the son of this grandfather, Peter Muhlenberg, which he did. And as an adult, he returned to Muhlenberg College to become Dean of Faculty for eight years, even though he was ill prepared to handle the politics that this position demanded.

Interestingly, although the sons of the original HMM became ministers, they devolved into other careers later in life. In 1801, Gotthilf Heinrich Ernest Muhlenberg became a botanist and discovered a species of bog turtle, named after him, Chemmys Muhlenbergii. (Attending a Sophia Grail workshop and gift store at the Kanuga Center near my home, I chanced to find a reproduction of this turtle because the name Muhlenbergii caught my attention. Apparently, the bog turtle lives in that area. The reproduction of the bog turtle is framed and hangs in the foyer of my home.)

HMM's second son, Frederick Muhlenberg, became the First Speaker of the First House of Representatives in America. The third brother Peter Muhlenberg is remembered as the namesake of Muhlenberg College. Peter Muhlenberg's statue, known as Pistol Pete, proudly holding a rifle at his side, graces the campus front lawn.

Like his brothers, Peter Muhlenberg also devolved. It is said that as the Revolutionary War was beginning, Peter Muhlenberg ascended the pulpit of his church to preach his last sermon. When he had finished, he said (and here I paraphrase), "There is a time to pray and a time to fight. Now is the time to fight." And with this declaration, he threw off his pastor's garment to reveal a soldier's uniform underneath. Off he went to battle the British, taking 300 of his countrymen with him. Later, he became a Brigadier General in the Continental Army during the Revolutionary War.

Like these ancestral cousins, my father's career also devolved. While attending Muhlenberg College in the 1930's, where he was to complete his schooling for the ministry, he was offered a scholarship in music at a school in Ohio. When his mother heard of this, she told him she would cut off his finances if he left Muhlenberg College. Fearing the worst, my father stayed at Muhlenberg where he was teased unmercifully about his name and his lineage. Having spent most of his young years playing organ and piano in church settings, he knew little about how to negotiate relationships with his peers. Knowing and loving music as he did, I think my father took refuge in the chapel at Muhlenberg playing the organ for services and for himself. Later during his tenure as Dean of Faculty and even later, in retirement, he continued playing the organ in that very same chapel.

He did graduate with his class in 1932, but with a degree in history, not in the ministry. He too had changed the course of his life and ultimately became a professor of economics. However, he failed to pursue his dream which was to become a symphony conductor. The burden of his background, of the yoke of expectation and the use of religion as a weapon of repression had done its worse to strip him of the self-esteem and the confidence, he needed to realize his true potential. Even in his later years, he admitted how much he hated his mother, and retained no positive memories of her or of his upbringing. This bitterness seared his soul and chained him to a history from which he attempted to free himself for his entire life.

The history of his grandfather and mine, Henry Melchior Muhlenberg, HMM, born 1711 in Germany, was entirely different. One of eight siblings, HMM came from a poor background and was able to attend the University only because a member of the community in which he lived subsidized his education. He loved his mother very much. When the call came to Halle University from America for a minister to organize the Lutheran Church in America, HMM was eager to go. Although he loathed leaving his elderly mother, he felt called to bring the Lutheran religion to America, in 1742.

During that time in his homeland, Germany, there was a great deal of religious unrest and conflict between the three main denominations: Lutheran, Catholic, and Reformed churches. Each vied for jurisdiction over the populations in the Hanover area of Germany. However, the people felt oppressed by pressure from the church for monetary support and loyalty without the benefit of providing spiritual inspiration and teaching to the congregations in general. The clergy were seen as *lax* in moral and spiritual integrity and people no longer looked to them for spiritual growth and inspiration. Out of this ferment rose a movement called Pietism. People who were drawn to Pietism felt they were missing the experience of their personal connection with Spirit or with God. They began to congregate in small groups, in individual homes, where they read passages from the Bible. They were looking for a spiritual experience within their own persons because they could not find inspiration from the clergy at large. This movement infiltrated the churches: some members remained in their denominations and became Pietists while others separated from their denominations and were call Separatists. This movement found a home at Halle University where HMM attended and where pietism had become a central part of the curriculum under the guidance of Professors Francke and Spensor. During this time, HMM became a committed Christian.

"…..the wounds of Christ healed my wounds, the merits of his death gave me life:

My thirst was quenched by Him the Living Spring." Stoever,[22] 27

At Halle University, HMM found himself fully immersed in Pietism. He was determined to do missionary work and at first thought he was destined for India. However, that calling fell through but a call to consolidate the Lutheran Church on American soil came soon afterward. HMM rose to this calling, even leaving his elderly mother in Germany, and sailed to America to begin the Lutheran Church, Stoever,[23] 42. Those at Halle University had been told that the spiritual state of our people in American is wretched to "cause us to shed tears of abundance," Stoever[24], 56. HMM set sail for American and reached Philadelphia in 1742,

HMM was imbued with the love of Christ and of the Bible. His schooling and relationship to his professors had reinforced the love of Christ and the Spirit of God which he reflected and mirrored in his sermons and in his relationships to his congregations. He felt that Christ was directing him to bring the word of God to those in the new world. He felt he was fulfilling his mission as an ambassador

---

[22] Stoever, M.L., A Memoir of the Life and Times of Henry Melchior Muhlenberg, Gettysburg, Theologicl Seminary, Philadelphia, 1911, 27.
[23] Ibid, Stoever, 42.
[24] Ibid, Stoever, 56.

of Christ, Stoever [25]46. HMM was seen by many as the "Luther" of America as in Martin Luther, the founder of Lutheranism in Europe. He was a representative of the Lutheran Church. But beyond that and more importantly for me, he was filled with the spirit of love, the love of the Christ impulse which he demonstrated to the people he ministered to. He had what R. Steiner calls the Christ Impulse, which is the sense of deep connection to the spirit of love that the Christ so represents and brought to the world through his presence and ultimate resurrection. Steiner, 2014.[26] This deep reverence for the love of Christ and the love of all that God created propelled him forward in America where he was able to engage and inspire people, not so much by religion but by his open spiritual connection to his experience of the love of Christ which was evident to those with whom he came in contact.

Henry Melchior Muhlenberg had not been openly revered by my father because his mother had weaponized religion and thus blocked any spiritual connection that might have developed. Through his upbringing my father's history of transgenerational trauma was siphoned and reinforced by his mother in the context of the Lutheran faith.

My father's parents were both born in the United States of America, but their roots began in America in 1742, before the American Revolution. From what I could gather, my father's ancestors were living in Germany at the time when Pietism was in full swing. As I came to understand it, Pietism was a movement born out of reaction to a demand for allegiance by clergy in Germany without spiritual roots or compensation.

According to Gordon,[27] the Rhine Valley Germany was in a state of great conflict and bloodshed because of a series of wars which included the Thirty Years War, the French Wars and the Wars of Frederick the Great. Three state churches remained after the Treat of Westphalia (1648) which were Catholic, Lutheran, and Reformed. Conflict, competition, and even persecution arose between these three

---

[25] Ibid, Stoever, 46.
[26] Steiner, Rudolph, The Christ Impulse and the Development of Ego Consciousness, Rudolph Steiner Press, 2014.
[27] Gordon, Ronald, Pietism in the 17th Century, Germany, 1998, 6.

church denominations. Out of these conflicts and a kind of totalitarian insistence on adherence to the rules and laws of each denomination came a fourth root, Pietism[28]. People were tired of following empty rules which left them unfulfilled. Pietists wanted to replace these rules and rituals with an intellectual and emotional connection to the spiritual world. The experience of spirit, through faith, through regeneration, and through a more internal, even mystical knowledge gleaned from focus on the internal or interior world of each supplicant became the move valued approach to religion. This new spiritual experience was fortified by Bible study and prayer to feel the effects of grace. Some remained in the domains of various churches, but others separated and became known as Awakened Souls or New Reformers. These insisted on a total separation from an "immoral society" and an adherence to the tenants of the Bible. Philip Jacob Spener was the father of Lutheran Pietism, who in his publication of Pia Desideria (Pious Desires) 1675 insisted on clergy reform for piety and cleansing of the soul. Spener wanted a re-introduction of primitive Christianity that would challenge the stability of Lutheranism. August Hermann Francke was an association of Spener who taught biblical studies at Halle University and the University of Leipzig, from which institution he was later expelled. He came to assist Spener in gaining a professorship at the University of Halle, which became a focus of pietist reform. Francke brough pietism to the community where he established orphanages to care for young children, hospital for the sick and schools to education pupils for the ministry and the sciences.

One very influential Pietist of the Separatist wing was Gottfried Arnold, a law student at the University of Wittenberg, who experience a spiritual awakening as a disciple of Spener. He later published "Wahre Abbildung", Real Images of Early Christians, 1696, which resulted in a position as professor at the University of Giessen where he met Hochmann, a leader in the Separatist Wing of Pietism. Hochmann had experience his spiritual awakening through Francke at the University of Halle. He followed the path of his mentor, Arnold, and said the only true church was a spiritual one that had separated from

---

[28] Frederick, William K., Henry Melchior Muhlenberg, "Patriarch of the Lutheran Church of America," Lutheran Publication House, Philadelphia, Pa. 1902.

denominationalism and especially from governmental interference. He later settled in Wittgenstein under the protection of Count Henrich Albrecht who promised refuge to persons experiencing harm for religious beliefs.

Alexander Mack, the son of a German miller, born in Schriesheim in 1679 was greatly influenced by Pietism. He asked Hockhamm to minister in Schriesheim who then used Mack's property for Pietist meetings. Pietism was a threat to the existing authorities and Hochmann was sentenced to hard labor while Mack escaped to Wittgenstein, a center of Pietist supporters.

Here the Pietists experienced communal practices, sharing goods in common, confession of sins, and spending many hours in prayer. Hochmann considered the pure church unnecessary while Mack believed the church and its sacraments still to be necessary. Gordon, 1998[29]

It was in this tumultuous religious atmosphere that my father's ancestor was challenged by his mentor at Halle university to begin the Lutheran church in America. In 1742, Henry Melchior Muhlenberg moved from Germany to America where he began a small congregation in an area outside of Philadelphia, Ephrata, and in other locals north of Philadelphia.

I don't know how many greats it would take to declare Henry Melchior Muhlenberg a great grandfather. Too many to count since he was born in 1711. Nevertheless, while doing research on his life I fell in love with him for many reasons. For one, his devotion and experience of his internal Christ Impulse resonated with mine. He was recruited by his professor Francke from Halle University to sail to America, to leave the comforts of home life in Germany, and to establish Lutheranism in the American colonies. At that time, American was Indian country with a few European settlers sailing to the continent to establish new freedoms for their spiritual life as well as their political and social life. As I learned from reading a condensation of HMM's

---

[29] Ronald Gordon, Pietism in the 17th Century, Germany, 1998,6.

condensed memoirs,[30] 1959, HMM encountered no asphalt roads, no housing developments, few if any inns, and no restaurants on his journeys. He traveled on horseback, through woods and across streams, in good weather and through rain and snowstorms, in the direction of settlements or individual homes that he was directed to. When those in small communities knew he was coming, they would arrange meetings so that they could hear him preach a sermon, at the beginning mostly in German. Sometimes it was in a private home and sometimes if a church building had been constructed it would be in that building.

As settlements evolved, and English-speaking persons congregated in their own communities, he also delivered his sermons in English. I learned too that he knew six different languages: German, English, French, Dutch, Bohemian (Czech), and a little Swedish. Mann, 1911[31]. He was also known to speak Latin who those who were educated and knew the language. He also played several different instruments including organ and harp (an instrument I also play). These skills and the kindness with which he treated people endeared him to them and helped him create an atmosphere of worship. Also, the settlers were hungry for spiritual teachings and HMM was able to deliver that to them gladly and with enthusiasm. As Mann, 1911[32], HMM went alone and was faithful to the trust (of establishing Lutheran congregations in America). Kunze, who was a minister as well called HMM the Luther of America (referring to Martin Luther). He was even compared to Elijah who was sent to redeem the Israelites just as HMM came to America to bring Lutheranism to this continent,[33] Mann, 1911. He was good natured, the master of many languages, was adept at theology, mental philosophy, medical science, and proclaiming the word of God. Mann,

---

[30] The Notebook of a Colonial Clergyman, Condensed from the Journals of Henry Melchior Muhlenberg, Trans and ed by Theodore G. Tappert and John W. Doberstein, Fortress Press, 1959.
[31] Mann, William J, D.D., the Life and Times of Henry Melchior Muhlenberg, General Council Publication Board, Philadelphia, 1911.
[32] Ibid, Mann, 526.
[33] Ibid, Mann, 525.

1911[34]. HMM often acted as an ombudsman in settling disputes over land or between clergy of the same or different denominations. As denominations were growing roots, they often teamed up, sharing the church facilities that were available. For example, the Lutherans and the Episcopalians together formed the Union Church in Salisbury NC in the 1800s. Personal conversation, Professor Freeze.[35]

HMM spent many years in the Philadelphia area, but travelled as far as New York, New Jersey, and as far south as Charleston, SC where he spent weeks preaching and teaching the word of God. He was acquainted with Benjamin Franklin, who ran the postal system and was in contact with the clergy and professors at Halle University in Germany where he was able to secure assist clergy who would come to America to help with the expansion of Lutheranism.

This was a time of the revolution in America and so the British troops were present as well as the American Indian, so it was not without danger that HMM travelled the countryside. It was said that some settlers were massacred by Indians. It was also said that the British were not welcoming to HMM as he posed a threat to them as a freedom loving man who did not align himself with their political tenants. Although he was conservative by nature, he believed in the freedom of all to choose.

This can be seen in his first-born son, John Peter Muhlenberg, who did return to Germany and was educated as a minister in the Lutheran Church at Halle University. However, as the revolution became very intense John Peter went to war and later became a Brigadier General in the Continental Army.

While this fighting was going on, HMM continued his ministry to the church. He came to reside in Trappe (Providence) PA and in 1784 was conferred a Doctor of Divinity Degree by the University of Pennsylvania, Mann,[36] 1911, among other honors which are may. He kept a diary of events which is how we know in detail about the hardships he endured while establishing the Lutheran Church

---

[34] Ibid, Mann, 528.
[35] Personal Conversation, Professor Freeze, October 27. 2021, St John' Lutheran Church, Salisbury NC.
[36] Ibid, Mann, 495.

in America, Henry Melchior Muhlenberg, 1959. Even though he was beleaguered by dropsy and swollen feet he continued to write daily. His last entry, dated 9/29/1787, included an extract from a verse written by Boehm (Kirchenbuch, no. 558) Mann, 1911[37].

> "A long road, before me lies
> Up to heaven'ly paradise
> My lasting home is there with Thee,
> Bought with Thy life blood once for me."

He died in Trappe Pa, at the age of 76, 10/7/1787.

Writing about social and ecological conditions of American in the early stages was his daily form of expression in which he was relentless. Without this care to detail, the reader would never know what the state of our land was in over 250 years ago, nor the travails HMM endured while following his calling to bring the spirit of Christ to this world. He was on a mission and was undaunted in that mission.

What I seem to have in common with HMM is the desire, the need to write about my daily life. Although I am not a pioneer in the way he was, still I feel called to write about the Christ presence in all of us and to support the opening of the connection to God in this time of darkness and struggle. In writing about HMM, I feel a long and deepening connection to history and a clearing of debris that encumbered my father HMM through his life. Hopefully, now he will be free to enjoy the love and self-acceptance, even though he is no longer in bod. I wish that he knows it is his birthright, to know that he can live *untormented* in his soul and his mind because he is a son of the ever-living Christ that resides within him even now as the Christ impulse.

Three hundred years ago, even more, my grandfather many generations ago had a heart opening, a transformation, an enormous conversion by the Spirit of Christ. And the love, the joy and gratitude he felt for the liberation of his soul he carried through his life as he strove to bring a religious body, the Lutheran Church to America.

---

[37] Ibid, Mann, 522.

Three hundred years later, I recognized his spiritual conversion, his heart-led journey because it resonated with my own spiritual journey. HMM apparently was awakened while he was at Halle University. There may have been a particular incident that began to open the door to his heart but that had not been revealed in the manuscripts I have read. I only know that it happened at that time and was an outgrowth of study and was highly influenced by his professors.

This resonance of love and connection with the Christ impulse is the thread that connects me with the past, with this paternal grandfather, and with my spiritual journey in the present time. This journey which is central to the development of ego consciousness and spiritual evolution is the path that has defined me and continues to inform and protect me in the current times. This is so because the journey delineates the internal movement of the lower self to the higher self, from the Lower Ego to the Higher Ego, from an ego- driven life to a heart-led life. This new life is a life that has emerged as one with the Christ impulse, with the integration of male and female aspects within the self and with the integration of the soul with the Divine.

Letter of Appreciation

Dear Dad,

I want to remember the times we had and the gifts of joy that infrequently occurred. These moments reside in my memory as special moments of a connection we had, even though it was fleeting. Once such moment happened when we moved to Jenkintown, a suburb of Philadelphia. While in the Jenkintown home, I remember we had a ping pong table in the basement. None of the rooms were finished downstairs, so we played in what had been the coal room. It was dark except for the two light bulbs that hung on the wall, and it was spooky there. Sometimes you and I would play while my mother was preparing dinner. You would serve up a fast ball and sometimes during the game the ball would hit the edge of the table and fly around the room with abandon. When this happened you and I would laugh so hard, holding our stomachs and bending over, sometimes to the point of tears. We were giddy with silliness as the ball would take off with a mind of its own, pinging against the walls and then even out into the coal bin. Although there was an element of healthy competition between us, our game was less about winning then about having a good laugh and we often did when we managed to play...which was infrequent. Sad to say.

And then there was Christmas when I was nine years old. I was really surprised to find a blue two wheeled Roadmaster bicycle beside the tree for me at Christmas time. I had no clue about how to ride it. At that time there were no training wheels. You got on the bike and hoped you could move it forward before you fell over. One spring day you casually remarked, "Why don't we go to the back and try this bicycle." I was eager to do this but afraid I would fail to keep the bicycle upright and would fall and hurt myself. Nevertheless, we went to the back of the house where there were driveways and a narrow road leading out to the main street. You told me how to stop the bicycle and then helped me on the bicycle seat. As I pedaled, you started to run behind the bicycle with one hand on the back of the bicycle seat. The bicycle went faster and faster. It felt like flying. Much to my surprise the bike stayed upright, and I was actually keeping it going. As I approached the street you called to me, "Don't forget to stop yourself!" So, I did and then found that my two feet had come to the ground on either side of the bike frame. Wow, I had done it. You and I did a few short runs after which he said to me, "Now you do it without me." At first, I was scared but after the first successful attempt, I realized I could do it. I was able to ride, keep upright, and stop the bicycle and get off without falling. This was a great accomplishment and I had succeeded in riding without aid.

Two years later we moved to Jenkintown, another suburb of Philadelphia. Balmy weather surrounded us in our new English Tutor home on Runnymede Street. I could not wait to get on my bicycle and ride through the residential neighborhood. Through the summer that year I rode every street, every alley, saw every tree and home and enjoyed the freedom of going where I wanted to without restraint or permission, a wild and wonderful feeling which lasted the entire summer. I even met one or two kids who also rode wherever they wanted. One time, I remember going into a garage which was open and finding some long bullets in an open compartment near the door. I thought this was exciting and dangerous and talked to my buddy saying that this was too dangerous to fool with and so we left without disturbing anything. Back then, it was easier to explore without restriction because in that community at that time, doors were left open enough that a kid could wander in, look around without being caught. That is what we did. I loved the freedom to explore and travel on my own. Now I am grateful to my father for giving me the wheels to travel.

Dad, probably the most long lasting and memorable gift was Trixie, my first friend. She came one day after Blackie, our cat disappeared, never to be seen again. You surprised me with this adorable little female dalmatian puppy, with a large black spot, we called a saddle and a black swirl over one eye. If she had been a human, she would have resembled Veronica Lake, a well-known actress at that time, who covered one eye with a wave of long jet-black hair.

Trixie and I got along from the start, playing together and rough housing, rolling on the floor. With a sock or old shoe in her mouth, she would growl holding it tight between clenched jaws, me holding tight on the other end. Around in a circle we would go, she growling and me laughing. She had a long tail which whipped from side to side with joy when she was excited, especially going for walks around the block, which we did daily. I had to stay out of the way of that tail because it could really sting if it hit my leg. You told me I was allowed to keep the dog on the condition that I fed, walked, and cleaned up after her. Although I did not care for the clean-up, to have a friend who seemed to love me without restraint no matter what mood I was in or what I had failed to do, was a gift.

Trixie had an unbounded spirit, something I admired. I wished to be as free as she was. One day, my mother made some chocolate brownies which made the house smell so delicious. Trixie nosed the air too and wagged her tail in expectation of a chocolate treat. "Not for dogs," I told her. When the brownies were finished baking, my mother brought them to the dining room table to cool. There the brownies sat for a time as my mother continued preparing lunch. It was Saturday so the whole family was waiting to eat together. You were out in the rose garden cutting some stems for the dining room table and I was helping my mother in the kitchen putting the vegetables on dishes. Suddenly, we heard Trixie running across the living room floor. Apparently, she had started from the front door and galloped through the living room and with one bound, she was on the dining room table, mouthing as many brownies as she could. My mother turned and called out, "Stop that, you bad dog." But Trixie kept on munching. You had just brought the roses in from the garden and had placed them in a vase with water. With a crash, the vase broke, and the roses and water spread across the dining room table. You heard the crash and come running in, saw what was happening, and reached to grab

Trixie who ran under the table. You spat out, "You bad dog…. you are going to your kennel, a kennel he had built under the stairs. Trixie evaded my dad's grasp and acted like she was playing a game. But you were very angry at her and in a stern voice, "When I get you, you are going to your kennel." You finally did corner her in the kitchen and picked her up by the scruff of the neck and took her to her kennel. I just watched her, quietly congratulating her for being so persistent, so unflinchingly determined to get what she wanted, but partly I was horrified that she was going to receive your anger, maybe even a spanking or maybe even get sick.

Trixie stayed in her kennel through the luncheon meal until we heard her groaning. So much chocolate did not agree with her. We knew that because soon there was an odious smell competing with the chocolate smell. You looked at me and said, "You need to go and clean her up." We all knew what that meant. I left the lunch table and collected some paper towels and a bucket of water and headed down to clean her up. It was hard for me to see Trixie feeling bad, but I had to admire her spunk. She had guts, although she was paying for it and so was I.

What I appreciated most about you is your true voice which was not your words or pronouncements but your music. I did not recognize your gifts at the time they occurred, but they have continued to enrich my inner landscape through the years. For this I am deeply grateful. In my head, I hear your organ music through the melodies of Mozart, Bach, Debussy and Gershwin. In my mind, I hear the rhythms of Gershwin's *Rhapsody in Blue*, or Concerto in F. These are treasured sound memories that continue to fill the hallways of my mind with their melodic strains and rhythms. You played: the Toccata and Fugue in D Minor by Bach, The Engulfed Cathedral, or Clair de Lune by Debussy to name a few that you played on piano and organ. Your music continues to resonate with me and is a most "spiritual" and important legacy you left with me. I have reclaimed it again as I now play on my harp. Music was a profoundly important outlet for him and has been a deeply soothing and healing energy throughout my life, but particularly for the last 20 years or more as I have played the harp.

While we did not have close communication ever, and especially during the final years when you were unhappy in your current third marriage and feeling abandoned and bereft by your wife, you still managed to return to Pennsylvania and create a life with your new wife. In the end, she turned to her sister and brother- in-law for refuge and companionship, leaving you with the alpha dog, *Fosig*, at home alone and lonely.

As I look back on your trials and tribulations, I see how disadvantaged you were by not having had the opportunity to socialize and to learn the give and take of friendships as a youngster. You were in a way like an only child, as I was for many years, alone, and trying to figure out what you needed to survive and who you could depend on for support.

Your struggle claiming your ground against forces that were eroding that ground was my struggle as well. You had to face and contend with the force of your mother as well as your second wife, Emma, who was my mother and my challenge as well. We both had to learn to say no to her, to stand our ground and to walk a different path than the one she desired or needed from both of us. In the end we both succeeded in finding new paths to one extent or another.

I think it took a lot of courage for you to walk away from your marriage to her in your mid-sixties as you did. I too walked away from my mother when I refused to return to Pennsylvania and subsequently moved to New York instead, but I could not have done it without the support of my analyst Dr. Gabrielle. I don't know if you had any support. You may have done it by yourself. In any case, I admire your fortitude for doing this.

We both chose this circumstance, this family, to work on developing our ego consciousness and freedom to choose. We both needed to find our own inner voices which would lead us toward our greater potentials. Your life circumstances and struggles remind me of what I encountered as well and draw me to you as someone with whom I can empathize because we have tread similar paths.

In the end, I am glad that you were there and found satisfaction through music, which I felt was your true voice. I felt honored and privileged to have been bathed in that luxury of sound which continues to resound within me. I am grateful and feel enriched by being able to share as much of life as we did. I am deeply grateful for my first friend, Trixie, our dalmatian that you brought into our home. She was a friend I desperately needed and deeply appreciated.

Let me not forget to mention the garden of zinnias and roses which you planted when we lived on Williams Avenue in West Oak Lane. As I tend to my garden now, I think of how hard you worked on the rose garden and how people admired his garden of zinnias which etched our long walkway to the front door. Your love of those flowers and desire to bring the beauty of nature into our home is a gift that I continue to cherish and that I enjoy as I bring my home-grown golden marigolds into my home.

As I did not communicate my feelings to you when you were alive, I wish now you can hear them and hope that you will be able to receive the sense of compassion and love that I feel for you. Thank you for agreeing to be my father.

Your loving daughter, Anne Elizabeth

My dog, Trixie, my first friend

Dear Trixie,

Luckily, my father brought you, Trixie, into my life when I was about eight years old and named you Trixie. You were the Luciferian force that brought joy and wonder into my life. A small, cute, no, adorable little dalmatian puppy with a large black spot on one side of your body which we called a saddle. My father chose you because you were short haired so you would not likely shed hair on the carpets and because dalmatians had a reputation for not bringing unwanted dog odors into the house. Unlike Blackie, our cat who ran away just after being spade, and who would scratch me when I tried to play with him, you were playful and full of enthusiasm and affection and did not hurt me. You loved to wrestle and sink your little teeth into anything soft, like bedroom slippers and soft leather shoes. When we left you alone in the house, we had to remove all our shoes from your eager teeth so we would not chew and destroy them. Often if one shoe or bedroom slipper were missing, I would look under the bed or in the closet and there I would find it, still wet with your saliva. You like to chew used tissues in the wastebasket so we had to make sure the wastebasket was empty before going out because you would never lose an opportunity to have a good munch.

My father made a kennel in which we placed a soft old bathroom mat and a rug for you to sleep on. Just like Harry Potter, you slept under the stairs with a door which we could lock when we needed to secure you. You did not like being in there as you preferred to rump through the rooms of the house and then of course outside, which was your favorite. I remember when we lived on Chew Street, we had a huge yard which sloped to a copse of trees. One evening we saw lights of a police car drive up our driveway. then flashlights shadowed the trees at the back of our home. We learned that foxes lived there, and one had been sighted in our yard, but usually you saw groundhogs, your favorite prey. Once spotted, you would run with tail circling furiously, and barking, as you chased the furry brown creatures into the woods. Often you would come back, your tail wagging with a small struggling creature in your mouth. Usually by then the groundhog was dead, but if not, I would tell you to let go which you reluctantly did and off the wounded groundhog would go with me holding you by the collar to keep you from rebounding to the chase.

You were not a huge dog, but big enough that I could give you a good hug and feel your soft warm body against mine. That was a real pleasure of mine. For you, my hug was soon too confining and when you squirmed free, off you would sprint to the kitchen where you could smell dinner cooking.

Although I took you for walks around the block on your leash, this was not your favorite activity. You wanted to run. Sometimes I would take you to the nearby field and I would take you off the leash so you could run. But often I would have trouble getting you to return to me and would have to run shouting your name and waiting until you were finished chasing an animal or rolling in some "wonderful" animal smell. Once you ran after a skunk and got sprayed. I had to drag "smelly" you home and give you the tomato bath which took most of the smell away, but not all of it. That remaining smell took several weeks to finally disappear.

Once you decided you wanted something like brownies or a groundhog, you went after it without hesitation. I liked your spunk and your resolve with no thought of consequences. Nothing would keep your spirit in check in those moments and off you would go with me chasing after you.

When I was eighteen, I went off to college and you remained with my parents and a one-year-old brother. While I did say goodbye to you when I left, I never thought it was a final goodbye. But when I returned for the holiday, you were not there. When I asked where you were, my mother told me you had been given to a farm because she feared your fur was aggravating my brother's asthma. I asked what farm in hopes that I could visit you but my mother either did not remember or did not want to say. I was not sure to this day if that is what really happened. In any case, I was devastated because I was given no chance to say goodbye or to negotiate decisions about your future. I was informed that they made a decision about your life, and I had no say in what happened to you. This hurt me deeply because I did not have that chance to perhaps make different choices for you, or at least to give one last hug. I am deeply sorry for this and want to acknowledge what a good and loyal first friend Trixie was to me, how you filled me with a sense of joy, and a feeling of not being alone. Trixie, you still live in my heart as my true and loyal companion, and I will never forget who you were and what you have meant to me. Thank you for being who you were for me.my first friend, one I could trust and love without any fear or reprisals.

Introducing my mother to my etheric mother, Mary

Dear Mother,

I want to introduce you to my etheric mother Mary, who became my friend, sister, mentor, and even friend. Certainly, she does not replace you. No one ever could, nor would I want that. But her mercy and her kindness were so profound that I hope you too can partake of her goodness in some way. I know that life was not always kind to you and that the loss of your father when you were just graduating from high school marked you deeply and shaped your life in a myriad of ways. I think also that your mother was overwhelmed, unwilling to learn very much English, and with a husband who no longer could work. In any case, I think you too had to survive without much tenderness or parental care. Mary can afford you this care if you will allow it.

At the same time, I know that you are agnostic and are not at all sure that God even exists. You do not have to believe in God to feel the care and protection that Mary can afford you. It is true that knowing Mary is a way to know God as it was for me, but it is your choice as to the path you take. In the meantime, I want to tell you about my second meeting with Mary, a meeting which changed my life...and might change yours even though you are disincarnate. Please follow me as I retread this path that I took many years ago.

At first, I met Mary at St Raymond's Church when I was eight or nine years old. She was a statue dressed in blue and white with a crown of seven stars around her head. Her gentle smile was comforting and welcoming and was often all I needed after a hard day at school. I treasured those moments with her.

Mary came to me as part of the feminine archetype, a goddess from the east which seemed fitting as I was studying Buddhism at the time: White Tara with the seven eyes, one in each foot and palm, her two human eyes and one in the third eye and Green Tara with one foot reaching to the ground and showing the importance of staying grounded. Then Sherab Chamma, Bon (Tibetan,) goddess of wisdom and compassion resided with me for five years after a ceremony that I witnessed at a monastery which was dedicated to the Divine Feminine. As Mary, the mother of God and Mary Magdalen returned to my life, I returned Sherab Chamma to the Bon Community where I felt she belonged. Tankas or wall hangings with White Tara, Green Tara and the Queen of Heaven still grace my walls at home. Over my bed is the framed poster of the three emanations of the feminine archetype Mary, the mother of God, Mary Magdalene, and the Mary Sophia.

Even though I have not always paid tribute to Mary directly, I have had the feminine archetype in heart through the years. When I reconnected with Mary at the Jesuit Center, I was overwhelmed with the deep friendship and connection she offered me. The Jesuit Center where I encountered her once again in the grotto, offered extensive paths through farm fields, and on one of those paths, the stations of the cross had been erected with small white plaques nailed to trees. As Mary and I walked slowly through the stations of the cross, I could feel the weight of her pain as she remembered Jesus's walk to the Mt. Caramel, the heaviness of the cross, the crown of thorns which leaked blood on the path, Jesus's falling and strained under the weight of the cross as he tried to return to his feet with the cross on his back. I felt the stream of her tears as they mingled with Her Son's blood on the ground as a sacred mystery, the mixing of blood and water in the earth. I felt her pain and her sorrow. I also felt the intense caring and resolve to stay the course with him even though it grieved her deeply, even broke her heart. Here was her son who had provided so many with teachings filled with love and light, healings that restored people to a renewed life, and even restoring people to life once again as in the case of Lazarus. I trusted her connection with me and felt she was joined with me in some way that nothing could break or change. She seemed to understand without me having to explain the deeper torments of my heart, the pain of betrayal, deceit and misunderstanding that I had endured. Not that I am alone in that regard. On the contrary, I am sure Mary does this for anyone, male or female, who appeals to her for wisdom and relief from the heaviness of past transgressions.

Mary was someone that I could depend on without any doubt. She was always present for me and held space for whatever I thought or whatever feelings came up which I dared not speak to anyone: feelings of shame, guilt, and unworthiness. All the above she held me in her heart with no judgement, no recrimination, and no attempt to fix it. She just accepted what I said and knew that I was contrite and grateful for the space she provided for me.

Mary was the one who took me by the hand into the circle of Christ where I felt the touch of Christ's love as a huge wind that doubled me over and immersed me in a power so pure and so overwhelming that even to this day it is difficult to find word which adequately convey the essential power and nature of this experience. I owe Mary a deep gratitude of thanks which again words cannot possibly convey.

So Mother, I hope you have been able to take this journey with me. I know it is not your journey, but it could be at some time in the future. I say this without pressure or promise, but with hope that you can come to know that Spirit lives deeply within you even if you cannot recognize it or own it. And I hope you can celebrate with me that I found help through Mary, who bridged the gap in fulfilling needs which perhaps no human person can fill. There is no blame or comparison between what Mary offers me and what you offered me as my mother. I hope that whatever mothering you may have missed as a child can be fulfilled through the presence of Mary in your life, just as it fulfilled the gaps for me in my childhood. I hope you can celebrate with me the profound gift that I received from Mary, the deep blessing that was gifted me during this moment. And I hope it is a gift for you as well.

Your loving daughter, Anne Elizabeth

Letter of Gratitude and Appreciation

Dear Mother,

After your second husband died, you invited me to take his seat at the Metropolitan Opera house. By that time, you became a kind of friend and companion with whom I enjoyed the beauties of the Metropolitan Opera. We heard the most exquisite operatic voices in the world singing on that stage. The resonance of those voices, the myth that they brought to life in full color, in full dimension was unimaginable. At long last, we were joined through the music and myth depicted in overwhelming splendor and beauty that opera provided for us.

At those times we would travel to New York and arrive for breakfast at the St. Pierre Hotel off Fifth Avenue. I would order the Japanese breakfast complete with miso soup, fish, sea vegetables, and a cold egg, the latter of which I never ate while you dined on the American bacon and eggs breakfast. Afterwards we hurried to Lincoln Center where we heard some of the best performances in opera that one could hear. We felt the opulence of the opera house with its rising chandeliers, heard the exquisitely beautiful voices singing arias that brought the house down more than once and walked on the red carpet that adorned the stairs and hallways of the opera house. The resonance of those voices, the myth that they brought to life in full color, in full dimension was unimaginable. We were joined through the music and myth depicted in overwhelming splendor and beauty that opera brought to us. In fact, as I speak of it now, those voices are still resonating in me. On the way home on the bus, you squeezed my hand, and I knew that you were moved the same way I was. After so many years of dancing around each other, we were finally dancing together, metaphorically speaking. The music of the opera brought us together in ways that had not happened in the past.

The other night I had a dream about being with you once again. There you were sitting behind me in a folding chair. You were smiling and had on a dark plaid dress, which you might have worn to teach at the University. I was smiling too and glad, more than glad, deeply delighted to see you once again. It appeared you no longer had Alzheimer's disease and were fully conscious of your faculties.

In the dream, I turned around to you and you were almost laughing. I said to you, "What is the plan?" You started laughing and so did I. We laughed and laughed and laughed, so much so that I was holding my stomach which felt like it would fall apart if I laughed any longer. You were doubled over with laughter as well.

There was no answer to this question because in effect there was no plan. Or another way to put it was that the plan was no plan. We both knew that, and we were both happy with that plan, the plan of no plan. We both knew that the best plan was to go with the flow and allow whether would happen would be just perfect or at least fine. We both knew that something mysterious and internal was happening to each of us. Your internal voice was present and communicating with my internal voice which was also very much present. I think my internal voice had been there all through my childhood, but I had not acknowledged it, pushed it aside because it did not seem as important or strong as your voice. Or perhaps I did not think you would respect my voice as you viewed your voice as a more accurate guide for decisions to be made.

I noticed in the dream that you sat behind me, not in front or to the side. This meant to me that in fact, I had claimed and honored my internal sovereign voice and that my voice was no longer eclipsed by yours. At the same time, our internal voices seemed to be working together on the same page as it were, contemplating the unknown, an invitation to be acknowledged and perhaps followed. No decision was made at this time, nor needed to be.

But then I ask myself why the laughter? Why were we both in gales of laughter, side-splitting laughter. I could feel the energy juddering through my whole body, my soul and I had the sense that it was juddering through hers as well. I think we both knew the ridiculous situation we were in, thinking that we had command over decision-making of any kind. We were in another dimension, but thinking in a third dimension. At the same time, our thoughts were coming from the unknown, perhaps the divine, and were synchronized in some mysterious way, which we realized was so much bigger in perspective than our own thoughts were. We wanted to bathe in the mystery that was so much bigger than we were. And so, we willingly and gladly surrendered to the higher voices from each of our souls, voices that met in that plane of consciousness without judgement of fear and we did this was great bliss and joy. A quote from the poet, Rumi says it all:

"Out beyond the world of ideas of wrong-doing and right-doing there is a field. I 'll meet you there."

You and I are definitely meeting in that field now, mother, without expectations, desires, or responsibilities for each other. We are free and we know we have arrived at this place for the first time and know each other as never before. We know we can love each other, respect each other, now unencumbered and without blemish or end.

This is the message from the dream that I want to convey to you. This is the message of love and gratitude that I have for you as my mother. I am your daughter, deeply grateful and fully free to be my sovereign self. We can stand side by side, respecting and loving each other without reservation and with reverence for the paths we each have taken. We have both been blessed by each other and by the Divine that has given us life together.

Your loving daughter, Anne Elizabeth

Introduction to my etheric parents

Dear Reader:

At the age of seven I felt very separate from and disillusioned with my parents. I did not feel comfortable in their presence and was always seeking comfort and protection in the home of my friends with their parents. That continued for a time until by "accident," I was led to St. Raymond's Church, which I passed while walking to and from my elementary school. Here is where I met my etheric parents which I now want to introduce to you. But first, I want to tell you about my home life with its lack of warmth and connection which drew me into the peace and safety I felt in the sanctuary.

It is true that home…should be a place where you eat and sleep, where you belong, where you are loved and accepted, even needed. Not the case for me. No, for me the home I lived in was a house, the place where I slept, where my personal belongings were kept, a dresser and bed, my clothing. I did not have favorite pictures or photos on the wall of my room. Pink wallpaper with ladies surrounded by flowers decorated my walls, not my choice. I was not offered a chance to select colors or wallpaper that would have made the room feel more like me or mine. I lived within these parameters which were defined by structure, by my parents with whom I lived with. This life resembled the life one lives in a boarding house.

We ate together, but rarely talked to each other. We slept under the same roof, brushed our teeth and bathed in tandem, each in our own separate worlds. We prepared for the day's activities, school, or work, as soldiers prepare for battle, taking our armaments, books, and a briefcase, or in my case a backpack, filled with schoolbooks and headed for the "trenches," (a word my parents used), the office, or in my case, school. At the end of the day, having done battle in our respective arenas, we returned to have a quiet meal, and then retired to our rooms, mine to complete homework. My father would sometimes play the piano or organ, and my mother, an English teacher, would work at the dining room table to prepare for the next school day's lesson. If my father played the piano, his music would eclipse the still tense silence that continued to occupy every corner of our house despite his music.

In those days I walked to school, about six blocks from my home. The sun shone brightly on the row homes, which were new. No trees had been planted on the perimeters of the sidewalks so there were no dark places to hide, for me or anyone else who might have been a danger to me. About three blocks from my home stood St. Raymond's Roman Catholic Church, a small brick church with a white cross above the door and several low riser steps leading to a large wooden entrance door. Inside the sanctuary it was quiet and peaceful, still fragranced by the remnants of incense used during the previous day or weekend services. The church was usually empty so on my way home I would find a seat during the entrance of the church and sit admiring the stained-glass windows. The reds and blues of the various tints would play across the wooden pews and would change as the sun moved slowly through the hour deepening the colors and spreading them across the tile floor of the sanctuary.

Flanking the altar at the front were two large columnar candles and two statues one was of Mary, in her white gown with a blue robe astride her shoulders and a golden crown on her head. A benevolent smile adorned her face, peaceful and serene. I loved to feel the energy of her facial acceptance spreading through me as I watched in silence.

On the other side was the figure of Jesus, in his white garment with deep red or vermilion cloak. His face, with a gentle smile and even a look of concern which continued to radiate from his face. He too had a crown of gold atop his head, sandals on his feet. Although they represented the holy family, Mother Mary and Jesus, her son, I saw them as my parents, accepting, loving and protecting me in a peaceful unsolicited way.

Even though the statues of Mary and Jesus were visible to me, I call them etheric because their presences lived in the ether of my being, behind the veil. I felt their energy inside me. These etheric parents, Mary and Jesus were extremely supportive to me psychically and to some extent replaced my need to depend on parents who were not available. I felt safe with them, and free to be who I was, a child, with no need to apologize. I was not an intrusion in their lives, which I felt at my parents' home, but was welcomed as a person, not equal, but unqualified in their midst. This was a home away from the home, a place I could come to for quiet refuge, safety, and freedom to breathe, to take in the beauty and to feel undiminished consistent acceptance each time I came to the sanctuary. It was a peaceful feeling I could count on.

When I was seven, my friend Kathy, who lived several blocks from me, decided to receive Holy Communion at St. Raymond's Church. I decided to do the same. I remember this because the family photo album shows me in my white veil, dress, and white shoes with a certificate in my hand. In the photo, I was looking to the left toward St. Raymond's Church. I felt a sense of belonging and inclusion at the Church. My connection was anchored by my belief in Mary and Jesus, as my etheric parents. and ultimately my connection to God. They had come to me through God and through the Church. I looked to them for protection, connection, and freedom. Emotionally they were closer and safer to me than my biological parents. In my mind I could count on Mary, Jesus, and God for unconditional support and acceptance. That belief sustained me for a long time.

As a Catholic, I was expected to attend confession. So, on Saturday's I went to the sanctuary, blessed myself with holy water from the baptismal font, and waited my turn to enter the confessional booth. A priest would be waiting to hear what I had to say. Often, I would think hard about what I had to confess because I was never sure what I had done right or wrong, what sins had I committed. Since I was under my parents' surveillance and bound to the notion of being good, I did not risk going beyond what I thought were acceptable boundaries. So, I had to make up sins that I thought would be believable by the priest, who would expect a penance of some kind. Sometimes I lied about what I told my parents about my homework, or I would make up a story about stealing money from my father's wallet, which I could not imagine doing because the penalties would be as severe as being disowned. I imagined I would be thrown out, shunned, never to be spoken to again. I would say these "sins" and wait for the priest to dole out my penance. He would say, "Recite three Hail Mary's or The Lord's Prayer, or once I think I was told to recite the Nicene Creed," which I was not sure I could remember. In any case, I would dutifully kneel at the pew and recite my penances while looking at the faces of Mary and Jesus. They were always smiling no matter what lie I had told the priest. That was very comforting to me because they did not seem to judge me. Reciting the penance was my way of having more time, taking in their quiet support. Being in their presence was well worth any penance demanded by the priest.

In the empty church, there were no barriers or hidden agendas. No suffocating tensions or threats of disapproval or needing to disappear into my room. No criticism and no sense of failing to meet expectations. I felt the relief of feeling accepted and acceptable. At church I was a free agent, supported by two loving parent figures: this was a piece of heaven.

Religion buttressed my emotional needs that were not supplied by my family. Sitting or praying in the church felt safe and private. My parents were not religious and did not regularly attend any church at that time. I had no fear of them visiting St. Raymond's or walking in on me while I was praying or listening to God. It was my sanctuary and mine alone. Nor did I want to share it with my parents. Here was my place to be free and to breathe easily without threat or expectation. I had a taste of what it felt like to be myself, whatever that was. It felt so good just to take that in for a few moments.

I later recalled through past life regressions that I had experienced many past lifetimes as a nun. During these past lives, I spent many hours in prayer and meditation, leading a monastic life, attending matins and other services, cleaning stone walkways and praying in quiet sanctuaries with the smell of lingering incense surrounding me. In this lifetime, my religious connections lasted for 42 years, until I left the church to follow a path of spirituality led by my inner voice.

During those years and beyond, Jesus and Mary were my ideal parents whose support extended into my adult years and have continued with me into the present. They guided me and sustained my hope in the possibility of a different life.

This meeting with Mary and Jesus was the fourth of several pivotal encounters I had with her spirit and the spirit of Jesus. The second encounter with Mary came years later at a Jesuit Center during an eight-day spiritual retreat. (See retreat at the Jesuit Center, Part 5).

Anthroposophy

INTRODUCTION TO THE SPIRITUAL SCIENCE OF RUDOLF STEINER

Dear Reader

I now want to explore with you the Anthroposophical Spiritual Science of Rudolf Steiner which has captured my intellectual, spiritual, and emotional mind because Steiner addresses the origins of thought and the relationship of thought to the Divine, to the Supersensible world as he calls it. Together, we can question where thoughts and how they spread through the generations. What does the word anthroposophy mean: *anthropo* refers to human and *sophy* or *Sophia* refers to wisdom. Anthroposophy is a term depicting human wisdom.

BRIEF BIOGRAPHY OF RUDOLF STEINER

Rudolf Steiner was a philosopher, educator, occult scientist who is probably best known now for the many Waldorf Schools which have spread throughout the country. Born in 1861, in the Austro-Hungarian Empire (now the northern part of Croatia), he began his studies in math and science, even read Hegel as a schoolboy, and later immersed himself in many philosophies and literature, particularly that of Johann Wolfgang Goethe (1749-1832) and occult science. Steiner became an editor of Goethe's work and wrote for the Deutsche National Literature publication project. Also Steiner became an archivist of Goethe's works and later entered school where he received his Ph.D.

in philosophy from the University of Rostock, 1891. His dissertation, Truth and Science (Wahrheit und Wissenschaft), became his notable work, Philosophy of Freedom, 1894, (Philosophie der Freiheit).

Steiner's interests deepened to include universal education and *spiritual science,* which grew out of his connection with the Berlin Theosophic Society. He gave many lectures on theosophy and developed his ideas of spiritual science which he labelled as anthroposophy. He inspired new ways of thinking giving at least 6,000 lectures which ranged from Christian themes, history, drama, science, agriculture, and education. He believed that human beings had three major components: Thinking, Feeling, and Willing. Further he asserted that the human being has four aspects that could be developed: a spiritual ego, the "I", which interacts with the astral, etheric and physical forms. Human development was overseen and protected by Archangel Michael and challenged by an anti-Christ figure named Ahriman who sought to prevent human evolution and to control humanity and by Lucifer, who believes in over expansion without boundaries. Unlike many Christian denominations, Steiner believed in reincarnation and that this process is pivotal in the lives of humans as it led to the purification and moral development of the soul as connected to the Divine. He remained a Christian but incorporated esoteric knowledge and the beliefs of the Rosicrucian Order in his philosophical system. At the same time the scope that he offered was different from and was often in conflict with Catholicism and Protestantism.

In the early 1920's, Steiner was attacked by the Nazi party because he supported independence for German province of Upper Silesia (now part of Poland). However, Steiner was also attacked by Catholic and Protestant churches, for his occult science and beliefs in reincarnation and by Marxists, and rival spiritual leaders. On December 31, 1922, his Goetheanum, in Dornach Switzerland was burned to the ground by the Nazis, an assertion that was never backed by evidence. A new one was erected and considered an architectural landmark in the twentieth century. Even under attack Steiner continued to give lectures to the public in which he emphasized natural farming methods and new system of medicine which he used to train physicians. Steiner died in Dornach on March 30, 1925, because of suspected poisoning, a possibility which Steiner never confirmed.

In the early 20th century Rudolf Steiner introduced anthroposophy to the world. Steiner went on to suggest that Anthroposophy is a path of knowledge which can be taken by anyone who seeks spiritual knowledge as a spiritual human being. Anthroposophy offers a spiritual science, a way of purifying ourselves so that we can experience the higher dimensions which are available to us. He suggests that Anthroposophy is a guide to the spiritual in the universe which arises in man's need to develop his ego consciousness and to elevate his soul. He further suggests that when man questions the nature of man and the universe that this spiritual path can lead a human being to the discovery of deeper meaning and revelations to these questions.

ANTHROPOSOPHY

What is anthroposophy as established by Rudolph Steiner in the early 20th century?

Many definitions exist all describing a philosophy of life whose objective is to make the human experience accessible and comprehensible of the spiritual world. The Waldorf school defines anthroposophy as a spiritual philosophy which responds to the spiritual questions of humanity, to basic artistic needs, to scientific attitude of mind, and to the need to for mankind to develop complete freedom based on unique individual decisions and choices. The process of spiritual progress is outlined within this framework which emphasizes the need for self-discipline to receive cognitional experience of the spiritual world. Inherent within this teaching is the belief that humanity can transform the world through arts, speech, drama, painting, sculpture, and music and the art of eurythmy, a system which Steiner crafted to stimulate self-healing through body movement to speech or to letters. Working in this system promotes rhythm, balance, orientation in space and in one's own body. It is said to strengthen life forces and to stimulate internal healing.

Steiner's philosophical and spiritual vision extended across the centuries and incorporated civilization as we have generally known it from the beginning. He outlines these changes in Steiner's book.[38] The Christ impulse is a culmination, a point of the spiritual growth of the soul which becomes impregnated with the Christ consciousness of love through the mystery of Golgotha, the death and resurrection of the Christ, the latter of which changed the world.

Steiner outlines the development of this ego consciousness beginning with the Egyptian Chaldean culture which develops the sentient (or feeling) soul with ego feeling from the soul force of the consciousness. Development continues through the Graeco- Roman culture through the development of the intellectual or mind soul continues the soul evolution. This culminates in the *consciousness soul* which we have been experiencing through the last several centuries. The ego or "I" was not apprehended in the Egyptian-Chaldean culture so much as the senses were expanded and used to ascertain reality. In the Graeco- Roman culture the development of the mind brought in much more of the ego and the "I" into prominence. In our evolutionary epoch the ego and the sentient mind has become integrated so that we experience the marriage of the two forces within our ego. Culturally we see these differences expressed broadly in the contrast between the Occidental and Oriental views of spirituality. While the Occidental view begins more with the external view, with the idea of service and deeds to humanity, the Oriental view tends to begin with the interior world, the sense of the Tao or the way with expands from within outward and with the sense of connection to nature and oneness with the elements of the natural world. Love of the Tao appears in the oriental east while conscience appears in the west, occidental.[39]

As conscience becomes stronger, an inner voice of conscience begins to be heard. This inner voice can feel like God's voice, or the voice of angels or the voice of the Higher Self directing and guiding an individual. The more a human being can transform a personal or Lower Ego, and to be open to hearing the voice of the internal world, the more one is able to receive higher wisdom, insight and higher knowledge coming from above or from higher consciousness.

---

[38] Steiner, Rudolf, The Christ Impulse and the Development of Ego Consciousness, Rudolf Steiner Press, vol 116 2014.
[39] Steiner, Ibid, 110.

Listening to this inner voice brings a relief from suffering, from anxiety, and from the chaos and troubles of the third dimensional world that humans live in most of the time.

However, the Christ impulse extends beyond religious denominations in the east or the west. Steiner claims that the Christ death and resurrection is a necessary event to inform all of mankind that man lives forever in God. Through the reincarnation of many lives, through the evolution of human DNA, man has the privilege of being eternal because man is an extension of the Spirit of God and made in the image of God. The Christ crucifixion and resurrection was instituted to affirm that limitless human transformation was possible and present for all humans no matter what religion, be it Christian, or Buddhist, or Hindu, or Muslim, to name only a few. This makes the mystery of Golgotha pivotal in the history of mankind as an undeniable and profound mark of change in the history of man's development.

Steiner goes on to say that we need to recognize that there is a spiritual science that exists and has existed for some time and that it is important to acknowledge this and to study spirituality as a science that has been the backbone of human civilizations for many eons of time. This is the case because embedded in spirituality are the morals and ethical standards by which man has lived. These standards have helped man to learn to live together, to ameliorate differences, and to learn to respect differences between individuals, cultures, and races. These standards are part of the ladder that reaches to the Divine, to the supersensible world from which are morals are derived. Although, unfortunately wars and conflicts still occur, it is the intention of spiritual science to support mankind as individuals evolve into higher states of ego consciousness and spiritual evolution.

Steiner also intended that humankind realize our oneness with the earth, indeed with the entire solar system, the relationship of our sun and it planets, the influence of the stars on our birth and being, and the ways in which our solar system is an integral part of who we are and has shaped us into who we are and who we are becoming.[40] Through this process man would learn to honor and work in concert with the

---

[40] Steiner, Rudolf, Cosmic Memory, 1959.

earth, replenishing what was taken and utilizing and acknowledging what earth provided as a gift to help sustain mankind.

As part and parcel of spiritual science, Steiner elucidated other forces which shape and grow out of the ego. He divides the ego into two domains: the Lower and the Higher Ego. The Lower Ego is composed of two conflicting energies which vie for power and dominance in the Lower Ego. Ahrimanic influences the materialism in man, the need for control, the need for power and dominance over other beings. Ahrimanic forces want to squash chaos, to dismantle, distort, or block thinking and to subvert aspects of nature which don't conform to expectation or to the criteria or system which has been put in place. Ahrimanic substances are connected to earth and water. The feeling of Ahrimanic forces is dense, cold, unrelenting. We see this *exemplified in the "dementors" in the later Harry Potter movies, for example, the Prisoner of Azkaban.* As the dementors fly over the earth, flowers and growing plants freeze on contact. The windows of the Hogwarts's train frost over. Even the water in the water bottle freezes at the presence of the dementors. The "kiss" of the dementors sucks out the very life, and soul of an individual.

The Luciferian force is also born out of the dimension of the Lower Ego. This force is based on the fallen angel, Lucifer, the light bearer who challenges the power of God and who would like to take the place of God as the object of worship. Luciferian energy came into being prematurely before its time. Too much information, too much stimulation which tended to distort the good impact it should have had on humans. We also see an example of Luciferian forces again in the Harry Potter, *Prisoner of Azkaban* which emphasizes magic, the magic wands, the spells, the ability to fly on brooms. the game of *quidditch* with its magic balls like the *bludger* and the *snitch* that fly self-propelled, the invisibility cloak, which makes all under its mantle disappear. Even a Marauder's map which shows the movements of individuals on the grounds of Hogwarts's castle, in the Prisoner of Azkaban is part of the magic that makes this story sparkle. This is just to name of few examples of magic which have enticed children and adults throughout the world over the last twenty-five years.

But the human race did not have the capacity or capability or spiritual underpinning to manage Luciferian energy at the time it was introduced. Therefore, Luciferian energy has often not be used in the best way possible in everyday life. Lucifer pushes humankind to go beyond their capabilities, to try anything, to enter chaos and learn to live with it or learn from it. Lucifer makes things sparkle so that humans are drawn to want to possess things or become possessed by ideas which they may not have the background or conceptual framework to understand or to critically assess. One notion may lead to many other notions about the nature of things, even the universe. But unless these ideas are tested in the cauldron of reality, based on a foundation of experience can be built, these ideas and structure on which they are built will eventually crumble. Lucifer is warm, stimulating, of fire and air, always moving and always wanting. Lucifer is very seductive, sensual, and enticing.

Both Lucifer and Ahriman have something in common: they want to be worshipped as God, take the place of God and they want to live forever. They want immortality at all costs. and they fight in the domain of the Lower Ego. They often work together, like hand and glove. We see this expressed in the attitudes of mankind about war, the use of aggression, in the way planet's resources have been used without regard to the impact on our earth, in the treatment of humans and disregard for human life through the poisoning of our environment which infects and poisons people, which often leads to illness and death. The earth's resources are used and abused without compunction, for the most part without replacing or acknowledging that the earth has given up a piece of herself to help man survive.

Eventually, another voice can overtake the Lower Ego, the voice of the Divine, of God or of Jesus. This voice is the voice of moral right behavior, or conscience, coupled with the voice of love and kindness to fellow men. That voice announces that we are connected to the earth and each other because we come from the same spiritual realm. Individuals may hear a nagging voice of guilt or shame, which may stop negative behavior for a time. Or the voice of love may begin to replace the dominant positions that Ahriman and Lucifer have taken in the lower soul. This can happen in a process called the

Dark Night of the Soul, a process of cleansing and purification that the soul goes through in order to come to know the true connection of the soul with the Divine. This is the journey from a self-serving Lower Ego to a Higher Self "I" from which a Christed ego can emerge. I will share my experience with the dark night of the soul, (Part 5) how Christ or spiritual love came into my heart, and how this began to form a Higher Ego in which Christ's voice became dominant and began to influence the thinking, feeling and willing aspects of my being. (See Appendix B).

Anthroposophy introduction continues

Dear Reader,

I want to introduce you to Ahriman.

According to Steiner, Ahriman is one of two forces vying for power in our universe currently, the other one being Lucifer. The Ahriman force or impulse is materialistic and wants to dominate and control. Ahriman is into biotechnology, artificial intelligence or AI, and into having an immortal life through the implantation of computer chips and other micro-technologies. Ahriman is dense like the earth. He wants to convince everyone that there is a new religion, a bio-tech religion which challenges the religion of the Christ, and the Christ impulse. He wants everyone to bypass the cleansing and purification process that are a necessary part of ego consciousness and soul development, connected with the Christ impulse, and lure them to take the chip. He says this way you will have instant gratification and won't have to spend one ounce of energy working on being immortal. You will be there as soon as you get the implant. Ahriman promises that through bio- technology, you can have immortal life. He has forgotten to mention or remember that those who are connected to the Christ impulse already have immortal life, through the process of reincarnation, different bodies at different epochs in history and the evolution of I-Consciousness.

Ahriman wants to invite you into the 8th sphere where you will be enslaved forever, like gerbils in a cage running the wheel which never stops and never goes anywhere: you will serve him forever and like it. Yes, Ahriman says you will like it because all your needs will be taken care of. You will not have to fight to survive, to pay bills, to work, and to feed your family. You will not need to own a home, a car, but can relax and just do the jobs you are instructed to do and live a life of obedience, following the letter of the law, and have no wants or desires, or dreams.

Ahriman does not want you to own your properties, your thoughts, your dreams, and your children whom he wants to keep as his servants and slaves. Ahriman does not want you to make any decisions, does not want you to be independent, and most of all does not want you to be sovereign. He wants to manipulate your thinking and your will, that you will replace any other spiritual beliefs with loyalty and allegiance to his scientific materialism, and to convince your family members, and others to follow the same.

Ahriman does not want you to expand; on the contrary he wants you to contract, to be minimalistic, to never go beyond the bounds of what materialistic science would suggest. You must not think, must not ask questions, must not challenge society, must be conformist like everyone else, must be like a robot.

In *A Wrinkle in Time* by Madeleine L'Engle, her three main characters, three children of different ages, find themselves in an Ahrimanic- like country as they travel to free their father from imprisonment from an Ahriman- like presence, a brain without a body. Their father is trapped in a veil of stupor from which he cannot free himself. As the three children travel in this Ahrimanic world, they see each child in that world bouncing their ball at the same time, each child jumping rope at the same time, each mother calling her child for dinner at the same time. These are robotic- like actions which each human captured by the spell of this Ahriman figure enacts. When one child fails to act in concert with the others, the child is taken to a central station where he undergoes rigorous and painful reprogramming. This represents a likely picture of the 8th sphere which Ahriman has created and which he is convincing some to join him there.

Ahriman has been instrumental in helping to irradicate our freedoms and rights because they conflict with his plans for humans. He does not want humans to challenge him. He wants to rule and promises to be the "father" to all, taking caring of all needs and all people, to be God. In schools, he restricts people talking, sharing, and getting to know each other as individuals. He doesn't like free speech because it breeds sovereignty and decision making which goes beyond the bounds of what he can control.

BREAKING THROUGH THE AHRIMANIC HOLD

According to Tomberg,[41] along with the clearing or purging of the Luciferic Double which inhabits the ego, the expulsion of the Ahrimanic double must also take place. The Ahrimanic double is the force that wants control, that is determined to constrict growth and evolution through new experiences and strangles attempts to explore what is unknown. This is a force that confines one to status quo, because it is fear driven and wants domination and order even though it may stymy or sacrifice growth.

A great deal of my father's contribution to my upbringing was about restraint, not going beyond what was expected even though expectations were not spelled out. As a teenager the perimeters of my life were defined by household chores and perhaps visits to a nearby tennis court. Travel, with groups of friends or by myself was outside his conception of rigid boundaries that comprised my father's expectations for me. Even in college at age 19, when I attempted to gain his financial support for a trip with a Presbyterian group travelling to India for 10 years, he refused to make any attempt to help.

I internalized those boundaries and did not venture forth into the community unless it was at the suggestion of a friend. Only later in life, much later, did I risk going beyond expected boundaries, dared to challenge expectations and to travel to unknown places with new acquaintances. Finally, when I could afford to travel, and was financially independent, I travelled to spiritual places of power and community in Hawaii, New Zealand, Thailand, Tibet, Nepal, Egypt twice, Peru, Czech Republic, Spain, France, Germany, Switzerland, Italy, Austria, Ireland, and England.

---

[41] Tomberg, Valentin, Inner Development, Anthroposophic Press, 1992, 47.

Even to this day, I wrestle with Ahrimanic influences which want me to play it safe rather than take risks at something new. Choosing appropriately is important as well as taking the challenges which occur. Failure, if it occurs, is an opportunity to learn and grow, sometimes even more than having success.

Probably the most significant early example of standing up to an Ahrimanic force was the moments of saying *no* to my mother's insistence that I attend an interview with a university to enter the Ph.D. program in English. Without my consent or input, she had set up the interview, time and date and insisted that I attend. I wrote her once saying *no*. Then a second time saying *no* I could not possible do that. And a third time, finally with one word only, "NO." I was only able to do this with my analyst's backing. And I waited breathless by the mailbox for weeks expecting a "howler letter" (like the one Ron Weasley received one from his mother in *Harry Potter, the Chamber* of *Secrets* film episode). Mine would berate me as an "ungrateful wretch." But only silence, no mail and no phone call followed. A part of me felt that I had disappointed her and was once again shunned. Another part of me said that I am free of her control, free to move on, and free to breathe once again. The second one was a little stronger at the time and grew stronger as I realized I could live without my mother's approval, or disapproval.

Through the years I have explored various other healing and meditative forms of spiritual connection. Among them is Taoist philosophy, which I found is not in conflict with various Christian or spiritual traditions if you experience the Tao, the flow of life, as the Christ impulse. I discovered this as I have engaged in Taoist Fusion exercises to integrate the five elements within myself, which are water (wisdom), fire (acceptance), wood (compassion,) and metal (integrity) into earth (trust). Doing the Taoist Primordial Exercise helps me to return to the personal primordial seed of energy with which I was born. This energy is pure and uncontaminated by life's stress, negative messages, and experiences which darken or delude the soul from its original purposes. The impact of this exercise had helped to clear away some of the debris which had insinuated itself into my soul through a variety of life events. My inner soul was now so much freer to breathe and to return to uncover and ignite the energy of trust and love which had been hidden by the effect of life circumstances.

The Taoist exercises have opened a new physical and etheric portal, the earth element, activated in my gut, which means I am deepening trust, trust in myself and my world. This combined with the Christ Impulse, living inside me on the etheric level, gave me confidence that I could do what was needed and that if I needed help or inspiration as to what to do, I would be guided as to the appropriate action. What a relief. I was not alone. The lack of confidence that had been a huge albatross around my neck was lifted. Whatever shame I had was gone. A new opening and a new energy lived within. When and if needed, I could be of service. I only had to listen to my inner voice to know when and what to do. Still, I reserved the right to discriminate as to which situations to respond to. But I would not be making these choices alone as I knew I was guided by my Higher Self. I was no longer encumbered by the Ahrimanic forces of control over money, or not having any money as in the past, or shame or guilt, but by the spirit of the greater good and what was morally inspired purpose through love.

Dear Reader, you see, I have been working on myself as I have been writing my memoir. This has led me to research into the formation of consciousness as explored in Anthroposophy, the Spiritual Science of Rudolph Steiner, where Steiner talks about the development of moral values.[42]

"And if we do not look at short time periods but larger spans of time when we can see that the conscience is something which entered the human soul at about the time that the Christ impulse gained ground in the soul. We might say that the conscience follows the Christ impulse almost like a shadow as the latter enters into the world historical development."

He states that eventually as *thought*, *feeling*, and *will* merge, they connect with higher moral values. Steiner also talks about the Christ Impulse and how each person has this impulse born out of love inside

---

42 Steiner, The Christ Impulse, Rudolph Steiner Press, 2014, 100.

them. Through morning meditations, a golden tree of life was formed inside me (Taoist teaching) in which the Christ Impulse and Sophia, the sacred masculine (the Father impulse) and feminine (Sophia) where conjoined in a ball of golden light, according to Steiner's Spiritual Science. Around this I used the golden pearl to complete the microcosmic orbit (Taoist teaching).

The doorway to the path of higher moral values was opened to me. Together these energies dispelled my initial impulse, to protect my own needs, and led me to see the value of the Greater Good, a higher moral value which is service to others.

Agatha Christie has written the Crooked House which I viewed on DVD, and which is a clear example of the way in which the Ahrimanic influence along with the Luciferian influences shaped the story she created. If you do not want to know the ending, please move to the next chapter. For those who are curious, read on and assess for yourselves what forces you think are at work here.

AHRIMANIC DISPLAY IN A NETFLIX PRODUCTION
OF AGATHA CHRISTIE'S CROOKED HOUSE

First published in 1947, this story is about a now-wealthy Greek businessman named Aristide Leonides who came to England penniless and built a fortune and how he fails to connect emotionally with his family members, leaving them at odds with each other. During the dinner hour when they gather for dinner, they bicker and compete, do their best to put each other down. There is no love shown and no compassion or understanding. This atmosphere of bitterness and resentment persists in their daily lives and treatment of each other.

The elderly Aunt Edith, who is dying, is the one person who is very protective and attached to her niece Josephine. Aunt Edith is the one who is aware of the evil nature of her niece as she has read her diary and knows that Josephine has killed her grandfather because Aristide has refused to allow his 12-year-old granddaughter Josephine, to take ballet lessons, a refusal which Josephine deeply resents and causes her to hate her grandfather. This resentment leads her to planning her grandfather's death by substituting a lethal dose of medication for glaucoma, which replaces his heart medicine, which causes his death.

Another person, her nanny also constricted her movements. Josephine laces her hot chocolate with rat poison which she knows the nanny will drink and Josephine enjoys the fact that she has murdered her nanny and has gotten away with it. Now we see the demonic and Ahrimanic force played out in the willful destruction Josephine has brought to the family, through the murder of her grandfather and her nanny. Furthermore, she is proud of her accomplishments because she has gotten away with both murders, has removed barriers to her freedom. This again is a sign that she is completely taken over by Ahrimanic forces and is mentally unstable to say the least. (This leads me to question to what extent Ahrimanic or Luciferian forces contribute to sociopathic and psychotic behaviors of individuals. But that question is for another time.)

Aunt Edith is also captured by Ahrimanic forces. She remembers Josephine's notebook within which are her plans to murder her grandfather and nanny. Aunt Edith hides Josephine's notebook, in a lime barrel. During the time of the murder investigation when no one is to leave the house, Aunt Edith lures Josephine to the car by telling Josephine that she is going for ice cream and then taking her to a ballet lesson. But as they are driving off the estate, Josephine knows the road they are taking will not take them to a ballet lesson and she is struck with fear, grabs her aunt's arm in terror. Aunt Edith has an Ahrimanic compulsion to protect her niece and herself from going through a painful death, is inextricably bound to a suicidal-homicidal act. Aunt Edith, with Josephine screaming beside her, drives into the quarry with the car bursting into flames as it crashes at bottom. Nothing will stop the cruel and incontrovertible impulse that drives Edith. This depicts the compulsion, the impulse to both save face for the family, to save herself from going through a slow and probably painful or pitiable death process and her niece from a life of imprisonment and humiliation. Edith sees no other alternative but to kill the one person that she loves deeply, her niece as well as herself. A chilling but true depiction of how far the Ahrimanic Force can lead a person even to commit murder and suicide.

What do you think, reader? If you say there are Luciferian forces here as depicted by the pride of Aunt Edith, I would say you are right. So many times, these forces work together and certainly in this case that is true. But I felt the Ahrimanic forces that were first set in motion by the controlling and restrictive pressure that Mr. Leonides put upon all members of the family, and especially on Josephine, the young granddaughter by refusing to allow her the ballet lessons she so desired set many of these forces in motion. Often it only takes one action or one decision that can set a cascade of forces which fall like dominoes into areas which no one intended and which often leads to tragic and undesirable outcomes. These are the forces that we must contend with every day. It is only through meditation and purification that we can transform these forces into benevolent outcomes for ourselves and others.

As I look back on all my spiritual travels, I made three spiritual pilgrimages to follow the trail of Mary, the mother of Jesus and Mary Magdalene. I found myself travelling through England, France and Spain visiting places Mary Magdalene was reported to have visited and churches that were named after her because one or both had spent time in the area. I want to share with you details about these three spiritual pilgrimages I made through England, France and Spain which follows in the chapter on Spiritual Pilgrimage. (See Part V on Spiritual Pilgrimages).

Introduction to Anthroposophy continues with Lucifer and the development of ego consciousness

Dear Reader,

Here I introduce you to Lucifer because Lucifer helped with the development of my ego consciousness, because he pushed me to go beyond my safe boundaries and to try new possibilities.

Again, according to Steiner, Lucifer is the other force working in both cooperation and competition with the Ahrimanic forces to subjugate and control humanity for its own ends. I introduce the Luciferian force because it affects all humans in one way or another. In fact, it affected me very deeply because I am artistic, intuitive, and mystical, and because I grew up with an enormous deficit in many areas of self-care and self-esteem. Primarily, I had never learned to love myself in a way that was balanced or supportive to myself and others. This lack triggered the seeding of the Luciferian force which played a large role in my early adult years, which then led to depression and the Dark Night of the Soul, the life-changing purge.

Luciferian forces were instrumental in helping me to develop my ego consciousness which was critical to my decision-making process and to my growth as an individual. Being able to make decisions was important to knowing myself, knowing what I liked and did not like, and discovering who I am. But it also had its downside.

LUCIFERIAN FORCE

The Luciferian force has several effects on the human soul: it causes one to be prideful, self- aggrandizing, egotistical, self-righteous and reckless. However, it is the Luciferian power that originally brings man finally, into a non-transparent state, in which the *ego* can enter the human body along with the physical, etheric, and astral bodies that help to form the physical body of the human being as we know it today.[43] This state is necessary in order for a human being to develop an ego necessary for evolution with the higher ego and Christ Impulse through many reincarnations.

The dark side of the Luciferian impulse attempts to disengage humans from their soul connection with God or Spirit, and to be totally sucked into the physical-sensory world. For an artist this absorption can bring energy to creative gifts, but also what is produced is not sustainable because it is not imbued with Spirit. The artistic product is a flash in the pan which leads to depression and loss as the spark dissipates and the artist is left with the ashes of desire.

The Luciferian force often emerges in relationships, particularly intimate ones. In my case, that Luciferian double was deeply embedded within me as I became involved with my first love at age 19. I was looking for love externally, for someone to love me, rather than looking inside myself to develop my own resources for loving myself. The relationship continued for about a year and a half during which time I became more and more needy of his attention and his time. At the same time, I substituted sexual feelings for love and wanted increasingly more time to be sexual with him. Not surprisingly, he seemed to want to spend less and less time with me and more time in the interests he had cultivated on his own. Our relationship slowly disintegrated over the year and a half we were together. I realize now that I had substituted sexual feelings for love which drove him away. Even though he had pinned me, by giving me his fraternity pin, which in those days was a sign of pre-engagement to be followed by engagement, and then marriage, he broke up with me saying he had

---

[43] Steiner, Rudolf, From Jesus to Christ GA 131, Lecture V1, October 10, 1911, Rudolf Steiner online library.

found a woman he felt he could live with for the rest of his life. (see photo at age 19)

Now my Luciferian energy overshadowed my entire life. At college, I was left despondent, with no interest in doing anything, meeting anyone, doing activities I once loved like going to movies or playing tennis, which I had also enjoyed. I found myself sleeping long hours, dragging myself to class as I was in my junior year at college, and taking eighteen hours or six courses which I could not handle. I was unable to concentrate, to read and retain, and had no interest in absorbing the material. In fact, there was no room in my mind for any information. I was empty of desire and joy. I was deeply depressed, drinking to excess. My choice of drink at that time was Scotch *neat* so when I got drunk, I felt I was on a centrifuge circling round and round, no stopping. I got drunk several times until I finally decided getting drunk was not worth getting dizzy or sick, too much commode hugging in the end.

My depression was so intense that where I had been on the honor roll, my grades dropped to mediocre C in my major. In desperation, I went to the Dean of the College at that time and said I needed to change my major from English to Art History. I knew that I had aesthetic sensibilities which could get me through courses in Art History, and which did not require the amount of reading and memory that I needed to finish in English. I was granted permission to major in Art History and so was able to graduate with my class.

However, I had no clue what the next step was for me and made an ill-thought-out decision to apply to enter a Ph.D. in Art History program. Continuing in school was a diversion from the real work that needed to be done, which was to get my head and heart straight.

However, Lucifer inspired me to continue as an alternative to returning home. I had no clue what the next step was for me and made a wild and reckless decision. I was admitted to a program at Bryn Mawr College but after one semester realized I had made a huge mistake because I was not interested in pursuing any of the work that was required of me. I could not concentrate, was dragging myself to lectures and was unable to do any justice to the assignments.

My art history mentor referred me to his analyst, Dr. Tony Gabriele at the William Alyson White Clinic in New York. With $90.00 that I had saved working as a waitress at the Princeton Inn, I left the Ph.D. program and moved to New York City. With only those limited funds I could not afford a hotel room, so I scoured the newspapers looking for ads for people looking to rent rooms to individuals. I would answer the ad saying I would only stay until they found someone more permanent. This happened at once. I started to see Dr. Gabriele once a week and to attend groups twice a week. Dr. Gabriele knew that I was searching for a place to live and made connections for me with another patient of his, Irene W. with whom I lived for several years. She had a small apartment on the east side of New York. A tall, beautiful Swede, with multiple talents, one of them being an operatic voice which was well trained. However, her psychological hang ups and her lack of confidence prevented her from trying out for the Metropolitan Chorus, which I felt she might have made. But she continued to work as a fabric designer and to welcome me into her three- floor walkup. Irene lived in chaos. Each piece of furniture had something on it so finding an empty seat was always a chore. She was curious about how her phone worked, corded black phones of the 60's. She took off the phone cover and left the phone naked and exposed on the coffee table. She was not unclean, but clutter was everywhere, and this was the environment she had lived in for many years. Nevertheless, I felt very fortunate to have a place to sleep on her sofa without having to pay rent immediately as I had no job. In fact, I had taken the test to work as a social worker for the Bureau of Child Welfare in January almost immediately after my arrival in New York, but the results of the test would not be forthcoming until April. So, in the four months before that job began, I had to eat and pay Irene what I could. I created resumes to work as an editor, as a secretary, or as an administrative assistant, although I had no experience in any of these professions. But I sent them out while applying to work as a babysitter. I would arrange to take jobs from 4-9 p.m. and would go into the refrigerators and would find the open packages of meat or cheese and take the bottom slice to hide the missing piece. Or I would take the piece of fruit that was going bad and cut out the bad part and have that for my dessert. This job then served both as a little income and offered a small meal to tide me over until the next day. It didn't cover my dental needs. I remember going to a Chock Full o' Nuts diner and ordering a cream cheese and walnut sandwich on raisin bread. I took one bit of the sandwich and felt a piece of my filling fall off into the corner of my mouth. I pulled it out and put it in a napkin which I placed in my purse. A trip to the dentist would have to wait until I had some money to pay for "luxuries" which is what medical needs were at that time.

Through the years I was in New York, I continued in therapy with Dr. Gabriel who helped me to break away from the hold that my parents, especially my mother had on me. It helped me to work though guilt and the sense I had of being an imposition. I began to learn that it was ok, even necessary to ask for what I needed.

ACUMEN: SQUARE GAMES

While the analysis with Dr. Gabriel was helpful in allowing me to uncover and express my feelings and to dissolve my mother's emotional hold on me, I felt a need for strengthening of my ego, holding my boundaries firm and being clear about my decisions in life. I knew I needed more help in continuing to know and to assert my boundaries without fear, self-doubt, or shame. Through a friend of a friend, I came to know Marv W, a recent "splitee" (one who leaves Synanon) from Synanon in California and who offered a self-help community which was another opportunity to reaffirm the strength of my ego and my decision-making processes. With a few friends, Marv started a self- help community modeled after Synanon for non-drug addicts, like me, called square games. We called ourselves Acumen.

Chuck Dederich had created Synanon after he had himself been a recovering alcoholic, and a member of AA. He was recruited to be part of an LSD experiment sponsored and funded by the National Institute of Mental Health NIMH to explore the effect of LSD treatment on treating addiction. Chuck experienced an ego breakdown after taking LSD and an opening which allowed him to take charge of his life. He was deeply affected by the essay by Ralph Waldo Emerson, "Self-Reliance", and felt a destruction or assault on the ego was a part of the method for self-recovery and rediscovery. If it could help him to conquer his addiction, it could help others too.

Chuck felt that one could achieve complete recovery, but that recovering addicts could never leave the structure of Synanon. Chuck created games which were central method by which people were aggressively confronted with their perceived maladaptive behaviors and thoughts and were attacked and humiliated for them. These group confrontations were an effort to break down the ego defenses so that the individual would finally surrender to a higher power and develop a new ego informed by the connection with a higher power. Once much of the ego was destroyed or dislodged, then new behaviors and new commitments to life could be made. Dederich's AA training stressed a surrender to a Higher Power to reconstruct a more consistent ego which was aligned with Higher Power.

Some of Chuck's techniques were brainwashing which were also utilized by the government for their own purposes. Once much of the ego was destroyed or dislodged, then new behaviors and new commitments to life could be made as was true for the addicts in Synanon. However, this kind of brainwashing could be and was used for evil purposes. In the case of MKUltra, under the auspices of the CIA, attempts were made to create "Robot Agents". People who were programmed by MKUltra to do the bidding of the programmers could be manipulated to perform nefarious deeds, like killing or sabotage, without their conscious consent or even their memory of the deeds done.

The Acumen community consisted of eight of us gathered in a small three- story home on the lower east side of New York for these confrontational sessions. Someone who wanted to work or who was seen as needing some correction was placed in the "hot seat." The rest of us would go on the attack, words which were meant to humiliate and to break down the barriers around the ego defenses. When people would finally break down and surrender their need to defend, we would say, *looking bad is looking good*. This meant that with your defenses down, you can now build new structures which are positive and more along the lines of self-reliance and self-determination.

The original eight of us became known as a live-in community, Acumen, rented a home in Brooklyn which became a community dedicated to the improvement and development of constructive decisions and behaviors which would help us evolve into better human beings. Marv, the leader, and his wife had the top floor while the other floors were divided into two apartments. I had the half the space on the street level and Kurt, my friend and his girlfriend had the other half of the space. Kurt had been my boyfriend for a time until I broke up with him. Even so it was difficult, painful to hear Kurt and his new girlfriend making love just on the other side of the wall which separated our bedrooms.

Square games took place twice a week and sometimes on weekends if an emergency session was required. The games were tense and intense; people smoked cigarettes so much so that we were choking with smoke at times. My friend, Beryl had a pot habit and was made to wear a pacifier around her neck as she was seen as a "baby" because she was addicted to pot. That was one example of a humiliation tactic that was used to shape her behavior. Pressure came from the group and was promoted through a duties roster. Each person in the community had a job to do. Those who were functioning well, managed the paperwork while those who were not, were given jobs cleaning the bathrooms in our original community house in the lower east side. A hierarchy of social responsibility was installed. Those who failed to perform well were demoted to the more menial tasks. When this happened, their demotion was made public to the group as a punishment and another form of humiliation. There was always hope of recovery, however, as being demeaned became incentive to perform better and to adhere to more positive behaviors for self and for the group.

I needed this community to learn to voice my feeling, to ask for what I needed, and to stand my ground when challenged with friends in the community I lived in. I had an opportunity to learn this on a regular basis during the games and as time went on felt more and more assertive and confident while I learned to purge stored emotional baggage, clogging my emotional and mental arteries. Even more important I was able to confront shame and humiliation and to learn that I was still ok when I did, even better. Feeling shame was not the end of the world, or the end of my being liked or likeable. On the contrary, when I admitted how ashamed I was about something or some feelings I had, I was supported and told, *you are looking good*. That shame and humiliation had been a huge stumbling block, one which had stopped me from trying, or even attempting to engage in new endeavors or new untried paths which I would ignore because I feared failure and the shame of someone saying shame on you. What lingered was the inner thought, *I should never have tried that*. All of those thoughts disappeared over the course of the two years I was in the community.

Eventually, I realized that I had done what I needed to do, had spent my time and energy helping the community and myself by engaging in blood sweating, tearful confrontations. Now it was time for something else. But since I could not "graduate" and leave the community with their blessing, I had only one choice, to become a *"splitee"*. My friend, Beryl and I planned to escape in the night when other members were busy with activities, we were not involved in. Secretly, Beryl had rented another home in Brooklyn which was ready for us. On a given day when it was dark, we loaded things into our cars and headed to our new home where we lived together for a year before I left to study Macrobiotics in Brookline Mass. That was 1970.

Without the backbone of the community to shore me up, I entered another dark place. No sign of God, no light, no air to breathe. I felt very alone and forsaken. I was like Sisyphus, dragging or pushing the ball up the hill, every morning. Every night I would disappear into an anxious sleep from which I awoke in the morning feeling almost as tired as when I went to bed. Every day I searched for some kind of opening, some kind of change, something I could hang onto, and nothing appeared. I felt a cloud of darkness, one could say a lack of luck, or even evil, following me day after day. I did not know who I was anymore and did not know how I could find out.

The Luciferian force oversaw my life, was holding me in its ever-pervasive shadow. And through this time, which lasted for about 17 years, I had to empty myself of all that I knew myself to be, all those voices that I thought were my own, and to clear the way for something unknown which I could not name or understand. I was captured by the dark soul, the Luciferian double, which had been fueled from the beginning by a lack of self-love and self-understanding.

In Harry Potter's *Prisoner of Azkaban*, in a dark magic class at Hogwarts School of Witchcraft, Neville Longbottom is asked what or who he fears the most. He whispers Professor Snape. Professor Lupin, Neville's teacher, whispers instructions to Neville to see Professor Snape in the clothing that Neville's grandmother wears. Neville's wand is "at the ready" as he says, "*Riddikulus.*" The closet holding the boggart (the object most feared by the person) opens and out comes Professor Snape dressed in Neville Longbottom's grandmother's hat, red purse, and dress, looking embarrassed and self- conscious. Snape is wearing a huge feminine dark hat with a large bird perched on top, perhaps a small eagle, complete with white head, yellow beak and wings in flight position. Also has some animal fur around his neck. The bird completely dominates the hat.

The great tempter, Lucifer has encouraged me to try various sensual and sexual activities, whether it was skinny-dipping in a lake outside of Dallas or having sex with a stranger in an empty building which happened to be unlocked (and where I lost my favorite teardrop amethyst earring in the process) or having a crush on a person and then realizing this person was demeaning and possessive, and not in my best interest. I wanted a relationship but not at the cost of my freedom. So, I stepped away still searching and Snape now appears non-threatening, even silly.

Lucifer is a clever clown who works on feelings, enlarging and magnifying feelings, making feelings chaotic, making feelings feel like the most pressing and undeniable force inside you. The feeling of desire, of must have something. These feelings took me out of my body, disconnected me from reasoning and thinking: they were so large that they often overwhelmed, or they obliterated choice or alternatives. Only this will do or that. Lucifer tempted me into thinking I can purchase that car or that house even though I didn't have the financial support to back it up. Or Lucifer encouraged me to go into debt to pay for the vacation that I felt I deserved; after all others will think *you are a nerd or not cool if you don't take the risk.*

Lucifer wanted me to go beyond myself, out of my comfort domain, even if the risks were not supported by the possible outcomes. Lucifer wanted me to be out on the limb, unsteady and insecure, to overstep my bounds, to go beyond what is reasonable or to invest in an unpredictable and costly outcome. The driving thought here is to invest every penny of my savings and see what happens. A recipe for disaster, even becoming homeless or worse, becoming ill and dying.

Lucifer always pushed me to go beyond, to take risks sometimes with reason and sometimes without reason, to try new and unknown place, to get acquainted with people who were daring and eccentric and to take a chance on goals that were uncertain but might just work out, and to ask questions when I did not know something. Some questions led to wonderful new beginnings, like a vocation as a psychologist, even though I had no money for school and had to work a full-time job as a schoolteacher while taking a full-time academic load. Lucifer's push led me to start a Certification as a Music practitioner playing the harp so fulfill my desire to play healing harp at hospice. Ultimately, I secured a part- job playing for the local hospice which was a great joy to me. However, other ideas led to an impractical decision to become a public-school music teacher. But after so many years away from playing the piano, which I had begun under my father's tutelage and then quit at the age of 11, I could not bridge the musical gap when compared with those who had invested so many more years in music than I had. After one year of music education, I decided to change to a more pragmatic plan of action, and so enrolled in a Master of Education, Clinical Reading Program which aided me in gaining employment as an elementary school teacher, teaching language arts and allowed me to sustain myself financially and return to school for the Ph.D. program in counseling and psychology several years later.

Lucifer was still pushing me to gain further training so that I could become financially independent and engage in something I really loved, to find a position in the world that I could identify with and flourish in. That turned out to be the study of consciousness, the clearing and emancipation of feelings, combined with clarity of thinking, as a psychologist. I was on a mission to heal myself and to help others heal as well, to find their potential. Enrolling in the program of counseling and psychology was a perfect choice. Even though I had many financial difficulties, still I was given scholarships and part time positions which helped me to pay my way. I was accepted into a Counseling/Psychology program that I knew would provide me with the education I needed, and in the end with a degree and ultimately a license to practice as a psychologist. This was a choice with risks but a choice which was aligned with my background, experiences as a seeker of truth and evolution of consciousness, as well as my ongoing need to facilitate others to realize their own potential.

The years of therapy did not end with completing my Ph.D. program but continued long after I received my Ph.D. Fragments of my psyche, and my soul were still needing to be integrated and healed where deep ruptures had occurred. So, I continued to travel to New York for therapy to further integrate my mind, body, and emotional aspects. I began to study Psychomotor Psychotherapy with Al Pesso who had created a therapeutic system which integrated feelings with movements and gestures of the body. As a teenager, Al had danced with the Martha Graham Dance Company, so he focused on tracking individual feeling through the movement of the body. His instruction concerned following the feeling trails through the body so that questions or comments would be generated by body language of the individual.

This therapy occurred in a group setting in which a "structure" was created. The person who wanted to work designated who would play the roles of a parent, or a virtue or a feeling that the person wanted to incorporate in life. The person conducting his structure would create the script that each of these roles would be speaking. The script would be in two parts: one part would be the injurious or toxic message that was heard in the past, the second would be the desired or benevolent message that was needed to neutralize that toxic message. These two messages would be paired and the person conducting his structure would have a chance to breathe in the new message which was grafted to the old. This grafting would be installed through the breath. Then the person would be given a chance to be alone for 30 or more minutes, as long as it took, for the message to be fully integrated into consciousness at that moment.

During one of my most potent structures, Al Pesso, who was leading my structure, suggested that I use some small stones that he had in his office to represent my DNA. These were placed in a basket and were offered to me. I had already designated Al and a female participant as the parent figures, along with representations of other aspects of my life: hope, despair, passion, and the missing DNA. I created a script which Al used in conjunction with messages that I had incorporated in my own psyche: you will never amount to anything, you are nothing, you are powerless, you are inadequate. With each stone we created a counter message: you are finding your power, you are becoming more and more adequate, you are knowing your gifts more and more.

Finally, the last enactment of the structure was this freeing message: *YOU HAVE ALL THE DNA YOU NEED TO DO WHAT YOU NEED TO DO FOR YOURSELF.* I took that basket with my "DNA", and I cried, (not something I do in public very often), feeling the power of that moment going deeply within me, saturating my blood and my bones. I felt a huge healing and Al expressed it by saying this has been a very deep internalization for you. His confirmation made it even more real. He had me escorted to a safe alcove where I lay on a futon for a long time, I think until it was time for lunch. Although I did go with the others for lunch, I was not hungry, did not eat, as I already felt filled with such love. Self -love and Self -acceptance. This is not narcissistic love, but a love that originates from a deep connection with the underlying depths that make up the components of who are. You know it when you feel it…and it does not go away.

The structure transformed the lifelong mantra, I am not enough *to I am enough* which has stayed with me and deepened through the years. Even as I write about this experience, I can feel the strength and power of that moment still pulsing within me.

RELATIONSHIPS: LUCIFER'S IMPACT

Addictions are also in Lucifer's realm. Whether it is alcohol, drugs, porn, video games, gaming, or marathon watching of mystery series, Lucifer is pushing and enlarging personal interest. Lucifer may entice through drama and intrigue, through personification of animals or robots or other artificial intelligence. In this sense, Lucifer may work with Ahriman to convince and cajole people into believing that artificial is better than natural. They often work hand in hand. I have been addicted to various DVD series and watched them nonstop until I grew so saturated with them that I finally moved on to something else. Always searching for some entertainment, some interesting story with a twist, or a series that where you become acquainted with the hero or heroines and long to follow their history as they were a relative or friend, as if you had a genuine relationship with them.

Addictions to real people can be a problem, driven by Luciferian feelings. Being in awe of someone who is so handsome or beautiful. Being smitten by a lifestyle you dream of with that person or being swept up by a feeling of being loved and respected, only to find out that the experience was skin deep and did not last over time. Lucifer is all about appearance and that which glitters, not about substance or working together to discover deeper connections together. Lucifer is not interested in building relationships, only in the momentary excitement of an encounter.

Relationships with real people which involve mutual understanding through communication about experiences is another story. I ended my first marriage after two and half years because I found out my husband was more interested in men than in me. My husband was incredibly handsome and all about show. You will not be surprised to know that our relationship lasted for about two and a half years. My second marriage lasted for seventeen years and ended because we grew apart or more accurately, I continued to grow, and he failed to grow with me. I took a chance and married a second husband, an older man, because I thought he was "mature," and could love and understand me deeply. But I came to realize that he was "married" to aviation, to building and reconstructing aircraft as well as to flying. As a gesture of love and loyalty, and as a way of ingratiating myself to my husband, I learned to fly an airplane and became a pilot. We would travel to a grassroots airport where I was offered lessons in an Aeronca Champion, a two- place, taildragger aircraft. The taildragger is a challenge to fly because the pilot must first get the tail in the air before take-off from the ground. After many hours, I mastered take-offs and landings and graduated to a Cessna 150, also a two- place aircraft but not a taildragger. This was the aircraft that I flew for my final cross- country trip which was successful (in that I did not get lost or killed) and with that I earned my pilot's license.

But the hours of investment and energy in my husband and his aviation was not reciprocated. Our lack of deep connection pushed me into a corner from which I could not grow or communicate other parts of myself which I yearned to share. Freeing myself from this marriage allowed me to explore the musician in me as well as other sides of myself. Eventually, I took up the harp and played for hospice patients as a CMP, Certified Music Practitioner. (see Spiritual Pilgrimages and Appendix B)

Dear Reader,

I define trialogue as a conversation between three beings or entities. This is a reflection on the Dark Night of the Soul experience. It also illuminates my developing "I" consciousness or Higher Ego and the conflict and struggle between three forces.

As I observed this conversation in my head, I noticed that three main characters were present and speaking about me and for me. Thoughts and ideas whirled and swirled around. At first, I heard Ahriman say, "She is not worth it, she doesn't add anything to our world in terms of power or influence." Lucifer chimes in, "This is not true, she is adding her caring and warmth to those that she meets. She should strive for the highest level possible and then figure out how to get the skills she needs to maintain it." The voice of the Higher Self says quietly but firmly, "She is worth as much as any human as she strives for clarity and for truth. She is a child of God." Ahriman sneers, "Well, she may be a child of God, but how long is that going to last? What are you getting from her anyway? Is she worshipping you? Lucifer adds, "Yes, she has been striving beyond the expectations of her family, even choosing a career path her father disapproves of but she hopes to fulfil. She is not addicted to drugs or alcohol, either. Ahriman pipes in, "But she does not know how to save money, always giving it away instead of consolidating her resources." Lucifer defends her, "Well, her mother never taught her or gave her the freedom to make choices about careful spending or spending within a budget. Neither did her father for that matter. She is just learning to exercise her right to make these decisions so she will make mistakes from time to time." The Higher Self-voice intrudes, "She has the right to make mistakes so that she can learn what is a good purchase and one that is not. She has the right to learn."

Ahriman chides the Higher Self, "You are always so willing to forgive and even forget but the fact remains that she does not think through what she needs to support herself in the future, what monies may be necessary, and what she needs to do to save money. Money is power and according to her bank account, she has no power. Nothing saved."

Lucifer responds: "She must begin somewhere and now she is applying to schools in the hopes that she can become certified in a professional by which she will support herself. She must take some risks, and sometimes they will not work out. But she must try."

The Higher Self, "If she listens to me, I will steer her toward making decisions that will sustain her. But she doesn't always listen or hear my voices because your voices are more prominent and can be more easily heard. She hears that she should not do something or cannot do something, and she does not know why because you do not explain to her what might happen. She is in a dark world trying to find her way."

Lucifer, "Yes, I am pushing her, have always been pushing her to find a profession whereby she can support herself, even if she does not get approval from her father. She has the right to find her way on her own."

Lucifer continues, speaking to Ahriman, "You just want to control and manipulate her to do what you think is best for her, to use her to complete some project you have in mind for her, in short for your own ends. Your energy petrifies and hardens the heart, makes one cold and uninviting. You want to get rid of all the chaos in the world. But what you don't understand is that out of chaos comes new growth, new energy and new ideas. Chaos is necessary if the world is to continue to evolve and mature."

Ahriman shakes his head, "You are all the same; you like chaos and can live with it. I hate it, makes my stomach turn. I like to see things in my control, orderly and manageable by various means. I am offering the world transhumanism, nanotechnology which can be used to help people live a healthier life."

The higher self speaks: "You want to take over the world, to convert humans into hybrid beings dependent on machines which will draw a wedge between humans and their divine origins. You offer everlasting life using chips and cyber technology as if everlasting life has not been available to all. Also, you are setting yourself up to be in control of all those who are infiltrated with nanotechnology. You are developing an empire for which you will be the leader in control. Where is your support for humanity? You are not concerned with helping but more of eliminating the human population that you cannot control.

Lucifer jumps on this, "You are trying to set up your empire, but I thought we were working together. Now I am suspicious about how you are setting up things so you can be in charge and in control and I don't know where I fit into this world.

Ahriman continues, "You have always been my helper and have helped me corral a lot of apeople to believe. We have been working together. But you have two sides to you. One side wants to guide and encourage people to potentiate themselves. But these go beyond what I want. I like the side of you that pushes people into addictions of one kind or another, helps me to gain the control the people. Your other side doesn't help my plan, so I hope you reign that in."

Lucifer responds: "You also have a second side which crimps my style. You encourage people to be disciplined, to be orderly and to achieve a goal. At the same time, you enslave them with your over control and unwillingness to bend and allow growth. I enslave through addiction, and you enslave through control. But I want people to enjoy the warmth and to feel free, even if they are not, while they head down the path which deceptively promotes freedom through access."

The Higher Self-remarks: "It is true that you both value enslaving others, you Lucifer through warmth and you Ahriman through cold control. What is interesting is that both of you offer a side of evil oppression through which each person can use to learn to reach for the true light of freedom, the true value of growth and living in the spirit of the Divine. In that sense you offer an important backdrop which humans need in order to sort out the truth from falseness. This will help humans to learn to discern through using the heart and their feelings as the chief organ of discernment. This is what I hope will happen with Anne who is now suffering an attack from both of you.

In the meantime, I hear few words but am burdened with the conflict and sense of struggle that surrounds me. A cloud of darkness envelopes me as I hear these mutterings and monstrasions I am absorbed by this cloud, this fog of unknowing that grows and lasts for many months and even years. Sometimes I think I am heading into a clearing but that fades into a dark space, a tunnel through which I grope my way. No light at the end. No sense of clearing. A heaviness invades my soul and makes me feel blind. Only fingers now feel in the dark, feel the edges of my space and guide me along the way.

That is until one day I hear the voice of the Higher Self-beckoning me to try something new, to take a chance. Even though I feel the Ahrimanic tendency to dampen down, to stay put to only do what is known, which at this point feels like nothing. But the Higher Self touches another part of me saying, "What do you have to lose by trying?" And so, I try. I head to New York to begin therapy with an analyst recommended by my art therapy mentor. I leave behind my default dream of getting a Ph.D. in Art History and take the test to become a Social Worker for the Bureau of Child Welfare. It promised to be a good paying job which would allow me to support myself, better than most jobs, and for which I only need a college degree which I had. The job appointment does not happen for three months, so I take babysitting jobs in the meantime. Since I have little money, I schedule time over the dinner hour where I can sneak a piece of cheese or a fruit from the refrigerator of my employer. I answer ads in the paper saying I will pay for the room advertised until someone else takes the room permanently. And I attend weekly individual sessions with my analyst as well as group therapy twice a week. My Higher Self in conjunction with Lucifer keeps pushing me to stay afloat. Over time I take a job as a typist for a lawyer and find myself working on the 53rd floor of the Empire State Building. Eventually I am hired as a social worker and find myself walking the streets of Harlem and also dilapidated areas of Brooklyn which are spooky and scary to say the least. I continue to pray that I will be protected. To disguise my purpose as I walk the streets, I hide my casebook by tucking it under my arm. I don't wear any jewelry and walk briskly so as not to draw attention to myself. My feet are often sore and wet from walking in the rain with no boots or cushions in my shoes. And at times when my contact lenses get cloudy from dust, I take the subway in the wrong direction and must turn around and head back to find the address I am to visit. I hear stories of female caseworkers being approached and attacked, even raped but I feel fortunate that I am not attacked on the job. My staying on the job for two and a half years was a record among my co-workers. But the wear and tear on my physical body as well as my emotions was great because I was frightened of being in deserted streets and afraid to walk in new areas where I was unknown and had no adequate protection from a possible attack.

But my Higher Self-more and more evident and has helped me to discern how and where to travel. I hear the voice saying to me, "Not that street" or "wait for the next one." I learn to respect and follow that voice which becomes my most reliable protection against unseen danger.

This heavy cloud began to clear when Lucifer pushed me to move from New York to Brookline Massachusetts to study Macrobiotics with Michio Kushi. I had no idea how I would manage financially. Ahriman was telling me not to go, but Lucifer encouraged me and eventually I worked cleaning houses while I shared a room in a large house converted into a dormitory in Brookline. There I met Mark R., a brilliant but crazy guy who was a college drop out because he wanted to explore the world. Or perhaps he was kicked out of school because he refused to conform. The mystery of what really happened was almost impossible to learn because Mark did not want to share his life story for several complex reasons which I never learned. However, he was very interested in the Apollo Rocket enterprise and convinced me to travel with him to Cape Canaveral to see the Apollo 14 shot.

With my one of my remaining suitcase filled with 50 bottles of his supplements we flew to Cape Canaveral and pretended to be press agents for the Erehwon Press. We roamed the facility separately as there was little security to scrutinize what we were doing. Neither of us had any money so we ended squatting down where we could for the night in the facility. I found a place under the chairs of a large auditorium. Where Mark slept, or if he even did, I still do not know to this day. In any case, the next day, we set off for Titusville where we could sit and watch the launch with a group of people. The launch was spectacular, like watching the Empire State Building rise in the air with flames trailing from the lowest end. The sound was indescribable, like a huge sonic wave that seemed to explode inside me and extend beyond this universe. This had to be one of the wonders of the world.

While Ahriman was telling me to return home to Pennsylvania and live with my family because I could not make it on my own, Lucifer was encouraging me to apply to school. I investigated and applied to two schools in Texas and found with loans and part time jobs I could support myself. I completed a master's degree in clinical reading and went on to be accepted and complete a Ph.D. in counseling with a minor in psychology. With the completion of this degree, that dark cloud that had been hovering over me for the good part of fourteen years.

What happened was that Christ came into my heart and opened me to loving myself and others through his love. This had come about through the Dark Night of the Soul and continued with the Auto Accident, and the Jesuit Retreat Center experience when I re-encountered Mary and Jesus. (See Chapter 5).

Four Pivotal Spiritual Events

FIRST PIVOTAL EVENT: ENCOUNTER WITH THE ETHERIC LION

Dear Mother

I am writing to tell you of an experience I had which I could not relay to you at the time. Although it would have been gratifying and more intimate to do so in person, it was not possible for so many reasons: I was too young, too close, to frightened and also too distant, because I did not have the benefit of life experience, and because the struggles of trying to raise myself were too painful and consuming for me to have objectivity or a more layered perspective of the situation. You had taken over my life and made all the decisions for me including and especially the clothes that I wore.

Do you remember the time when you were furious with me about what I was wearing, an old pair of jeans and a tee shirt, that you came into my room and insisted that I chose a skirt and blouse you had purchased for me? When I did not respond immediately, you began to kick me and kicked me right into the closet. Do you remember? And I sat in the closet, frozen in terror and outrage that you had attacked me physically for not immediately cooperating, for resisting wearing the clothes you had chosen for me and for not reflecting you or what you thought I should be. I have never forgotten this moment because it clarified why I was so terrified of losing your love. You could turn loving attention on and then turn it off without warning or provocation. When you did turn it off, as in that moment, I felt so alone, so shunned, so lost. I am sure you do not remember this, or perhaps don't want to. But it left an indelible impression on me even to this day. It might help you to know why I did not want to reveal myself to you at that time. I was so frightened of you even though I loved you then and still do. This was one side of you but there were so many other sides that it was hard to see you as one person. Rather you were different at different times, so I was always on edge as to which person was in charge in any moment.

In writing this letter, I am not only knowing myself better but, in some ways, knowing and appreciating you in a more comprehensive way than was possible while you were alive. The letter has helped me to meet the challenge of joining the puzzle-pieces of our lives into a picture which seems to explain what happened. Through this process a new lens has captured the contents of our lives, that makes me feel I know you more intimately than I did before writing this, as well as knowing myself more deeply, an outcome that came as a complete surprise, and very illuminating and rewarding. It has deepened my appreciation of you and the lives we shared or tried to share, through which we came to free ourselves from the confines of backgrounds and hindrances which surrounded our mutual and respective beginnings.

The one lesson that I learned from you and that you achieved through a great deal of effort and endurance was sovereignty and freedom. You modeled the freedom to think for yourself, and to make the decisions that you needed to make in part for security and position in the world, but also for the freedom to choose the outcomes that would lead to a more realized self, because that is what you did for yourself. But you did not seem to realize that I needed to find my own voice to climb the ladder to freedom. I struggled to build my own structure from scratch so I could discover the ingredients of sovereignty for myself.

Not surprisingly, I know you as my mother and I have called you mother when speaking to others, but you were never a mom to me. This term, mom, suggests a familiarity and a touching intimacy that I never felt. You were more like a statue or even an institution that I could and did admire from a distance. But never did I feel I was invited to snuggle against or touch you. Even when you touched me, I felt a pull, that you wanted or needed something from me which I could not or was unwilling to give. This created a physical distance between us which remained with me through the years. You were the first one I remember knowing in my life and the first one I had to break away from to find my own voice. Not an easy task. In the interest of addressing you in some way, I will call you mother, even though the word only describes a prescribed role and does not reflect the true nature of our relationship, a name or word which remains unknown for me at this time.

Now, I want to share with you an experience from my past that I could not share with you at that time. This was such a pivotal moment for me because it began my consciousness quest. At the age of four, I had an encounter with something sacred which terrified me. It was with the image of a lion. At that time, I could not talk with you about as I had no conscious awareness of my feelings or words to describe them. Here is what I remember. I will tell this story as I remember it happening because I want to relive it now with you.

You and I lived in a one-bedroom apartment on the east side of New York City. Our living room faced the elevated train running daily on Third Avenue. The subway trains clinked rhythmically along the tracks outside our window at regular intervals. The roar and growl of the iron cars crossing the metal tracks filtered the air against the cacophony of buses and taxis grinding and honking their way through the streets below. The whitish, now greyish living room curtains shuddered in the breeze even with the windows closed as the train clattered its way down the track creating dust and wind which inflated the curtains like balloons against the windows. Except for the squealing and shrilling of the train, these sounds clinked rhythmically along the tracks outside our window at regular intervals. Slowly the metallic noises would grow faint as the train rounded the curve on its way to different neighborhoods.

You were busy studying for your exams or making supper. My father had been away during the war and had just returned to the household. He returned from the war when I was three years old and did not know how to connect with me. I felt uncomfortable and tense in his presence. But at the moment of the lion encounter, my father was at work or at school, not at home.

The single bedroom was behind the kitchen and a bathroom was attached to the rear end of our bedroom. To use the bathroom, I had to pass through the bedroom to the room's end where the bathroom is located. Little privacy existed in this small apartment with my single bed across from the double bed you shared with your husband. As a young child, I created a haven under the dining room table covered by a large white tablecloth which draped to the floor. (You may remember that.) The table was in the living room opposite the windows facing Third Avenue where the train tracks were.

On a day in late winter, the apartment was filled with grey gloom. You were cooking dinner in the kitchen adjacent to the living room. The kitchen light reflected like a white lighthouse beam on a black sea and silhouetted you stirring beans in a pot on the stove. The single bedroom was behind the kitchen and a bathroom was attached to the rear end of our bedroom. I needed to use the bathroom but was afraid to go through the dark bedroom to get to the bathroom. So much fear of the dark, I sucked in my breath, held it, and ran through the bedroom into the bathroom, quickly turning on the light in the bathroom and closing the door. Once I had finished in the bathroom, I took a deep breath as I planned to hurry back through the bedroom without breathing. While I scurried across the bedroom floor something happened, like a dream but not a dream…. very real and threatening.

As I reached your bed, I felt a presence behind me. It felt like a lion. I sensed it had a very large dark mouth. It was so close to me that I could feel it breathing down my neck. I reached for the bedpost which was carved like a pinecone and wrapped my fingers around its ridges, the only thing that tethered me to this world. In an instant I sank to my knees because my legs were like rubber, trembling and unable to hold my weight. I could not speak or move. I was immobilized with fear and paralyzed in a kneeling position. I tried to call you in the kitchen, but no sound came from my mouth. It was like I was encased in a force field with no sense of control of my body. My voice, my breathing seemed to have stopped. Time passed and I was still kneeling, wanting to move, but afraid to disturb the lion that was already so close to me. It might attack, swallow me up.

Similar to a lucid dream and yet it was not a dream because I was unable to move my arms or legs, even a finger. After a time, I struggled to move very slowly but my limbs now weighed a ton. So much weight. I was going very carefully because I did not want the lion to see that I was beginning to free myself. First with my arm on the bedpost, I began to slowly lift myself to a crouching position. Then I painfully pushed one leg forward, and then the other. As I did this, the force field seemed to slowly loosen its hold. I took advantage of this by taking the next step, in slow motion. This step seemed to find purchase on the ground. After a few minutes, I sidled my way crablike toward the open door. The light in the kitchen pierced the darkness where you were cooking dinner. The light from the kitchen still like a lighthouse beacon was shining across a dark hallway, lighting an exit path for me.

What has just happened? I felt very alone and terrified. Something big entered my life, without my knowledge, or without warning. Something, a lion had immobilized me, brought me to my knees. I had no idea why or what it meant. At the time, I felt I must live with this experience and try to figure out what this means on my own. I had no clue about how to deal with my terror. My feelings went underground, into the catacombs of my interior world where they found a niche in which to wait until some doorway or some knowledge came to me about what this experience means.

Now that I reflect on the lion, I can imagine a new voice and a dialogue with the lion which I might have had, if I had a voice and consciousness, at that time, enough to have a conversation with the lion. This is how it might have gone:

I speak: "You frightened me so. Why did not come to me in the dark like that? You brought me to my knees. I was so scared that I could not talk or scream or even move. I was so paralyzed with fear that I was immobilized for some time. And my whole body was shaking for some time afterwards. Why did you do that to me? You are a very big presence in my life. I thought perhaps you might want to swallow me whole…but you did not. You did not show teeth or growl. In fact, you were silent. And that too was scary. What did you want me to do or say? I cannot imagine. And why in the dark?"

The lion responds:

"I did not mean to frighten you, but I did want to get your attention.

You always seemed to be distracted by other things, by other people, that I had to reach out to you when you were alone. Also, I chose to seek you out in the dark because my presence is better felt in the dark rather than in the light. I was determined to find a way to let you know that I am in your heart and that I want to protect you even though at first you felt so vulnerable. But you are young and in need of protection and at the same time you need to have confidence in yourself to go into the world and explore the unknown. I want to encourage you to think for yourself, to listen to me when I suggest that you might find pleasure and fun by going beyond what has been suggested or demanded by your parents. Nor do I think you should do this without getting information about what might be happening as a consequence. Not every opportunity ends up being helpful. But if you don't think and ask questions about what might be there, then go beyond the boundaries you have already traveled, you cannot learn more about yourself and about the world. It gets dull and boring, doesn't it?"

I continue, "You are right. I was so startled and afraid that I did not think about what you might have to offer me. Now I see that sometimes I am afraid to start new things, but that I need to move beyond my fear and shame. Always I am afraid I will fail at learning new things because they are new and because I will feel humiliated when I don't do it right the first time."

The lion continues with words of wisdom, "Even though it may feel bad, there is nothing wrong with failing if you have earnestly tried. Allowing yourself to take a risk is important. Even if you fail you can always learn something about yourself and about the situation. You can see all opportunities as a chance to learn. But I find that failure provides the greatest opportunity for learning and that is important. Because you are here to learn and grow."

I query, "But often when I fail, I feel ashamed and am scolded for not having done the task correctly or completed."

The lion adds, "Sometimes parents or adults respond the way they were responded to. If their parents shame them, then it is likely they will shame you. But if their parents said, "Good job", then it is likely that your parents would tell you that you had done a good job.

When this happens, you can tell them you are learning and would like to have another chance to get it right. I am hopeful that most of the time they would understand and give you a second chance. They would be learning to know you and to provide opportunities for you to learn and you could eventually make them proud of you because you tried and succeeded."

I laugh and say, "That would be wonderful. I will try to ask for that second chance and see what happens. Thank you for being a part of my life. But next time if you appear to me in the dark, please give me a warning, send me a heart message or a message in a dream that you will be coming so that I won't be so frightened."

The lion insists, "Now that you know I am here, I will not need to come as a large presence in the dark but will be a voice in your head that will make suggestions and comments. How does that feel?"

I respond, "So much better because I know you heard me and do not want to scare me so much as be with me. So, I will listen for your voice in my heart and know that you will help me especially when I need protection and direction. And now maybe I feel a little relieved because I do not feel so alone."

The lion claims "I have been with you since your beginning and will continue to be with you as long as you are living and growing through your lifetime here."

Dear Reader,

Here are some of my reflections on the lion image.

I call this moment the Lion's Gate because the fear I had associated with the lion continued to live with me, and to haunt me from time to time during my growing up years. It has become a portal to new understanding. The power of seeing and experiencing this image stirred my desire to investigate what was happening. The symbol of the Lion became an invitation to incorporate aspects of the lion into myself. Why a lion? I do not know. I did not have a lion toy or remember seeing a lion at the zoo. Nor do I recall dreaming about lions. In fact, I only sensed it was a lion and, in fact, did not see the figure of a lion, only felt it…. a huge presence with a large, opened mouth. I do not remember any teeth, just a large black hole like a void, which seemed ready to swallow me.

When consulting with a friend, a retired art therapist, she suggested that I draw the picture on paper, my image of the scene. Even as an adult, I experience some apprehension about drawing this figure. While it may not be what I would have drawn as a child, still the essential elements that the lion held are still captured in the image and resonant a feeling inside me.

(See lion drawing p. 153). This drawing shows a large animal lion head with no teeth and a large black hole for a mouth. It also showed one eye, not unlike the Horus eye that is seen in profile in Egyptian paintings. The head is huge, and the open mouth and the breath are still palpable to me decades later. Also, the lion seems to have this all-seeing eye. I am not sure I saw that as a child, but it has emerged in the present-day drawing, perhaps as a morphing of the original symbol which symbols can do over time almost as if they have a life of their own. Each part of this image is important, especially to compare original and newer additions to the image. All these need to be explored.

As part of my desire to understand, I decided to do some research. In my research of the lion image, I was led to explore the appearance of the lion image in various cultures. For example, to the Egyptians the symbol the eye of Horus means protection and good health. I was surprised to find this eye on the lion's face as it seemed like the eye of Horus, all seeing and more friendly than not. To have an eye seeing things which I should not be seeing left me vulnerable, like the distance between my mother and father which I did not understand but made me uneasy.

As I reflect on the image now, I know I felt loneliness because of my father's absence because I felt my mother's loneliness and desire for him to be with us. And yet, I was glad to have my mother to myself during these early years because when my father did return home, he brought tension into the household. Home from the service in WWII, he seemed unsure of himself and lost, my mother did not seem comfortable with him. I could sense my father did not know what to say and would leave her alone much of the time. Likewise, he did not know how to deal with me. If he wanted to be alone with his wife, I felt I was in the way. At the same time, I remember that I too wanted to be with my mother and try to comfort her so she would not feel so alone. (I could not verbalize this at the time but only feel it.) I came to resent my father's presence in my life.

If I see the lion as an archetype, Jung[44], 1956, 388, representing, my mother, then it explains why I could not imagine facing my mother with my words. For me, my mother was so many things: an anchor in life, my container, my source of nourishment and the lack of it. In any case, I was dependent on her and immobilized by the force field that she inadvertently created around me. I was her captive on many levels. So, facing her was like facing the lion image and would have involved an act of courage I did not have. It might have resulted in a complete rupture in the family, or of me disappearing completely. Or the other alternative that I would become invisible. As a way of defending myself against the negative forces that I faced in our home. I chose to become invisible by not speaking up until much later.

Here I am reflecting on my unexpressed rage and fear.

So much rage and fear built up under my cloak of trying to balance being invisible and sneaking in bits of my own thought and desires about what I might want. I was never sure because I did not have the courage to test out my desires in the cauldron of everyday reality. So much was still a mystery to me. When I saw others asking for and getting what they wanted, I felt growing resentment, followed by white flaming rage. A deep anger when I saw others being able to get what they wanted, and I seemed so locked into a cage of my own making. Even when I asked for what I wanted from you, it seemed I got substitutes and excuses about why my request could not be fulfilled.... a lack of time or money I was told. Only as an adult did I learn that my mother tried to purchase a coat with a little fur collar and that my father objected to the idea saying that I did not need that. I know my mother was hurt and resented that her husband denied her the opportunity to help me feel special by giving me the coat with the fur collar.

At that time, my parents did not have any excess money because money was being spent on their education, more "important" things at least in my parents' eyes. In the end it seemed futile to ask because

---

[44] Jung, C.G. Symbols of Transformation, trans, R.F.C. Hull, Bollingen Series XX, Princeton, N.J., 1956, 388.

I was uncertain about how they would respond: and they seemed incapacitated by my requests. Nevertheless, the rage that grew, was smothered by overeating and through dissociating or distancing myself from my feelings. I began to disconnect. Not just a disconnect between me and you but between me and my own feeling and memories, thoughts. The psychological term for this is dissociation. I could feel it happening, the separation between me and what I was feeling, thinking, and remembering. It was a way to handle the extreme stress of the moment. Inside I felt evacuated, empty with nothing to remember that was pleasant or fun. Where was the fun? Where was the sense of making decisions about what I might like or want to do? Gone. I had no sense of knowing what I was thinking or what I was feeling. Desires evaporated quickly and left that empty space. I lost the sense of who I was.

As you might imagine, I continued to store huge amounts of pain, rage, anger, guilt, and shame. Not to mention self-loathing. Each day another layer or a new root would attempt to climb through my cold interior. These roots were surrounded by freezing water which continue to thicken one layer on top of another. I so longed to shake free of the ice, longed to be free of carrying this heavy burden. And you know how heavy ice can be, it can break of limbs of trees; it can tear apart a road. So heavy and destructive. I was like the tree with frozen limbs, drooping and ready to snap. As it turned out, I became an observer waiting and watching for the moment when I could breathe and thaw.

But as hard as dissociation was on me, it was also a life saver. It helped me weather the emotional storms that would rage from time to time. In the end it helped me to cope with the icy cold. It helped me to develop a survival mode which I could use whenever I needed to. Dissociation as a defensive tool helped me to become self-sufficient because I knew that I could not depend on another human being to show me the way. I had to do it myself, had to learn to cope, by myself. Yes, if there is a gift here, that was it. To learn to depend on myself, to learn how to create my own world, to learn to rely on my own inner strength to create a world that I could live with. My creation, no one else's. A hard way to go and yet, the sense of satisfaction which came ultimately when I had success was very fulfilling, but it took a long time.

The question remains: "Why did this Lion come to me at that

time?" Even today, many years later, I am still uncertain that I know all of the answers to that question. However, I know it is important to continue to ask. I know that Jung also believed in synchronicity. That an event happens in the external world which links with some aspect of the events in a person's internal world. One thing doesn't cause the other. But there is an association, or deeper unseen connection, a synchronicity which links these events. In my case, I am not sure what prompted the visitation from the lion at that time. I also know it was a sign from my spiritual world that I was being supported and protected by some power that was sequestered in the image of the lion.

Nevertheless, this image from the unconscious leaves me with an unsettled and often distressed feeling that something foreign has entered my personal interior world and is waiting for inclusion or extraction. And so, it is with me and the lion who visited me. At the same time, this image was a gift that has continued to hold the essence of something very important to my understanding of who I am. Through my imagination, I now can continue to explore this image and the unconscious parts waiting to be claimed. (See Appendix D for further research)

Second Pivotal Event

Dear Reader,

I want to tell you how grateful I am for this transforming event. The adage that I had lived with and been bound by, *I am not Loved or Loveable*, was challenged and broken apart during this event. It allowed me to release much of my Lower Ego and to allow the Higher Ego to take a firmer hold on my being. It would not have happened if I had not experienced this *Dark Night of the Soul*

When I was twenty, a Divine force there at the time I was visited by the *Dark Night of the Soul;* I was not seeking the Divine nor was I a religious or even a consciously spiritual person. I was not conscious of Jesus, but I felt he accompanied me through this process. This began as a depression, which I experienced when a man I was deeply in love with broke off a relationship with me. I was engaged to be engaged as I had received his fraternity pin, so I was "pinned." (See photo of me at age 19 where the pin is barely visible on my left breast.) My lover was a very bright and articulate guy and was a planning a career in his field of etymology at the time. Ironically, much later in life he dropped the study of bugs and insects and became a child psychologist. Go figure.

In any case at the time, I was devastated, felt abandoned, unloved, and unlovable, all the feelings one goes through when the object of one's love disappears. My social world and my spiritual world dissolved, and I no longer wanted to apply myself to my courses because I found it difficult to read, to remember, and to sustain any interest in what I was trying to learn. I had no desire to meet people, or to explore the world. In fact, I was content to stay in my dormitory room, to sleep, to listen to music and to brood. I remember trying to read the texts that were required for the courses I was engaged in but found I had no interest in any of it. I was in a world of torment.

I was pulled into the endless cave of darkness and the unknown. Much like my father who was directed to enter college, a socially bewildered person, I also entered college with little clue about who I was or what I was thinking. I was eager to leave my home where I had felt so confined and suppressed, eager to explore the world outside of the confines of my upbringing. I began my second year of college on an upbeat note.

Mid-way through my junior year, my lover left me. My mental health was in shambles. I felt my spiritual life had died. I could not sleep or eat properly. I was being led by a Luciferian force (as defined by Rudolf Steiner) which was pushing me into a fantasy world, where I lost touch with my true feelings and with the sense of the Holy Spirit in my life. I was also oppressed by the Ahriman forces which had taken over my will and were forcing me to restrict myself, to deaden myself and my senses, and my intuition. I was in a cave of my own making caught between two forces, the Luciferian and Ahrimanic forces because I had lost connection with the Christ impulse inside me, the love impulse. I had to let go and surrender the old Lower Ego, so that higher forces, the Higher Ego and will, the voice of Jesus the Christ could once again rule my inner world. I was being led into the Dark Night of the Soul.

My dive into the *evolution of ego consciousness through spiritual self-love began with the Dark* Night of the Soul journey. Although I did not realize it, my heart was not opened to loving myself and others. It was torn into shreds and scattered to the winds. Only later did I realize that I could not think clearly because I did not love myself or the world enough. The relationship between an open heart and open mind was a portal which I was missing. In retrospect, I had to open my heart before I could claim my mind. Or more accurately, I had to learn to love myself (and others) before I could distinguish between my own thoughts and thoughts that had been grafted onto me by parents, family, school, and community rituals from my own thoughts. Only then could I test what was truly coming from my mind as different from what had been injected into my thoughts and awareness.

The anguish and pain that accompany the dissolution of the trappings of the personal or lower ego were very difficult and at the same time each moment of surrender to the higher force of the Divine brought greater light and some relief. When in the depths of the void, I was confronted with death itself, a sense of dismemberment, a loss of ego, of self, and all that I identified as my being. Prokofieff[45] talks about this as a meeting of Lucifer but who disintegrates and is replaced by the sense of a Christ figure during this process. He continues that in this moment when Christ takes the place of Lucifer, the earthly ego is preserved from this sense of obliteration.

The film *V for Vendetta* has a remarkable depiction of the death of an ego and a joining with the Eternal, love. Presented in 2005, *V for Vendetta* is a dystopian film directed by James McTeigue based on a screenplay by the Wachowskis. The film takes place under the rule of a fascist totalitarian regime in which V is a masked freedom fighter bent on starting a revolution and unseating the powers that are in charge. Evey Hammond unwittingly is caught up in the narrative when she is discovered after curfew by the "gestapo" police and is about to be sexual and physically abused. V successfully defends her and proceeds to hide her in his well disguised refuge. V wants to protect Evey and V places Evey into a "mock prison" where he will set up the

---

45 Prokofieff, Sergei, Riddle of the Human I, An Anthroposophical Study, Temple Lodge, 2017, 32.

circumstances of her "execution" and challenge her to betray him until she can find her own internal strength. During this mock incarceration, she is told she will be executed unless she reveals the whereabouts and knowledge of the revolutionary V. She withstands the torture and deprivations that V puts her through. She is stripped of all that she was holding onto, even tortured with cold water, and all her hair is cut off. Finally, she indicates that she would rather accept execution than betray V and is released from the "mock prison." While in "prison" she discovers an account written by a young woman which is hidden on a scroll of toilet paper in her cell, in which the writer displays her passion and love for her partner and for all who read her narrative. She says, "I love you even though I don't know you." Evey is very moved by this narrative and feels a new love for herself growing within her.

In the end, she comes to realize that she was incarcerated in V's self- constructed prison. At first, she is furious with V because of what he has done to her. She hyperventilates, needs air and V takes her to the roof of the building, to catch her breath. It is raining on the roof and V offers her a protective cape which she shrugs off and moves forward. She holds her arms open, accepts the rain, her own ability to love herself. In the gesture of embracing her eternal world, her new-found strength and courage, she offers herself to the outside world. She has surrendered to a higher power that now lives within her, the power of love. She has gone through her own dark night of the soul, enduring suffering and in the end finding an eternal life beyond fear and death that she now lives within her. She has no fear. She cries because she knows she is FREE. She has won her freedom. She has emerged whole and purified by love. Her love extends to V whom she now sees as her partner. She supports his revolution against the draconian establishment, his final act. V offered to her the chance to execute the finishing touch, which I knows he will not be able to manage because he is mortally wounded and is unable to participate with her in the final blow. He entrusts this act to her because of her new-found courage within herself. He knows that she will finish the job (of blowing up the parliament building) and she does.

The symptoms of depression overlap with many of the attributions that accompany the dark night of the soul. However, the one major distinguishing aspect of the dark night is the search for the Divine, for God, a hunger for connection that began when I was about four years old with being touched by the lion and continued in a variety of ways through my teenage years.

I had pushed the hunger aside and decided to follow a conventional way of learning to survive by finding a professional place in the world, as my parents had done. In this sense, I was very much still entrapped in their ways of thinking, hoping for their approval, acceptance, and respect which I did not feel I had up to that point. When the dark night of the soul came upon me, I did not recognize myself as an initiate. Yet much later, I discovered I was following the trail of initiates. The first step was the trial by fire, the purification of the ego.

"Why me?" was a question I have been asking myself for some time. In Steiner's *Esoteric Christianity*[46], Steiner talks about the work of Christian Rosencreutz (CR) who as the 13th great master, synthesized the teachings of twelve great masters of the east that came before him. CR calls upon those he chooses (for whatever reason, not specified) to undergo a cleansing of the soul[47]. This occurs through the purification of the soul where the ego of a person is laid bare of all secular trappings, an exceedingly terrifying experience, and gradually this naked ego is replaced or inhabited by the will of the Divine being.

In Steiner's *Way of Initiation*,[48] he talks about the first trial being one of purification. In this trial, all the debris that surrounds the soul is burned away. All that I could rely on was no longer of interest. I felt that I was disintegrating, being torn apart, bit by bit with no sense of an ego guiding me to one thought or another. Just pain, and the sense that I was in an emotional sea without a rudder or even a boat. I was floating on an inner tube which was a desire to survive---simply survive somehow and find a way to reconstruct my inner life. I know that this process was many layered, the first being the experience of depression. The underneath layer comprised a spiritual crisis, one that separated me from a spiritual being that I was aware of and that I connected with from time to time. The most prominent of these

[46] Steiner, Rudolf, Esoteric Christianity, Rudolf Steiner Press, 2000, 225.
[47] Steiner, Rudolf, Ibid, 226.
[48] Steiner, Rudolf, The Way of Initiation, Compass Circle, 2019. 72.

beings were Mary, mother of Jesus, and Jesus himself. So, I ask myself now, why me? Why did I go through this experience when others did not seem to. Or at least if they did, they did not speak of it. As of late I came to read in Steiner, *Esoteric Christianity*[49] that if a person finds oneself in this kind of spiritual crisis, that it may be because Christian Rosencreutz has placed in the impulse of will a force that leads to this experience. Perhaps a contract from even before birth, that a person desires to be purified to become more closely aligned with Christ. In any case, I was not conscious of such a contract but was determined, nonetheless, to fight my way from the darkness that I experienced into the light. Indeed, it took years to complete the process during which time I felt I had a black cloud of ill luck over my head. No matter what I did, the dark cloud still lingered.

After *the first phase* in which all the debris is burned, I, the initiate, entered the *second phase* which is the water phase or second trial (Steiner, 1994)[50] During this phase the initiate is deprived of overt support from outside circumstances. The initiate stands alone, feels alone, as I did, with no concrete intervention from God or anyone else for that matter. What I did during this phase was to put one foot in front of the other. I had no hope of reprieve, or no desire for reprieve because someone I knew that I had to endure, to gain self-control, to direct my focus to my internal world even though that world seemed desolate and without any resources to draw on.

Furthermore, my internal world seemed disgusting, with nothing to offer, no valuables, nothing to love inside I felt. Focusing on the inside world was painful because I felt so much shame for what was there, and what seemed to be the paltry essence of me which was not life sustaining. I felt I had nothing to offer myself or anyone else for that matter. And I was blown to pieces as if an atomic bomb had gone off inside me. Pieces of me were scattered in my world all around me. When Gigi Young in her June 5, Question and Answer[51] described the feminine initiation through the Black Sun, I felt that she was describing my experience. For

---

[49] Steiner, Rudolf, 73.

[50] Steiner, Rudolf, How to Know Higher Worlds, Anthroposophical Press, 1994, 74.

[51] Gigi Young, Question and Answer, internet, June 5, 2022, her response to my question regarding the Black Sun.

the feminine initiate on spiritual journey, going through the Black Sun, without being prepared with an immersion in self- love and the ability to love others in the world, is catastrophic. he indicates that the soul of a feminine initiate is torn into pieces and that these pieces return to her inside out and upside down. That is certainly the way the parts of my soul seemed to return to me, if at all. This for me was the time of tears, of deep sobbing for what I was both losing and gaining.

During the *second trial* [52]of water everything is flooded, covered in water and like Alice in Wonderland, one has to swim in an ocean of tears. I was immersed in tears during the second phase after I returned to PA and moved into my stepfather's farm. There I prayed and wept daily as I experienced the replacement of the lower ego with the installation of the Higher Ego. The sense of remorse of having failed to love myself and others coupled with the sense of gratitude for a lighter self which was not alone but was accompanied by the presence of the Divine was overwhelming. It was difficult for me to get through the day without dissolving in tears as I navigated the shoals of my new inner world.

The *third trial* is one of air. During this trial Steiner,[53] says the initiate must find his or her way alone. During this process, the initiate begins to develop a sense of trust and faith that some spiritual guide will eventually come if only one is patient enough to wait for it. During this time, a sense of Spirit or God began to enter my consciousness, a feeling of being known and loved by some force much larger than myself. As the initiate, I began to follow an inner voice which I did not recognize as my own but coming from a higher place, an intuitive place. As I began to move into the world, not with any personal assurance of doing right but with a sense of trust that the voice inside knew what was best and I needed to follow that voice. I needed to allow that voice to become my voice, to honor that voice as my own ego had taken a back seat, even disappeared to a large degree, and did not seem to carry the same love for me as this larger voice held for me. By

---

[52] Steiner, Rudolf, How to Know Higher Worlds, Anthroposophical Press, 1994, 74.
[53] Steiner, Ibid, 76.

extending myself in the world, following the urge of the inner voice, I was beginning to recreate myself, to learn who I was or who I was becoming. I was not the same person that began the journey, nor did I know where it was going. Just as a boat on a dark sea would follow the light from the light house, I followed the inner voice because it was the only light that seemed to know the best way for me. It was the first time I felt secure enough to follow a voice from within, a voice that I felt had my best interest at heart. I came to love this voice and to incorporate it as my inner voice, the one that was guiding me, and encouraging me to make decisions that were in my best interest. The proof of that being the right voice, came to me as I opened to new relationships and new challenges which allowed me to blossom and grow as a human being. It set my moral compass in a direction which resulted in my ability to love and to be loved on levels I had not experienced in the past. This was affirmation enough that I was on the right path. But always I knew I had to continue checking how my decisions as guided by my inner voice, were resonating with reality. When they seemed skewed, then I had to rethink or reassess what I had done and make changes. But that was part of my discernment process which I also learned was an integral part of working with my inner voice.

The recovery from the *Dark Night of the Soul* experience took about seventeen years as it meant reconstructing my world, letting go of the old attachments, the old ways of thinking and the old expectations. There were still moments of darkness, of anguish and of feeling completely adrift. I desired to find a niche in life, where I could help others alleviate their pain and grow into their potential selves. As I matured in my profession as a psychologist, I began to find satisfaction through my work. At the same time, I struggled through two marriages: one very short and the other for seventeen years, only to find that I had misplaced my spiritual needs for love and intimacy onto my partner. In each case, the intimacy that I desired, failed to materialize. My spiritual ideals could best be satisfied as I connected to Spirit, to the Divine within myself.

Written by St. John, a Spanish mystic, between 1577 and 1579, the poem is composed of eight stanzas, five lines each. In the poem, St.

John outlines the journey of the soul as it moves toward the Divine. He expounds on this journey in the Ascent, written sometime between 1578-85. The Ascent of Mount Carmel is divided into three books that outline two phases of the dark night. The first is the purification of the senses titled the "Active Night of the Senses." The second and third book go into detail about the purification of the Spirit, entitled the Active Night of the Spirit. St. John enumerates ten steps on the ladder of his mystical journal.

The ten steps are as follows: Dark Night of the Soul.[54]

1. First step causes the soul to languish, the soul swoons, loses its taste for all things

    Soul begins to climb the ladder of contemplative purgation. The soul finds no pleasure or support, no consolation or abiding place.

2. Soul seeks God without ceasing, it can only think of the beloved, seeks the beloved in all things.

3. Soul considers what it does as small, soul suffers because it does so little for God, soul considers itself worse than other souls.

4. Soul has habituated suffering without weariness, soul wants to please God, to render service, soul burns with desire.

5. Soul longs for God and is impatient, every delay is painful.

6. Soul runs swiftly to God; soul begins to feel purified and feels immense love.

7. Soul feels the heart emboldened and enlarged with love.

8. Soul seizes God without letting go.

9. Soul now burns with sweetness; the step is that of feeling the perfection of God.

10. Soul is assimilated with God, by reason of clear vision of God (in everything).

    Nothing is hidden from God; soul feels a total assimilation with the will of God.

---

[54] Dark Night of the Soul, trans E. Allison Peers, Dover Publications, New York, 2003, 19.

1.

In a dark night,
With anxious love inflamed,
O, happy lot!
Forth unobserved I went,
My house being now at rest.

II.

In darkness and in safety,
By the secret ladder, disguised,
O, happy lot!
In darkness and concealment,
My house being now at rest.

III.

In that happy night,
In secret, seen of none,
Seeing nought myself,
Without other light or guide
Save that which in my heart was burning.

IV.

That light guided me
More surely than the noonday sun
To the place where He was waiting for me,
Whom I knew well,
And where none appeared.

V.

O, guiding night.
O, night that hast united
The lover with His beloved,
And changed her into her love.

VI.

On my flowery bosom,
Kept whole for Him alone,
There He reposed and slept;
And I cherished Him, and the waving
Of the cedars fanned him.

VII.

As His hair floated in the breeze

That from the turret blew,
He struck me on the neck
With His gentle hand,
And all sensation left me.
VIII.
I continued in oblivion lost,[55]
My head was resting on my love;[56]
Lost to all things and myself,
And, amid the lilies forgotten,
Threw all my cares away.

St. John declares his yearning for God in the Stanza where he mentions the burning of his heart. He talks about the light that is provided for him so that he can find his way without candle. He talks about being deeply at rest, resting on the Lord as he would rest on the body of a lover. He talks of all cares that are gone and the sense of peace that pervades him just as we forget about the lilies of the field and do not worry about them either. He indicates that he feels totally at peace and at rest as he has come to meet His Lover, who is the Lord himself. And that, through the Dark Night of the Soul, he comes to know the Lord intimately as one might know one's lover. It is a declaration of merger and oneness with the Divine which is both secret and which happens as part of the spiritual quest of a human being. It is mysterious and also deeply joyful because it fulfills a deep longing in the soul of St. John. I include it here to demonstrate the power and surrender that takes place as the Divine takes over the lower soul and infiltrates it so that it becomes unified as the higher soul with the Divine dimensions of God.

Below is a summary of some attributes that can occur when one is experiencing the Dark Night of the Soul. This is not a definitive list, but these are some of the experiences that I had when I experienced this process.

---

[55] Peers, Ibid, 22.
[56] Ibid, Peers, 24.

1. First the loss of someone dear, a source of love and affection, a connection to the living world, to belonging, to being a part of society, a part of a couple, the loss of someone you came to trust as having your back no matter what, a sense of betrayal, of the self or of himself.

2. Then the loss of desire for reaching out into the world, a withdrawal of interest in participation in the world. The world is too much. Every breath draws in energy from the world that reminds one of loss, there is only pain, and an attempt to retreat, to avoid the pain of living.

3. Then there is darkness, a not knowing any light. Like living in solitary confinement without reprieve. Food does not interest, the usual distractions no longer distract.

4. No sense of a future, no sense even of a past, no sense of meaning in anything, no sense of any investment or need to invest in the world.

5. Where is God, Search for God, for the Holy Place. What happened to the promise or the question of rescue, what happened to my safety to the sense of protection that I once had?

6. There is no relief, and nothing can ameliorate the situation no matter what is tried. The usual past pleasures are meaningless.

7. The landscape holds no beauty, only vast expanse of nothingness. A vacuum. A void

8. The connections with people which were once important and sustaining like lifelines holding one in place are gone. All the threads of connection are cut, lying dormant and broken on the ground.

9. Time is endless, no sense of movement or progress, no sense of passing. Like space it is a void.

10. No voice can be heard distinctly. All voices are like murmurs in the background and whatever they are saying is meaningless. No news from the outer world makes any difference. Nothing that people say mean anything.

11. Where is God? Why can't I feel the presence of the Almighty? Where has the sense of protection and presence gone?I am

ALONE and no one to bear witness to what is happening. I am disappearing.

12. One foot in front of the other, but why? Living in hope? That something will emerge. The heaviness of the movement of each foot one after the other. Why? No answer. Just moving to move because there is nothing else to do. The wasteland of my mind and soul becomes my "I".[57]

The exquisite beauty and sense of peace, of love, and of coming into a sense of one's wholeness for the first time, defies description. The inexorable pain and ecstasy join hands in a spiraling dance which encircles the soul and creates a kind of cocoon in which the soul is reborn. Even though feelings are extremely intense, this rebirthing process is so sacred and so not of this world, that to disturb or to try to alter it in any way would be unthinkable. This passion is so involuntary and so encompassing that one feels immobilized into surrender, into the journey of simply taking the steps that unfold without trying to change anything. To attempt to do so would obliterate the soul in some very dark and irretrievable way. And who would want to as passion eventually outweighs pain, or the pain is so infused with passion that it is nearly impossible to separate the two.

While I did not immediately seek God, I came to reach out for the divine in desperation, as a reprieve from the pain I was experiencing. Only through time did the desire for God emerge and come to be present within me. For me, God's gift to me was in knowing him, being connected with the divine and the love that came with that through an opening in my heart. What also came with that was a tremendous sense of freedom, sovereignty, of being able to be, clearly myself, without apology, because the self I felt connect to now was different, on a new level and guided by a Divine Inner Voice.

The sense of closure of the dark night of the soul comes when one becomes one with the earth, nature and with humanity through a sense of love and acceptance. Prokofieff describes it as an experience of reaching out into the whole world and becoming one with it, though

---

[57] Ibid, Peers, 25.

without losing one's own essential being,[58] This is called "blessedness in God."

Perhaps the largest gift was the sense of eternal life, of no death, no fear, of living with the guidance of the internal Light which is always present and the sense of never being alone again.

In any event, the process of going through the Dark Night of the Soul, prepared me to walk the path which led me back to my spiritual connections, to trusting my connections with the beings that have been supporting and guiding me: Mary and Sophia, Jesus, God and the Holy Spirit. After another seventeen years had passed, I had the third encounter with God through Mary, the mother of Jesus and Jesus himself. This came in an unexpected way during and after an automobile accident. (Part V 3rd pivotal experience).

---

[58] 1Prokofieff, Sergei, Riddle of the Human I, An Anthroposophical Study, Temple Lodge, 2017, 48.

Third Pivotal Spiritual Event: Auto Accident

Dear Reader,

For seventeen or nineteen years, the dark night of the soul continued. There were moments of pleasure and moments of disturbance but overall, I lived under a very dark cloud. This cloud felt like an albatross around my neck that did not allow me to be free, to travel, or to have a life of comfort, even to breathe. This is until I had a second life-changing event: an automobile accident. That is when the darkness began to recede, and a new light entered my life. My heart was split open and allowed to drain free. It was like the lancing of a boil which could only heal after it drained.

During those post dark night years, I went through a gradual purge. Who can say what moment or incident will *open the door to your heart*, as Steiner, 2014[59] would say *to the Christ Impulse*? What was different for me is that the opening incident occurred completely outside the domain of any formal religion or church, or institute of learning. Nor had I been studying religious texts or attending church. On the contrary, I was steeped in writing a dissertation, the final requirement for my Ph.D. in counseling and psychology.

At the beginning of my final summer at University of North Texas, when I was 39 years old, I thought my only task remaining was the completion of my dissertation. My boyfriend at the time suggested

---

[59] Steiner, Rudolph, The Christ Impulse and the Development of Ego Consciousness, Rudolph Steiner Press, CW116, 2014.

we take a vacation to visit some friends in Virginia to which I readily agreed.

We left in my Honda Civic, small hatchback like an old VW bug. On the way to Virginia, our vacation destination, we were stopped at the Tennessee River Bridge because of an accident ahead. One white van pulled up behind us, but then after a few minutes, a truck from the Tennessee Black Top Company came barreling down the road with no breaks and slammed into the back of the van behind us, thrusting us forward ten feet. My car's hatchback window was shattered, and the steering wheel was freely turning because it had become detached from the steering column. There was gasoline and radiator fluids covered the road. A man started to light a cigarette and a woman in another parked car yelled at him to stop because of the gasoline spillage and danger of fire. I was sitting in the passenger's seat watching and listening but could not move. My leg had not moved, but I knew something was wrong with my leg because it hurt a lot, thought my leg is broken. There was no skin puncture or visible injury, but I was unable to move my leg at all.

Suddenly as I was contemplating the situation, a voice from inside my head came to me. It felt like a Divine voice because it was so calming and took over my entire being. The message was, *Do not be afraid. You are in my hands. If you are committed to me, I will take care of you.*

Whoa. I knew I was committed. Afterall, I was a captive audience. At the same time, something in me surrendered to the power and impact of this voice in me. I felt I had been touched by God, by the presence so powerful that the experience permeated my entire being. After a few minutes, a minister poked his head through the hatchback window and said he would pray for me. I almost said, "You are too late, as God has already been here." But I did not want to downgrade the experience by adding a voice which might diminish this moment so sacred and precious that had just happened. I also did not know if he would take my experience as less important to me than it was. Rather than risk that I thanked him and kept it to myself.

After a time, the ambulance arrived and put me on a hard, unforgiving stretcher to transport me to the hospital. By this time, my leg was really hurting. I figured that it had to be broken. At the hospital, they began to prepare me for surgery with an IV in my right arm. They asked me if I had an orthopedic doctor. Dr. Boswell, the orthopedic physician who had been recommended to me for my feet while teaching in an elementary school, responded to their call. When the nurse standing next to me lying on the gurney called, I heard Dr. Boswell yelling over the phone, "Don't Touch Her!" He told them to put a cast on my leg and to send me home. Dr. Boswell had been the doctor treating the Dallas Cowboys, knew how to treat this spiral break, and was already barking orders about treatment to the medical staff in Tennessee. I am so grateful that he did.

My boyfriend's brother-in-law, who happened to be in the throes of moving to Tennessee, not far from the hospital, took us to his new home, still filled with boxes needing to be unpacked, and the next day transported us back to my home in Denton, Texas. I had been given Percodan, a strong pain medication which helped me endure pain on the ride home. In fact, that drug disturbed my memory, so that whatever I was thinking disappeared in a fog a moment later. Finally, when I did see Dr. Boswell, he immediately told me to stop the Percodan because of its addictive nature and gave me extra strength Tylenol instead. This did almost nothing for the pain. Thank you, Dr. Boswell, I think, even though it was right, I didn't appreciate being in so much pain.

For ten months I was on crutches and then a special leather leg support. I never had any surgery. That is right, no surgery. Using X-ray, Dr. Boswell followed the progress of my leg's healing. When he noticed that the bones were not lining up because it was a spiral break, he blocked the cast. This meant he cut a slit around the cast and repositioned my foot so that the bones would line up. He said, "We could do this in his clinic or in the hospital." I said, "Go ahead," and without anesthesia, he moved my broken leg and foot, and then wrapped the cast with my leg in the new position. I almost fainted but grit my teeth and swallowed hard. I preferred facing the worst in his clinic rather than in a hospital where I would have to deal with white lights, many medical personnel surrounding me, and a lot of confusing energy. So, I sucked in my breath and survived the procedures right there in Dr. Boswell's clinic.

I had this car accident two weeks before starting a new job as a school counselor in the Texas School System. My supervisor wanted to help me keep my job and suggested I stay with her in her home for the next few weeks, which I did. She recruited her elderly parents who were staying with her to look after me while she prepared for work to begin in ten days. Her father had been a minister in a small church in Texas and did what came quite naturally to him, which was to read Biblical scripture to me. I was in a lot of pain and was only able to sleep for two hours at a time before the pain woke me. Nevertheless, my supervisor's father continued to read the verses to me each evening. I had heard some of these verses through the years in church, but those words never moved me the way they did at that time, and still do. This resonance moved me deeply as if they were coming from me. That surprised me. I felt these words inside me like a living water, washing through me completely. Although I had physical pain, my soul felt protected and clean. I was being cleansed and healed from the inside out. My heart was opening, and the words of the Bible were irrigating my heart and soul in the deepest way possible. I was filled with love and radiance that defies definition.

I felt and knew I was in the hands of the Divine. I had no fear, and no doubt that everything was happening for a reason and that I was going through a healing of my body and my soul which would change my life….and it did. The protective shell around my heart was split open to a well of tears and I was able to feel a deep love for myself and for others that I had never experienced before. I was transformed deeply by what I now call the Christ impulse[60]---this same impulse that my ancestral grandfather felt 300 years earlier and carried with him to America where I was born. This same resonance connected me to this ancestral grandfather born before my time that I never actually knew. Yet, I felt I knew him deeply in a way that I had not experienced with any other relative living or dead.

This experience left me with the sense that *I Am Worthy of Your Love*, the second transformation of the two themes that shaped my

---

[60] Steiner, Rudolf, The Christ Impulse and the Development of Ego Consciousness, Rudolf Steiner Press CW116, 2014.

life from the beginning. This "accident" began a process of healing my soul on a deeper level.

This heart opening was not a once and done occurrence. The healing process, which was occurring in my leg, was mirrored in my heart. My heart had been broken into a thousand pieces during the dark night of the soul and now my higher self and ego were undergoing a reconstitution from fragments of the old combined and reconstructed with new pieces of the new soul's light. This was brought forward by the power of love and reinserted into my heart creating a new fabric for my being. It is hard to imagine that this could be happening because the healing of the heart was all internal. The broken leg I could see and feel because it was painful in the cast but the casted leg was heavy so that when I went to lift it, my leg felt like a twenty-pound appendage that had been added to it. The healing process was gradual and continued even when I was out of the plaster cast and in a leather brace and had moved back to my home in Pennsylvania.

Since my mother had remarried and her husband had left his farmhouse to live with her in her duplex, I was invited to live in the empty farmhouse while I looked for an apartment. While at the farm, my heart continued to heal. Each day I collapsed to my knees, with tears of gratitude. I was living through the second stage, Steiner's water stage of initiation. Christ had taken over, had found a place in my heart, and was directing me from within. Day after day, I felt the fissures of my heart closing, the seams being knit together, and the awesome and fearsome impact of my soul's disintegration being rejuvenated and rebuild from the ground up. I had a new soul, a new awareness, a new perspective, and a new light that shone from within. I learned I could depend on this new inner being, this new voice because it was the voice of Christ connected to my higher self that was directing my life and stirring me in the right directions. It had joined with my higher ego consciousness and was integrating thought process which seemed to be for my most benevolent self. I also found that my voice was connected to this new inner reality and that we, my higher self and I, were co-creating together as a team. I felt I had a companion, my higher self. After this experience, I never felt alone again. This was indeed the beginning of a new life.

PART 5

FOURTH PIVOTAL SPIRITUAL EVENT: ENCOUNTER WITH JESUS AND MARY

Dear Reader,

This experience highlighted the reinforcing of *I Am Worthy* through the meeting and connection with Mother Mary once again and light of Jesus.

Seventeen years since the Dark Night of the Soul experience, and I decided to return to my Pennsylvania hometown and start my clinical practice as a psychologist. At the age of 51, I was still going through the remnants of the Dark Night of the Soul experience and had found a position as Educational Coordinator at a Pastoral Institute nearby. My mother was happily remarried, and I was looking for a place to rent in May of 1981. My new stepfather's farmhouse was available, and I was invited to stay there until I find more permanent lodging. I was still cleansing from the Opening of my heart by Spirit.

It was a time of adjustment to my stepfather's family and to my new position at the Pastoral Institute. As I investigated the area I was now living in, I noticed that the Jesuit Center for Spiritual Growth, a center where Ignatius doctrine is taught, offered eight-day silent retreats as well as other spiritual retreats for the general community as well as for the religious. An eight-day retreat intrigued me as I was wondering if I could be quiet and satisfied for eight days without running home or going crazy. I decided to give it a try because I was in the need of some spiritual direction since my intense experience around the car accident, broken leg, heart opening during the Bible readings. This retreat offered eight hours of spiritual direction, one hour each day which I looked forward to.

I arrived at the center, which is in middle of farm fields of eastern Pennsylvania on a blue-sky day. The tree-lined entrance driveway was distinguished by a black wrought iron gate which road extended into the parking lot just in front of the Cathedral and dormitory buildings. The complex rested on eight acres of ground stretching to farmlands and gentle hills. I parked the car and as I climbed the stairs to the main dormitory I smelled the boxwood bushes, a distinctive fragrance which marks this space as sacred for me because my mother first introduced me to the fragrance of boxwood. I was surrounded by this fragrance throughout my stay there. I entered the huge stone building which is dark inside and cool. The ceilings are high with wide corridors which are granite. Hallways are lined with stained glass windows. The cubicle where I slept for eight days is small and spartan, with one cot, a small table, wooden chair, and a desk lamp. There is a stand-alone two door closet near the door. I opened one door at night and secured it next to the opposite wall to allow the cool breezes from the opened window to flow through the room and still offer plenty of privacy. The coolness of the air was so refreshing that I found myself sleeping naked with the closet door opened to the wall to secure privacy so that my skin will be fully exposed to the caress of the cool breezes.

Buffet style meals were taken in a large dining room where those of us who were on silent retreat have our own quiet table. You needed know when it was time to appear in the dining room for the meal hour otherwise you might miss your meal. There were no bells, TV, or phones allowed upstairs but I had an internal clock which let me know the meal hour. When the grounds seemed emptied of all attendees, that was another sign that the meal hour had begun. There was a phone and antique phone booth on the lower level, where there were board games and a library of sorts where you could read or hang out. Also, there was an open Olympic size swimming pool with cool spring fed water, splashing out from a large pipe seemed to be spring-fed because it was so cool.

Over eight days, each participant was assigned a spiritual director who suggested three verses of scripture to read and meditate over each day. During the scheduled supervision with the spiritual director, I shared what I read, or thought about. That was the one hour of the day I was permitted to speak. On this first of eight days, my spiritual director gave me verses Isaiah 55, 2-3 to read. The section is called the final invitation and the words are: "Pay attention, come to me, listen and you will live."

In this first day of meditation and prayer, I was reintroduced to Mary. I say reintroduced because as a child I knew her at St. Raymond's

Church, as a beatific in the church sanctuary. Here I was having a chance to know her as an adult in a very different environment. This happened in a very indirect way, through my discovery of a grotto dedicated to Mary on the grounds of the Center. The grotto was a physical place in a knoll area, below the entrance way level, and sheltered from public view. At one end of the knoll was Mary, a white stone monument, placed in a shallow stone crevice, by a stone altar, surrounded by trees and with a black wrought iron gate enclosing her space. Four apostles were stationed at the four directions of this grotto. There was a stone stairway that led up and over the top of this little "chapel" and down the other side. Mary's chapel resided at the top and center section of this grotto. Around this knoll were trees and shrubs which acted as a backdrop or canopy, sheltering her from immediate view. It was a personal and intimate space to hang out with Mary.

Facing this grotto, maybe eighty to one hundred feet away was another area bordered by various fir trees positioned in a semi-circular fashion. Astride the trees on two separate sides were benches which were set at an angle to each other but both facing the grotto. There was a large opening entering the grotto space from the main buildings into the grassy area. At the opposite end was a much smaller opening leading to another circular grassy area where a figure of Joseph rested placed.

The grotto was self-contained and very private because it was lower than the road and surrounded by trees and bushes. One could sit on the benches meditating by the statue of Mary and on the beauty of this peaceful setting and not be seen by others walking the paths or the driveway. This was the first area I was led to, a place where I returned through the entire eight days. As I sat in quiet meditation and prayer, there was a sense of blindness, that I had to see with another part of my being, to see from my heart. I needed to connect with Mary, with the maternal protection and kindness that she offered deeply. With my eyes closed, I felt the perfect sense of being in her rhythm of peaceful calm. This flow gave me hope that I could receive what I needed, what I came for, in whatever form that took. I needed to feel that I was connecting once again with a higher spiritual presence. I needed to have the experience of surrendering myself to Spirit.

I continued to visit Mary daily and to become more and more imbued with the sense of peace and love. Eventually I began to explore the grounds and discovered a path out near a farm field where I walked quietly feeling Mary's presence. There on that path I discovered the stations of the cross. Each station was attached to a tree and was white in color except for the smudges of dirt and an occasional leaf that had fallen to it. As I walked, I felt Mary communicating with me telepathically about her experience through each station, how she longed for the life of Jesus, how she bore the pain of his suffering, and how he wished he had been allowed to continue with his teaching ministry. Yet she understood why this path had to be taken. She offered me support and companionship through my past suffering and let me know that she would remain with me into the future. She offered me unconditional acceptance and love. She offered me friendship and a sisterhood for which I felt deeply honored and grateful. She offered me her presence for a long as I as I needed her.

Each day Mary and I continued to walk together during which time she was sharing and listening to me. Sometimes I would pour out my heart about feeling of loneliness or despair but always she would give me hope for a future, that there was much more to come if I would only have patience.

On a sunny day, I think it was day six of this retreat I chose to sit under a small apple tree in a field near the grotto. There was no bench on the field, so I was on the grass with my notebook and my Bible ready to read the chosen verse for the day and to meditate. As I sat in the sun with my eyes closed, I heard Mary in my mind say, "Are you ready?" "For what," I asked. She said, "We are going to the Light today." I continued to sit there. Suddenly, there was a tremendous light that came into my being, blinded me. It was like a wind it was so powerful that it forced me to bend over. There in my mind- space was Jesus, a brilliant light being surrounded by his twelve apostles, also as light beings. They glowed in a mist of faint hues, different from each other and yet as one brilliant light of a thousand suns. I could feel energy all around me in an orb of light. It elevated my spirit and flowed through me as if I did not have a material essence, no boundaries. I could not believe what was happening, that I was for that instant part of the circle of the disciples. Mary had brought me to this circle. It was her hand that guided me to this light of a thousand suns, so powerful that it bowled me over. I was breathless and blind but could see using my heart. I learned in that moment that the heart is the true organ of perception, much deeper and more infallible than the eyes. The heart sees into the depth of the soul and knows what is true and what is not. I was stunned and elated.

I sat there for a time as the experience melted slowly into thin air and just felt the lingering vibrations which were still resonating within me. I stayed there for some time as the hour passed, not opening my notebook or Bible. I just allowed the immensity of this experience to permeate every particle of my being. I was taking it in as much as I possibly could. Finally, as the sun was shadowing my apple tree, I knew mealtime was approaching so I slowly gathered my things and set off slowly for dinner. I did not feel hungry as I already felt full, deeply fed, and satiated. I thought that taking in food would dispel the experience, the feelings I was having. But I went to the table and drank some tea, nibbled on some salad, and returned to my room. I wondered if I was going to share my sacred encounter with my spiritual director. I tried to sleep that night, but found I was still so energized that sleep was not what I needed. I returned to some scriptures and read through them, but didn't really take the readings in. I just lay in bed waiting for the dawn to come and allowing my body and soul to be completely and immersed in this sacred energy.

The next day I saw my spiritual director at the appointed time. Slowly, I relayed to him what happened. He listened and thought about it. Finally, he said, "This is not the orthodox way to come to Jesus." That was all he said. I understand now why he said this because "he like many clerics do think it is possible to know God within ourselves" Cinamar, 2007.[61] My spiritual director was skeptical about my experience because it came without the intercession of a cleric or other religious person. I was disappointed, let down, to say the least by his lack of understanding or awareness of my elation. I had had contact with the Divine, with Christ, with Mary and the apostles. He did not seem to believe that this could have happened in this way. He did not understand how

---

[61] Radu Cinamar, Mystery of Egypt, The First Tunnel, Sky Books, New York, 2007.

momentous this was for me. I felt I was in the presence of Jesus, the Christ, the Divine and this was all he could say? In the end, it did not matter because it was my experience and had I left an indelible mark on my heart and soul, a mark that could never be erased or forgotten.

On the seventh of eight days of the retreat, I walked along the driveway toward the entrance gate. Suddenly I felt quite heavy. As I looked down, I saw jewels sparkling on my arms and then on my chest. These gems were all colors, red, blue, green, and yellow, even gold. They were pressed against various places on my skin, light beacons gleaming in the setting sun. I was amazed and walked slowly as to not disturb them. But also, my limbs, my body seemed so much heavier that I could not go faster even if I tried. I felt that I was in a special space-time zone that was sacred and magical, and I wanted to remain there forever.

After some time, the heaviness began to lift, and I went to the colonnade and sat for a while allowing the feeling and sensations to deepen into my body. When it grew dark, I made my way to my room and say quietly and a peaceful meditative state. This was a memorable and sacred end to an incredible encounter with Christ and Mary for which I was and am deeply grateful.

I returned to Steiner's cosmology of Spiritual Growth, to locate and make sense of this experience. It seemed to be represented in the third state of Consciousness where one is literally touched by the Divine, as I was. This stage of consciousness, of ego development, is one of Intuition. At this time, I am touched by the Light of Jesus as it entered me as a wind, doubled me over and filled me with Divine light, with love. It was so powerful a force that it left an indelible mark upon me and continues to fuel the Jesus impulse that resides in my soul.

According to Steiner, in the development of ego consciousness, stage 3[62]: is that which is led by Intuition.

Here the higher ego from the realm of Life Spirit comes one with all other Christened beings in the world ego of Christ which manifests in the realm of Spirit Human (Atman). The world ego of Christ is the third, the true ego. The true ego is found outside the body and only through personal effort, where the earthly and higher ego are extinguished.

[62] Steiner, Rudolf, Theosophy, Anthroposophical Press, 1994, 61.

All the effort to develop the ego and become selfless and Christ-like must be surrendered and annihilated until nothing of the Self remains. The embodiment of the true ego (world ego) fills the hollow sacred space surrendered for the reception of this being. In its place, a spherical temple called the zodiac. Become a sphere of stars and can become-co creative with the Trinity (through Christ) to give birth to the new zodiac of ego beings who will, in time, come to their birth and development as Christened beings. The stage of intuition is one where the will of the initiate becomes one with the will of the world ego of Christ. It is from the realm of Spirit Human (atman) that the earthly ego was born and thus returns, but now as a creator equal to his own creator over the course of evolution. This mirroring of the true ego (world ego of Christ) in the earthly ego is the basis of consciousness in the physical realm becoming self-consciousness, higher consciousness and consciousness aligned with the cosmic Christ ego. [63]

Where to go from here? I had experienced the penultimate moment of being in the presence of divine energy, of Christ and his disciples. This energy made its home inside me and has not left me since that time. I was bursting with this energy and wanted to share it with someone who could understand and join with me in the exhilarated orb that lived in my heart and wanted to spread into the world. I no longer looked to the clergy as an appropriate place to share this "miraculous" experience. Instead, I began to maintain an openness to the energy of various people I had contact with. When it was appropriate, when there was a receptive audience, I would know I would follow the wave of resonance and share my experience with people where it would mostly likely be favorably received.

My most pressing need was to share this experience with my mother because I felt she could perhaps "enjoy" the resonance of love and acceptance that I felt. I did not share this experience with her when she was alive because I was still processing and integrating what had happened. I did not feel confident that I could transmit the sacred essence of the experience which I was still distilling in

---

[63] Rudolf Steiner, Part 111, Wisdom of Man, Lecture on Imagination—Inspiration—Self Fulfilment—Intuition—Conscience, 12/15/1909, Berlin, Steiner Online Library, 2021-22.

my heart and soul. But now, it has been years since she has entered another dimension and she no longer has the responsibility for me or anyone else in the family. Through writing to her spirit, I am now ready to communicate this experience to my mother. But first I want to introduce her to Mary, mother of Jesus and then perhaps to this sacred experience. (See Part 3, letter introducing mother Mary to my mother).

Sacred Pilgrimages: Tibet

For several years, I studied Buddhism as it informed me about meditation and the values of using the breath to still the mind. Singing bowls, gongs and toning enhanced the healing process and I became certified as a master of the singing bowls. Using sound for healing was not a new idea as it was utilized in the construction of some temples in Egypt. However, when Tom Kenyon advertised a trip to Nepal and Tibet to tone with the monks and to visit Nepal where many singing bowls are constructed, I did not want to miss this opportunity to visit this sacred land.

TIBET TO TONE WITH THE MONKS IN MONASTERIES

Traveling to sacred spots was one Luciferian desire that I continued to fulfill. A long journey to Tibet and Nepal but I could not wait to tone with the monks in the monasteries and to see Lhasa, the Dalla Lama's former home of 999 rooms, a white mansion in the mountains. To acclimatize to high altitudes before travelling to Lhasa Tibet we stayed overnight in Nepal in a small cabin overlooking the Himalayan Mountains. We had a small heater but what kept us warm was a German rubber water bottle filled with hot water. Amazingly that bottle when place under the sheets and blanket kept me warm all night. After a day or so we took a plane to Tibet where we found cases of water that we were encouraged to drink. At 12,000-foot altitude it was easy to get altitude sickness. Since travelers had become frequent in Tibet, remedies were offered in the form of small pellet like berries which were very effective as well as an abundance of bottled water.

The days were spent riding buses to visit monasteries, to tone with the monks, to drink yak butter tea, to learn new mantras using different hand positions, and trying to find a place to pee where you would not be surprised by a wandering yak. One woman was not so lucky as she ran toward the bus pulling up her slacks. We laughed and said, "She was having a "yak attack." But she too was laughing and safe after all. Most of the places to pee were deep holes in the ground which you crouched or stood over and hope you would not fall in. No toilet paper, you had to provide your own tissue or whatever was handy…and hold your nose.

We also visited orphanages and nunneries, as well as many stupas where sacred remnants were housed. We swirled prayer wheels, filled with hundreds of hand-written prayers, their energies scattered to the winds. We watched prayer flags fluttering freely in the wind over the rock hewn mountains, now bare of trees. We visited a cave where the monks had meditated for long periods of time and felt the thin air, the refined atmosphere of the very high secluded meditation "sanctuaries" of the monk. After ten days, I returned home with swollen lips from not enough water and tired feet which I had to soak nightly for a time. I brought home tankas which I framed, and I wrote a poem which was published in the Schuylkill Valley Journal of Arts, Fall, 2005.

> Spiritual Pilgrimage
> To see the Sakyamuni Buddha
> Smiling infinite peace,
> Pilgrims hasten through
> darkened hallways,
> lit by yak butter cauldrons
> and one light bulb.

The image of one light bulb has stayed with me as a signifier for the soul's journey. This one small light is enough to reveal my path and the sacred spark within me.

I was living three lives: one following the trail of Buddha, one following the trail of the traditional church, with allegiance to the Marys' and to Jesus, and one following the philosophy as written in the *Keys of Enoch* downloaded by J.J. Hurtak, Ph.D., Ph.D. in 1973. When I began to study this book, I realized that information relating to the Sacred Sciences and ancient scripture dwarfed the current approach to the teachings of spiritual wisdom from the conventional or traditional church. I dove into Dr. Hurtak's teachings, led my own study group for several years, and spend ten years incorporating these teachings into my thought process. For me the Keys of Enoch was an inter-galactic bible which integrated teachings of our earth world and earth sciences with the scientific discoveries of the current time and beyond. Here is a portion of the *Prologue* which drew me into the teachings which came to replace my reliance on traditional interpretations of the scripture of the church.

These Keys of Enoch, as a written testimony to the Father, are given so that the faithful of the "collective Messiah" will gird up their loins to help the Messengers of the Father's Kingdom and prepare every man, woman and child to be freed from suffering and universal discord, anxiety, and confusion.

This manifestation of the 64 Keys of Enoch and Metatron is showing how the Hand of Divine power has firmly laid the foundations for the new heavens and the new earth, revealing both spiritual and scientific signs for the breaking of the Seven Seals of the Book of Revelation. Through the knowledge of the Keys, beloved, you will be prepared to go through destructive fury of earthquakes, floods, storms, pestilence, famine, the mysteries of birth and death, change and permanence, and find your place in the universe.[64]

In the *Introduction,* Dr. Hurtak was told the following:

"I was told how those who govern the power upon the earth are those who have fallen from the higher heavens and now indwell in the stars known by earthman as Ursa Major. From this threshold gate, they control one of the major entrance points into our local system from the higher heavens.

I saw how the Masters from previous cycles were cast down to these stars from which they now govern the lower planetary worlds and the karmic penalties that were assigned to each. I was shown how

---

[64] Hurtak, J.J. Ph.D., Ph.D. The Keys of Enoch, Academy for Future Science, 1977.

earth was part of a biochemical testing zone using both fallen and divine thought-forms in determining what type of intelligence could eventually free itself from the countless physical rounds of existence controlled by the fallen hierarchies inhabiting the regious of Ursa Major, Ursa Minor, Polaris and Thuban. These realms contain beings in imperfect bodies of Light who use their power to establish themselves as gods in the lower realms.

And I was taken from this region of the stars into the Mid-Way station of Arcturus, the major programming center of the galactic Council serving the Father on this side of our galaxy, which is under the direction of the Council of Nine—the governing body of our local universe. There I was shown the network and the courts used by the spiritual Brotherhoods who adjudicate decisions pertaining to the planets involved in our region of space."[65]

In response to the section titled: *How are we to use the Keys?*

"The Keys themselves were given on January 2/3, 1973, to prepare mankind for the activation of events that are to come to pass in the next thirty years of "earth time." Enoch said this will be seen as the Brotherhood returning to earth to repair and resurrect humanity. Within this time frame, the preparing of the Office of the Christ and the Keys of Enoch are to precede Yahweh's Kingdom—giving sufficient knowledge for activity in the new worlds as we proceed in His Name. [66]

These ideas plus the world-wide explorations of sacred sites that Dr. Hurtak combined with studies of Gnostic texts as well as the Apocrypha were fascinating and filled in gaps of knowledge and answering questions that I had in my mind. His explorations of various temples and ancient monoliths around the world where evidence of the reality of the ideas he spoke about was compelling and reinforcing of the information he was transmitting to us. This book as well as the books that followed his interpretation on various scriptures and books of the Bible deepened and enlarged my understanding of the scriptures in a way that made sense and in a way that the church had

---

[65] Hurtak, Ibid, 1977, vii.

[66] Hurtak, Ibid, xiii.

not done. But it left me with nurturance for my mind but little for my heart and soul.

However, I felt overall that the concentration on the Keys alone was patriarchal and had placed the feminine contribution and archetype in a very minor position. Moreover, the studies were primarily intellectual without an integration with heart knowledge which would translate into service for healing the earth and working with nature as implicit in the development of sacred science and technology. With that oversight, I felt more and more drawn to seek Mary and nature in other formats. So began the spiritual pilgrimages seeking Mary the mother of Jesus and Mary Magdalene through travel.

Spiritual Pilgrimages: following Marys' Trails (Mary, the mother of Jesus and Mary Magdalene).

I had little money for the first half of my life to pursue places of spiritual or cultural interest. During the second half of my life when I began to earn some money and could afford to travel, I visited many places of spiritual power and beauty. Lucifer was still involved but was now connected with a need to immerse myself in architectural places of spiritual importance to connect with my own spiritual power.

The Luciferian force had overseen my life, was holding me in its ever-pervasive shadow just as my higher self was growing in Christ. Through this time, I had to empty myself of all that I knew myself to be, all those voices that I thought were my own, and to clear the way for something unknown which I could not name or understand. I had been captured by the dark energy of the Lower Ego-soul, the Luciferian double, which had been fueled from the beginning by my lack of self-love and self-understanding. This force has been slowly eroding, eating at my soul over the years. However, as divine forces began to move in during the Dark Night of the Soul and following, more and more light began to illuminate my path. This Dark Night experience was pivotal in preparing me for the transforming light of Christ that came to fill my soul and my life. It allowed me to seek the sacred in places throughout the world.

TRAVELS IN ENGLAND: PURSUING THE VIRGIN
MARY AND MARY MAGDALENE

In ENGLAND, I travelled with Claire Heartsong, who was researching a book later published in 2002 as the *Anna the Grandmother of Jesus*.[67] Twelve of us accompanied Claire and stayed with her at the Chalice Well Trust near the Tor where Joseph of Arimathea was to have buried the Holy Grail, the cup used at the Last Supper by Christ. We toured Glastonbury which is near the Bride's Mound of the old Magdalene Chapel where a Blue Bowl was uncovered in the early 1900's. Located at this Mary Chapel of the Glastonbury Abbey is a sacred stone inscribed with the names of *Jesus and Maria*.[68] According to Ani Williams, these same words were inscribed on a banner carried by Joan of Arc during the crusades. Some experts date this bowl between the first century to about 700 A.D. The Blue Bowl is now housed at Chalice Well and we were permitted to use this bowl as part of our meditation and commemoration ceremonies dedicated to the Mary the mother of Jesus and Mary Magdalene. We also used Frankincense, Myrrh and Spikenard, sacred oils which Mary was to have used in anointing Jesus as she cared for him. In this location of the Chalice Well, when she travelled, Magdalene sowed the land with the essence of her presence, the energy she held and transmitted as the beloved disciple of Jesus Christ. Even by the Roman Catholic church she is no longer considered a prostitute or undesirable.

In Vatican City, 2017, Pope Francis declared "Magdalena, the apostle of the new and greatest hope."[69]

---

[67] Heartsong, Claire, Anna the Grandmother of Jesus, Spiritual Education Endeavors Publishing Company, USA, 2002.

[68] Williams, Ani, Maria Magdalena, Article posted for Sound Alchemy World Awake Conference, 2021.

[69] Williams, Ani, Ibid, 2021.

We spent time in the Chapel of Mary Magdalene on the grounds of Glastonbury Abbey and were directed to a sacred stone which was used as a meditation stone on the grounds nearby. I collected some of the ground in the sacred shrine to place it on my altar at home where the energy of her presence could remain with me and continue to bless me.

Each of us took a turn sitting on a sacred stone on the grounds of the Abbey so we could feel the energy that was transmitted through the stone to each of us. It was another moment affording us the opportunity to connect with ancient energy not of this time or age but with the power that left me breathless and a little dizzy. The stone has continued to gather and hold energies of sacred prayers over time and to transmit those energies to those who are perched on the stone requesting transmission.

Toward the end of our stay in Glastonbury, several of us walked to the top of the Tor where the remains of an ancient medieval church, a tower, which was built four or five thousand years ago still stands. When we reached the top, we meditated, toned, and felt the immense energy come from beneath the ground where Joseph of Arimathea was to have buried the Holy Grail, which was reported to carry the blood of the crucified Christ. Now a spring known as Chalice Well, the name derived from that famous cup, brings the waters (laden with iron) which is associated with menstrual blood of the female and the white line, the male line signifying sperm. These conjoining of streams represent the sacred union of male and female. I saw the white pipeline, a small spring coming from a stone wall to one side of Chalice Well and carried some water to our meeting from that stream.

The red line pooled in one of several cauldrons, this one not for drinking, but for external healing. I thrust my feet into the cold red waters to allow for a healing process to occur. My feet immediately felt renewed and alive in a way that they had not felt in a very long time. And I gave thanks and gratitude for that healing moment.

CLAIRE HEARTSONG AT CHALICE WELL TRUST, ENGLAND

Claire Heartsong, with twelve "disciples" accompanying her through England as she collected material for her book, *Anna the Grandmother of Jesus.*[70]

The following is an excerpt from the above-named book written in letter format addressing the reader as: "My Dear Friend." Claire distilled this information through a process of meditation and metaphysical journeying during this time in England and has written it for the reader's elucidation. This excerpt comes from Chapter 1 titled, "A Letter from Anna of Mount Carmel":

"My Dear Friend,

I offer you my version of a complex, compelling and life-transforming story, among many, that presents Jesus, the human, and Jesus, the Christ. Along the circuitous path that leads us to meet with the Christ "face to face," much will be revealed about the ancient Essene initiations that I mastered. These same initiations I facilitated for Mother Mary, Yeshua ben Joseph (Jesus), Mary Magdalene, and other adepts who embodied and exemplified the Christ or the "Way of the Teacher of Righteousness," (the way of rightful use of energy). I gave these wisdom and high alchemy teachings (internal energy practices) to many, and now I pass the secrets of physical and spiritual immortality, resurrection, and other mysteries on to you. This I do because, you, my dear friend, have asked for freedom and empowerment. You are well prepared to use these gifts for the benefit of all as we move through a perilous passage during Earth's birth changes."[71]

Since meeting Mary years ago, as a child, and later as an adult when she took me to the circle of disciples, I had not been focused on my connection or my history with Mary. But the presence of Mary filled a gap, a need, for the feminine presence within me to be reinforced and nurtured. I had forgotten her presence, her strength, and her love,

---

[70] Heartsong, Claire, Ibid, 2002.
[71] Heartsong, Claire, Ibid, 2002, 1-2.

forgotten that I could depend on it, take refuge in it and be nurtured by it. A deep part of my soul called her forth, unbeknownst to my conscious mind, and this calling led me to join the trip to England with Claire and the other women who were also seeking connection with Mary. (See Part 3, Encountering Mary and Jesus at the Jesuit Center).

The Harp that played air music in the Merlin Cave

The Entrance to Merlin's Cave

FRANCE: ON MY OWN

In France, I travelled alone to visit Chartres and the Chapel devoted to Mother Mary where I played my tuning forks to celebrate her presence. On that day it rained heavily and the skies were grey. But I took my *F Sharp* tuning fork which is the tone or note for the opening of the heart to the empty chapel area and played my tuning fork. Even though the day was dark with clouds, the chapel seemed light from within as I continued to play there. The *F sharp* sound resonated across walls of stone and swirled through the space in a kind of vortex. I continued to play softly until I felt the area was fully infused with the sound. Then I thanked Mary for her presence in my life and left the church, filled with her love and her essence.

ENGLAND, FRANCE, AND SPAIN

Another Spiritual Pilgrimage across three countries following the Virgin Mary and Mary Magdalena under the leadership of Ani Williams. Two harps accompanied us on journey with Ani Williams as we traced the steps of Mary mother of Jesus and Mary Magdalene from England through France and into Spain

ENGLAND

The Cornwall Coast

The Ani Williams group engaged in ceremonies to cultivate a reexperience of the travels of Mary and Michael and to experience part of the Arthurian legends at Tintagel and the Caves of Merlin. In a cave across from Merlin's cave, the ceilings were high, and the open ends allowed strong currents of wind to waft through the tunnel. Here I first heard the sound of a solo wind harp. A harpist who was along on our trip, had brought a small harp which she lifted into the wind and the sound of the air harp so delicate and precious filled me with awe. The music was sacred and unworldly. When I returned home from that trip, I vowed I would reconnect with music through the harp and began harp lessons which I have continued up to the present day.

Playing Harp on the Cornwall Coast, England

THE MARY MAGDALEN TOUR WITH ANI WILLIAMS

FRANCE: Still on spiritual pilgrimage with Ani Williams

We visited *Les Saintes Maries de la Mer* on the French coast where the three Marys' (Mary Jacobe, Mary Magdalena, and Mary Salome who were fleeing from persecution in Rome) found refuge. Here the sun welcomed me as I stood on the shore, my eyes squinted almost shut in the power of the light reflected off the sea. I felt honored to walk in the shadow of the footsteps where it is said that Mary Magdalene walked and saw the same beautiful light on the shore of the east coast of France that she had seen many hundreds of years before. The light was strong and infused me with its warmth and power. I felt it resonating through all my cells and my bones. It was energizing and deeply satisfying to the very depth of my being.

MONTSEGUR AND THE CATHARS

I felt "called" to visit Montsegur, Southwestern France because of a past life as a cathar which was deeply moving and highly emotional for me. Here we the cathars lived and were burned to death at the behest of the Catholic Pope. Memories of being burned alive have continued to spider their way into my dreams and into current day fears of being burned by fire. The visit was a kind of homecoming where I was welcomed by those who had long passed away.

Montsegur was known as the seat of the Cathar church and provided a haven for those who had their lands and goods taken by the Roman Catholic Church. Montsegur was sanctuary for at least 500 persons. There was a two -week truce after many attempts to siege and capture the castle. Those 225 who refused to accept the Roman Catholic faith were schedule to burn. Pens were constructed for these victims, and they were burned half naked in these pens.

Nevertheless, Catharism continued to be practiced in Languedoc for many years but lost its leader during the years of the Inquisiton. A second Montsegur was destroyed and a new French castle, a royal fortress was built on the site known as Montsegur 111 which guarded France's border. Stories exist that say the Cathars themselves built Montsegur III as a solar temple aligned with the rising sun. One can see a plaque "Pret dels Cremats (Field of the Burned in Occitan) at the base of this mountain. Also in Occitan, "Als ctars, als martirs del pur amor crestian, 16 de marc 1244, translated The Cathars, martyrs of pure Christian love. March 16, 1244.

In Summary the cathars were the gnostics of France who threatened the authority of the pope and the Catholic Church because we did not feel we needed any intermediary as a conduit to God. We felt that the direct relationship through our prayer and devotion was all that was required. And we acknowledged Mary Magdalene as the disciple of Christ as well as his beloved consort. This was an anathema, a heresy in the Catholic church at that time.

"The gnostic of South of France, the Cathars, left their mark in the form of both castles and fortresses. But their fortresses did not protect them from the Albigensian Crusade. This crusade was started by the

Catholic Church of Rome to wipe out the gnostic religion. The Cathars believed that direct experience with the Divine was far more important than the written word. What do the Merovingian Kings, the Knights Templar and Cathars all have in common? They all acknowledge Mary Magdalene as the Beloved of Christ, and this was heresy for the Roman Catholic Church. Location 96 of 263"[72]

When I visited Montsegur, I felt a sense of gentle reception for those I felt I had known and those with whom I had experienced the burning death. It was an anniversary of the burning March 16 and I felt deep sadness as well as joy in being able to return to the site of our martyrdom. The mountain on which the now castle stands is very steep and very barren with no trees, just dry brown rock. I would have like to climb it, but seven months earlier, I had experienced a heart attack and did not feel strong enough to attempt such an arduous climb so remained at the foot of the mountain quietly thanking all those who accompanied me on that most painful day. And I experienced a huge sense of pride for those of us who held firm, not given way under tremendous pressure from the Church and from some of our companions who did not want to leave us and wanted to avoid the torturous burning. We had remained loyal to our faith and to the Christian love that we felt was the appropriate legacy in memory to leave to the world.

But being there reminded me of the constrained relationships between men and women. Sex and physical contact were definitely frowned upon and considered in compliance with the devil.

Regarding Mary Magdalene, Jean Markdale says this about Jesus:

The earthly Christ who died in Jerusalem was no doubt evil, and the licentious and adulterous Mary Magdalene, whom he defended, was undoubtedly his concubine. The true Christ, however, the celestial Christ who neither nor drank, was born and crucified in an invisible world. Strange concept. The assertion of the existence of an earthly Christ who was the sexual partner—or husband –of Mary Magdalene inspired, much later, strange stories centered around Rennes-le-Chateau and the church dedicated to her there. According to obviously

---

[72] Abbot, Raylene, A Mystical Journey to the Sacred Sites of France, @ 2010.

unverifiable stories, Mary Magdalene, wife of the earthly Jesus, moved to Razes region with her children—thus with the children of the earthly Jesus—who united with a Frankish line to become the ancestors of the Merovingian lineage. Cathar mythology sometimes leads to mysterious domains.[73]

Markdale summarizes the differing view about Christ's reason for being on earth in the following way:

Markdale says Christ's reason for being on earth that all Cathars, whether radical or moderate, accepted that Jesus bore a message and that he showed thee way of renunciation, a way that was truly necessary to assure salvation. While the fall of the angels constituted the departure point of the Cathar doctrine, the return to Heaven and the complete liberation of matter were its clearly expressed goals. Thus, the human being lives on earth to pay penitence, to expiate his rupture from God, and to win back his angelic status. On this point there is no divergence among the different currents of Cathar thought, which leads to an eschatology and the formation of morality.[74]

Human beings are the descendants of fallen angels and are thus angels themselves, either by heredity or by the transmigration of souls. The radical dualists arrived at the proposition: "My soul is the soul of an angel, that since the Fall, had transmigrated through numerous bodies as if through numerous prisons." The moderate dualists claimed that these multiple generations of soul and body would continue until the end of time. Only the perfect were spared the need to reincarnate, their souls waited in a kind of temporary paradise for the Judgment Day when God would separate the good from the wicked.[75]

The Roman Catholic Church was incensed by several things. One that the Cathars did not feel the need for a pope or a priest. They felt

---

[73] Markdale, Jean, Montsegur and the Mystery of the Cathars, Inner Traditions, Vt, 1986, 170-171.
[74] Markdale, Ibid, 172.
[75] Markdale, Ibid, 172.

that God spoke to them directly and no intermediary was necessary or even valued as the direct experience or communion with God was what was valued. Further they did not feel a compunction to solidify relations between two people through the sacrament of marriage. Sexual relations were no better in marriage compared with those outside of marriage, even though it was considered sinful to submit to venal or lustful urges. All sins were mortal.[76]

It was for this belief that the Cathars were accused of laxity and permissiveness. Actually, they made no distinctions between legitimate and illegitimate unions, free love, homosexuality, adultery, incest or even bestiality. But their accusers should have been able to recall that in the early days of the Church, which was heavily influence by Saint Paul and the other Church Fathers, the same concept existed.[77]

This distaining of physical and or sexual contact as an aberration in contrast to connection with Jesus and loyalty to the church was an unconscious law shaped my sexual behavior through my teens. Even though I experienced sexual feelings, I did not become sexually interactive until the age of 22 when I arrived in New York City and began a new life there. Lucifer was very much with me and was behind what happened in this phase of my life.

As a virgin, I was encouraged by my analyst who said, "It is time for you to get laid." I decided he must be right and so I took a chance with the first man who seemed to take an interest in me. Only after having a sexual relationship which was a committed relationship for a time, did I realize that I had been constrained by an unknown force to avoid sex and men for much of my teenage life. To do this I had to push aside my sense of devotion to the church and to Jesus and to conjoin my sexual feeling with love. In this first relationship, I learned to do that although I trembled with fear as I was approaching the loss of my virginity.

However, once lost, I enjoyed sexual experiences because the experiences contained many pleasures of the flesh. I found that sex was different with different sexual partners. Although my love for

---

[76] Markdale, Ibid, 173.
[77] Markdale, Ibid, 173.

Jesus the Christ remained strong, I compartmentalized my sexual experiences as being an important part of growing strong as a woman and a part of fulfilling my role in society as a woman who might have children one day. Although that never happened, still I never had the sense that Jesus left me. Rather I hoped that somehow in the end, that this experience would be incorporated into my person as an attempt to love and be loved which included being sexual. In the process however, I confused sex and love. Only after a number of failed relationships which had been sexual for a time, did I realize that to be loved was not at all the same as having sex. And I had failed to love myself enough to see the difference. I had to learn to wait to see if I was truly loved and loving before sex was part of the relationship. That took a good deal of patience, observation, and some testing before I could again surrender to my own sexual feelings.

RENNES LE CHATEAU

Nearby we visited the Rennes le Chateau where many mysterious and unexplained occurrences happened. The legend of hidden treasures and mysterious connections to the Knights Templar is deeply connected with this Chateau: it's strange and unusual energy is still there.

It is said that Mary Magdalene moved her family to Rennes, and because she lived in the area for a time, the church at Rennes le Chateau was named after her. During one of the many renovations the church underwent over time, ten stations of the cross were installed in 1897. At some point four must have been added making 14, the usual number of stations of the cross being ten. Mary Magdalene is displayed prominently and is positioned between the 12th and 13th stations of the cross. The 12th station shows Jesus the Christ as he is dying, and the 13th shows Jesus the Christ being taken down from the cross. However traditional in composition these two stations are other stations are not so traditional and have puzzled people who compare these stations with the traditional depiction of Jesus.

For example:

All stations have the sign of the Masonic Rose-Croix sculpted on their frames.

Station 1 A Golden Griffin is depicted there.

Station 2 there is a gold helmet lying on the floor and a small ladder reaching the sky.

Station 3 reveals an arc in the sky which could have a double meaning if translated into French as Arche or Ark of the Covenant.

Station VI has the Tour Magdala seen through the opened door.

Station X has a soldier who throws two dice, one displaying and 3 and a second 4, other a 5. If you add the first two you get 7 and the number of stations 10 equals 17 which is a number that appears frequently at the Rennes le Chateau. This may be another mysterious clue, of which there are many at Rennes le Chateau.

Station XIV has a square white cloth in the background. It also shows Jesus with a wound on his *left* side, while the Bible states Jesus was wounded on his *right* side. Also, it looks like Jesus is carried out of the tomb by full moon rather than in it.[78]

The bas relief of Mary Magdalene has the words of a prayer in Latin which is translated.

below. This prayer is said on July 22 which is considered the feast day of Mary Magdalene.

> Jesus, remedy against all our pains,
> The only hope for the penitent
> Through the tears of Magdalen,
> Thou washest any our sins.

In addition to these departures at the entrance and to the right side of the church is a very scary depiction of the devil with bulging blue eyes and holding a holy water vessel. The original head was stolen, never recovered, so the head is not original to the statue.

At the top of the entrance door is the inscription:

"Terribilis est locus iste"[79]

---

[78] Markdale, Jean, The Chuch of Mary Magdalene, Inner Traditions, Vt., 1989.
[79] Markdale, Ibid, 255.

The translation appears to be terrible is this place if my Latin is correct. The inscription combined with the bulging- eyed devil conveys an uneasy feeling to those who enter. This combined with the aberrations from the traditional depictions on the cross and the many codes, ciphers, and cryptograms, most of which remain a mystery, leave the visitor very uncertain, even wary of remaining in the atmosphere of this church. For me, it left me with a spooky feeling, an unsettled feeling, even foreboding rather than a sense of peace. Yet it was in name a church dedicated to Mary Magdalene, so I pushed aside any foreboding feelings and concentrated on the depiction of Mary between Station 12 and 13. She was the reason I was there and the presence of the devil or not, I was determined not to be scared off because of a threatening figure or of irregularities that were depicted on the stations. However, it was not a peaceful visit and although I remained long enough to see the stations, I was relieved to leave the church and breath in the fresh air from the surrounding country.

IN SPAIN

Montserrat: I continued touring with Ani Williams and her group following the journey that Mary, the mother of Jesus travelled when she was alive. According to legend it was thought that Jesus requested of Saint Luc to carve a statue of the Virgin Mary. Later Saint Paul carried the statue of the Virgin Mary by boat to Barcelona and gifted it to the local Christian community. In 718, Barcelona was besieged by the moors and the Christians hid the sculpture in a cave in the mountain of Monserrat. Over the 80 years the moors held dominion over Barcelona the location of the statue was forgotten. In any event, in 880, she was found by a group of shepherds who saw a light coming from a mountain cave, accompanied by music. When they investigated, they saw the statue of the Virgin Mary surrounded by angels who were singing and playing instruments.

The bishop came to claim her but because she became so heavy, the Bishop realized that this sculpture needed to stay on the mountain and not be moved to town below.

In 1025, the Abbot Oliva ordered a monastery be created for her. By 1100, the statue because well- known and pilgrims began to visit her from many locations. In addition, a boys' choir, the Escolania was permanently based in the monastery to sing to Our Lady of Montserrat daily. That boys choir continues to sing to Our Lady of Montserrat, and many come just to hear the beautiful sound of the boys' choir.

The original statue is no longer there because of the ravages of attacks. Instead, a Romanesque carving from the 1100 or 1200's has taken her place. No one really knows what happened to the original one. But this mother of Jesus has the Child Jesus on her lap. She is seated on a throne. Her skin is dark and in contrast to her cloak, robes and crown which are golden. She holds a sphere in her right hand which appears to be the symbol of the universe, a symbol of power. Jesus holds a pinecone, symbol of eternal life.

Because of her dark skin, she is named the Black Madonna of Montserrat and is one of 51 Black Virgins in Spain. She is the patron saint of Catalonia and was dedicated by Pope Leo XIII in 1881. Apparently, the Catalonians celebrate her birthday on April 27.[80]

The Black Madonna is secured in a niche behind the altar surrounded by a plastic bubble of sorts. Visitors gather into a long line and parade down the side aisle on the right of the church and exit either out the left side or directly to the outdoors (can't remember which). When you reach the Black Madonna there is one portal which allows the visitor to reach in and touch the sphere that she holds but not much more. People pause, say a prayer or two and move on. That is what I did as I stood in front of her, touched her sphere, and felt the power of so many prayers from so many visitors. The Madonna had a serene smile on her face and the infant Jesus on her lap seemed quite content. I felt a great sense of peace and love coming from the experience of being with her presence for the brief moments allowed. And I thanked Mary that I had the chance to be in her presence once again, along with many other people who had come to pay their respects, to honor her presence, her energy.

Indeed, according to Raylene Abbot, there is a close association between the Black Madonna and Mary Magdalene.

---

[80] Ibid, Mardale, 257.

Black Madonnas have been associated also the cult of Mary Magdalene. It was she who was the Most Beloved of Christ and applied the balm before his death. She was the first to witness his resurrection. Location 138 of 2631.[81]

In Montserrat, the dormitories and other structures have been etched out of solid rock. In the front of the church is a huge courtyard. And on the grounds are large rooms for making jams, crafts, tools, and other creations which the monks who live or lived there used to support themselves. Since Montserrat is high up a mountain, it is not easy to access so the monks by necessity had to be self-sufficient to a large extent. I think there may be dormitories for the monks as well as for the boys in the choir. There are also shops for selling the products that are made there but that may be a later addition.

I found the setting of the monastery to be other-worldly because it was so high in the mountain over the city of Barcelona and so embedded in the rock face of the mountain, it seemed close to the ineffable. Because we stayed overnight in one of the rooms, I was able to look from the small porch and touch the rough edges of the rock face from which the walls of the room seemed to grow. It gave the sense of being close to the power of nature and of God. Its inaccessibility gave it a sense of mystery, and awe. Its huge size was inspiring coupled with the delicate singing voices of the boys' choir coming from this megalithic sanctuary made it seem not of this world and at the same time magical. I treasured the opportunity to again pay homage to the Virgin Mary who had been with me and led me to so many sacred and life-changing moments in my life. The remnants of her presence were again seeded deep within me, and the feeling of her energy remains with me to this day.

---

[81] Abbot, Raylene, *A Mystical Journey of the Sacred Sites of France*, @2010.

Conscious Relationship with Nature

Dear Reader,

I want to talk about the impact of nature on me. Born in New York City, my only contact with trees and grass was at Central Park where I played in the shade of trees and smelled the flowers in spring. Not until we moved to the suburbs of Philadelphia, did I have the chance to really absorb the smells of flowers in particular the smell of roses that my father planted at the front yard of our home in West Oak Lane. These twelve rose bushes varied in color from red, to white, to a yellow-pink rose, all with strong and lovely perfuming fragrance. And in summer I tried to protect them by removing the Japanese beetles which were also quite fond of those roses.

In our next home in Jenkintown, I had the intoxicating experience of a balmy spring. At that time the rhododendrons were in bloom along with the honeysuckle which formed a border behind our home where the local train ran. My father was on a ladder trimming the hedge and fell over the bushes to the grass next to the train tracks. When I went to see if he was ok, the scent of the honeysuckle embraced me and "assured" me that he was ok. I guess the ground was soft enough to buffer any shock to his body.

In our backyard in there lived a huge catalpa tree which in bloom appeared like an enormous white bridal bouquet. The air was so scented with the natural fragrances of new growth, which replaced the gasoline exhaust smells of motor vehicles from the city, that the air felt light, buoyant, and free. That was my first uplifting encounter with the power of nature.

The college I attended in New Jersey was situated in a wooded area. Travelling from my dormitory to the commons and dining hall,

I had to cross a short bridge which was naturally sheltered by trees shadowing the walkway. I felt embraced by their extending limbs and leaves which surrounded me in a protective way and still remember their beauty as I write now.

Still, I did not feel a need to be close to nature, to huge trees until I returned to Allentown Pa. and began my practice as a psychologist. Close to my home was Trexler Park where the statute of General Trexler resided, overlooking the park of 1,108 acres. He had endowed and created this park as a refuge for endangered bison and elk at the close of the 20th century. In the center of the park is a duck pond where many geese and ducks established residence. Numerous trees had been planted along the many walkways separating large grassy areas where all manner of wildlife could roam. I admired the huge canopy that these enormous trees made and how they resided peacefully in a well-manicured environment, not a formal garden, but well preserved and cared for. When I walked these paths, I could view the ducks and geese cavorting on the water, see the occasional fox or groundhog running for safety into the bushes while I walked the circumference of the park as many times as I needed to feel I had gotten enough exercise for the day. Being in the company of the trees, these mighty tall beings and smelling the scents of the earth, was refreshing, and rejuvenating from the stale air that I usually encountered in old buildings or even in my home.

Now I live next to a pond which I view out of my bedroom window. Geese, ducks, and blue heron live here along with snapping turtles and carp. Many squirrels, chipmunks, and lots of birds of different varieties fill the air and eat from my bird feeders which hang from my screened in porch. These creatures are my daily companions as are the trees which border the pond. I now claim my feathered friends and leafing trees as part of my family for which I am deeply grateful. I want to thank them and show my appreciation for their shelter and presence without which my life would feel incomplete.

Connection with Nature continues.

Dear Reader:

The phase we are moving into is co-partnering with the earth. It is because we are from the earth and are part of the earth that we must claim our home as our responsibility and learn to care for it, just as we learn to care for ourselves. In the past, we have dominated the earth and taken from it what we need. Now we must recognize the earth as an equal and important partner, a living being with home we must negotiate and honor so we can live together in peace.

To really know who we are can only happen when we recognize ourselves as having a spiritual origin, when we recognize that we are connected by our spiritual roots, and that we are also connected to the earth which gives us sustenance. In this sense, the earth is our mother who feeds us, even though we have defiled her and used her without thought about the effects upon her. We belong to mother earth as she is our home and our domain. She supports us as we continue our spiritual journey, the development of our ego consciousness which elevates into our higher soul and into more and more refined frequencies and dimensions.

It is time to do this. Really, it is overtime. Steiner said it is time more than one hundred years ago. The earth has endured rape and pillaging since the Industrial Revolution and before. Only the American Indian and other indigenous groups have lived to honor the sacred relationship that humans have on the earth. It is because we not only depend on the earth's resources for our own sustenance, but it is also because we are a composite of the earth and heavens created by our

God, by the Divine. The being of Sophia is re-emerging to join the Sacred, to join the love of Christ to renew and resurrect a relationship with the world. It is not that we are here to dominate the world but her to partner as caretakers of the earth. Sophia is coming as the Rose of the World to lend her energy to us so that we may reclaim our right relationship with the earth.

According to Robert Powell and Estelle Isaacson,[82] from remarks made by Rudolf Steiner it is evident that Sophia ("Wisdom"), who spoke to the people of Israel through Solomon, was worshipped in the ancient Egyptians as Isis. He indicated that the decline of the ancient Egyptian "culture", the cosmic wisdom, Isis-Sophia, became "buried" or "killed," but that in our time She may be found again. She may be found in spiritual realms as the Cosmic Virgin, and if She is found there, She communicates to us a new wisdom of the stars. In the New Age, the age of Christ's Second coming, Mary Sophia may be sought also here on Earth, manifesting from within the Earth's etheric aura. She may reveal Herself to human beings not only in churches and cathedrals, such as the great cathedral at Chartres, but also in the stillness of Nature, in harmonious union with Mother Earth.

The Rose of the World is arising through the approach of Divine Sophia toward the Earth. Her approach is calling forth the following basic qualities or attributes of the new world culture that She is creating and inspiring: 1-7.[83]

Powell and Isaacson name seven ways in which the Rose of the World is inspiring and calling to us to honor the earth once again.

Finally, Sophia is working for the transformation of the planet into a garden. In their striving to live in cooperation and harmony with Nature, human beings are to take up their responsibility for the spiritualization and redemption of Nature's various kingdoms.[84]

But who or what is Sophia? From the anthroposophical point of view Valentin Tomberg describe his encounters with Sophia as a being

---

[82] Powell, Robert and Isaacson, Estelle, The Mystery of Sophia, Lindisfarne Books, 2014, 143.

[83] Ibid, 146.

[84] Ibid, 148.

of wisdom according to the Gnostics of many years ago and offers the plan for building the new earth. How appropriate now that we are in the midst of building a new earth as the old patterns crumble away.

Solovyov gleaned his knowledge from a different path than the one he follows to make it understandable to others. He speaks of the three suprasensory experiences he had in 1862, 1875 and 1876. The first experience came to him as a boy during divine service in church. The being appeared to him then whom, fourteen years later, he came to know in another form as the mother of God. He had the second experience while doing research in British Museum in London on certain questions related to the sources of human spiritual history. On that occasion, he heard the inner word, which directed him to Egypt, where in the loneliness of the wilderness he had his third, decisive experience. He saw—and immediately understood what he saw—the cosmic Sophia being as a revelation of the Wisdom of God. This experience was the true source of Solovyov's "philosophy"; the remainder of his work was merely a struggle to form his thoughts so that the essence of what he has seen might be told.[85]

What did Solovyov see in the Egyptian desert? Who is the Sophia? The Sophia is not an abstract concept or merely a pious, mystical state of mind, but an actual archangelic being who performs a particular spiritual task. A part of this special mission is the anticipatory *manas* revelation, given through certain individuals. Various other beings are also involved in this *revelation*, but it is Sophia who brings about the revelation by means of which the *Unity Of the Trinity* (and also the unity of the three occultisms) becomes perceptible. For humankind, Sophia does not represent separate cognitions in distinct areas, but the knowledge of what gives meaning in all cognitions.[86]

That being of whom Solomon speaks, and whom Solovyov saw, is the same hierarchical being who, during the first centuries of Christian era, was called Sophia by the Gnostics. For humankind, the "house" of

---

[85] Tomberg, Valentin, Christ and Sophia, Steiner Books, 2006, 140.
[86] Ibid, Tomberg, 140.

Sophia is the complete knowledge of the plan for building the universe and one with the goals of evolution.[87]

The part of the cosmic intelligence that has descended to the *"I" am being* and even lower is the "fallen Sophia," the Sophia Achamoth of the Gnostics. The pure Sophia remains in the heights of the spirit worlds. During the present era, her work of revelation is under the protection of the Archangel Michael, who is the "administrator of the cosmic intelligence" in the sense that he guides the whole revelation of the Sophia so that it may be absorbed by the best forces of the human consciousness soul. He creates the bridge between the *manas light* and the consciousness soul by pouring strength of will into the moral essence of thought revelations. [88]

The "faith" that Jesus Christ found surrounding him was the work of Sophia. And the imperturbable certainty conferred on souls of the disciples by the recognition of the Pentecostal flame was likewise bestowed through the cooperation of the Sophia Being.[89]

Mary is shown standing among the twelve, with the Holy Spirit in the form of a dove hovering above her head pouring a stream of revelation directly upon her. The resulting tongues of fire shoot up over the heads of the twelve. Mary Sophia is represented in a bright purple robe (maphorion) over a blue tunic (chiton). The whole group is surround by a design of flowers in bloom, while above is the enclosing dome of an inverted chalice. The picture of the circle of twelve with Mary Sophia in the center leads us to a question that must answered before the Pentecost can be understood; What is the nature of Mary Sophia and her role in bringing about the Pentecostal revelation?[90]

The first encounter with the reality of Sophia in our age occurs in human thinking when it strives to comprehend the Trinity as the cosmic revelation of a unity of three different principles. The recognition of

---

[87] Ibid, Tomberg, 141.
[88] Ibid, Tomberg, 141-142.
[89] Ibid, Tomberg, 152.
[90] Ibid, Tomberg, 303.

the Unity of the Trinity revealed in the cosmos is an event in human thinking that extends beyond the mere life of thought. It points to a meeting on the far side of it—one that favorably determines thought life but is not really a product of it. This meeting in the depths of thinking may be the first experience of the Sophia's reality. In particular, the Sophia manifests human consciousness by bringing about the harmony of all spiritual hierarchies, through which, in effect, the Father, Son, and Holy Spirit reveal themselves. What is called "synthesis" in the practice of abstract thinking becomes an experience of cognitive knowledge when the ascension through life meets the Sophia being. Sophia causes cognitive perception of harmony in the spiritual, divine world; she does this in a literal way since she is a being of inspiration, with whom the ascending human thought can meet. Before such an encounter can occur, however, consciousness must ascend (if only for a moment) two stages above ordinary objective consciousness. The ascent is needed because Sophia is without speech, both for objective consciousness and for imagination consciousness. She has no speech in these spheres because she does not possess the force of imagination, the faculty for creating imagination. She does not possess this faculty because Lucifer robbed her of it. This happened during the period of Earth's spiritual history when the fall of humanity took place. Lucifer took for himself Sophia's imaginations by using them himself instead of serving her. And he used her imaginations as she materials he needed to create a world.

This world, however, was to be constructed from Sophia's imaginations so that it would not reveal the harmony of the divine world but the grandeur of Lucifer himself. Thus, Lucifer transformed the imaginations of Sophia into their opposite, and a world of lies arose.

The Luciferic sphere is a false paradise or false spiritual world, the source of those visions of egoistic bliss that manifest so frequently in popular religious life. The danger of that sphere is not so much that it encourages the egoism so deeply rooted in human nature, but, because it is made up of Sophia's imaginations, or pictures of comprehensive cosmic truth, it can have a tremendously corrupting effect on the faculties of knowledge that are not (yet) fully awake. A cosmic lie is not just a wild fantasy but abused truth. And the truth of the imaginative revelation of Sophia was abused so that it was first broken into pieces and then reconstructed in a different pattern. The shining wisdom of God was change into a glittering garment for Lucifer.

In this way, Isis Sophia, the "Wisdom of God," was killed for the lower worlds, since Sophia became a being without speech regarding the two lower realms of existence. The creative force of imagination was taken from her, and, as a result, she became colorless, ineffective being, barred from any activity in relation to earthly events. The figure of mater dolorosa, or the mourning mother, is the best expression of the tragic state of Sophia. She is generous in nature and inwardly filled with the gifts of wisdom, but she cannot give those gifts to human consciousness unless it rises to her sphere.

The gifts that the Sophia bears within her are quite different from those of other hierarchical beings. She carries concentrated inner wisdom that is not only light of the Godhead shining through her being and not just the vista of the cosmic chronicle, or akashic record. The wisdom to which this being owes her name is neither a direct revelation or a higher divinity nor the epitome of the cosmic memory from the akashic record as presented to the gaze of hierarchic beings; rather, it is the memory of soul ascending from within; it is the wisdom of the soul's pure creativity, and at the same time, such that the whole experience of the past cosmos arises from the inner being as the primal intention, or "plan" for the present cosmos. Hence Sophia, is for humanity, the spiritual archetype of the soul—not just in the sense of the tragic destiny of the soul growing more and more mute in the world, but also in the sense of the concentrated wisdom that is only possible in and through the soul.[91]

There is a similarity of destiny between the true human soul being on Earth and Sophia's soul being in the spiritual world. In earlier times, human beings were aware of this similarity; consequently, an astral (or

---

91

sentient) body was so purified from the sheath of egoistic interests that the true soul being could come to expression as the "Virgin Sophia." In this sense, Mary the mother of Jesus, was also the "Virgin Sophia." Because of extremely complicated influences coming from the spiritual world, Mary had an astral body that was so purified it could receive the revelations of Sophia and pour them out again in inspirations of the soul. This faculty was the very reason why, at the time of Pentecostal revelation, the Virgin Mary occupied the central position in the circle of twelve.

Through the cooperation of Mary, however, something more could happen; the disciples' heart beats in harmony with hers while they experienced the Pentecostal revelation as personal human conviction. Through this experience, they became not prophets but specifically apostles.

A great event occurred in the spiritual world at the hour of Pentecost; the Sophia's silence ended, and she regained her ability to reveal herself through speech. Moreover, she could reveal herself in such a way that not only could certain initiates rise to her sphere and receive her inspirations, but she herself could also descend and pour her influence into the ordinary day consciousness of earthly human beings. It was not that the Sophia had been reached by a certain group of human beings (which had happened before); the point now was that for the first time, on her side, she could reach down to a group of earthly human beings.

At Pentecost the barrier Lucifer had erected between Sophia and the realm of human day consciousness was cleared from the path.[92]

Then, between the area of the Sophia's inspiration and the imaginations of the life tableau of Christ, we find the Luciferic sphere itself. At the time of the Pentecost event, however, the sphere became pervious to the Sophia revelation descending from above. This happened because Lucifer's inner conversion at the Mystery of Golgotha. A penitent Lucifer became the humble bridge over the realm

---

[92] Ibid, Tomberg, 306.

of lies he had created in the past. Thus, the path of Sophia revelation led through the realm of Lucifer and, in fact, through the being of Lucifer himself. At the hour of Pentecost, Lucifer surrendered entirely to the Sophia impulse; he united with it and led it through his own being down to the life tableau of Christ, where it reached human souls.

The Paraclete is not just the Holy Spirit as the third hypostasis of the divine Trinity, but a revelation of the third hypostasis such as was affected by the combined influence of Sophia and Lucifer when Lucifer humbly submitted to serve the Sophia impulse.[93]

In the area of *intuition*, she (Sophia) is united with the Christ, and, through this union, brings about in the spiritual world what she must also bring about in the realm of earthly humanity—the realization of Christ's words, "Ye in me, and I in you."

The path that the Christ had to walk would lead from an outer position to living within. This happened at the Pentecost when the Christ entered the disciple's souls. And he did this in such a way that he was, as it were, born a second time; through the "heavenly Mother" Sophia, he was born into the souls of the disciples. Thus the" I" being of the disciples was filled with the Christ, who became the Kyrios, the group "I," as it were, of the disciples. That "I" was sheathed in the communal astral body of Sophia, in the ether body, however, they bore the combined experiences of the life tableau of Christ; and physically, the disciples represented a circle formed to become the means of the Pentecost revelation, with Mary as its center, who esoteric name was the "Virgin Sophia."[94]

Pentecost was the resurrection of the soul in the sense that it brought to life wisdom that had united with the soul. Soul life did not arise out of mere feelings, but from powerful perceptions of the Christ mystery—perceptions that arise from the deepest ground of the heart.[95]

---

[93] Ibid, Tomberg, 307
[94] Ibid, Tomberg, 308.
[95] Ibid, Tomberg, 309-310.

As a city girl, I was drawn to the city's cement forest filled with tall skyscrapers, all lit at night, streets bombarded with taxis, cars, buses, and trucks and wind rushing between the buildings as if going through a wind tunnel. The constant cacophony of sounds from horns and squealing of train wheels down the tracks was a natural backdrop for me. These were the sounds that lulled me to sleep each night and created the tapestry of noise each day, most of which I tuned out unconsciously.

Moving to the suburbs at age seven meant I had to become accustomed to the quiet of the streets, especially at night. No background noise except the occasion dog barking or maybe even the hooting of an owl. The trees, the flowers and all the grass were foreign to me. To have them always around, and to walk on the grass, or under the shadow of the trees was beautiful and yet unnerving. Just getting accustomed to things growing all around me took some time. Just to realize that at night there only a few lights and they would go out leaving a very dark world, dark sky, and silence was hard to accept at first.

As time went on and I began to relax and enjoy the sounds of nature, the rustling of the tree leaves, the soughing of the wind in the pines, the smells of mowed hay or grass just cut, and the quiet song of the mourning dove, which often greeted me in early morning or serenaded the sun as it began to set. Eventually, I began to listen for these sounds as they appeared to be friendly and gradually welcomed me into their unseen web of contentment.

Years passed before I felt secure and safe enough to begin to see the presence of trees, birds, and insects as a gift, something to honor and to embrace as part of my world.

The idea of living things like plants and trees have an intelligence was at first foreign to me and gradually became a part of my consciousness. Taking walks just to be in the shielding shadows of trees, listening to the sounds that the forest made, and watching the insects swarm and move in the air was magical.

A friend of mine and I went to Blue Deer Center in Margaretville, New York for a five- day retreat with Eliot Cowan to study plants as allies and resources for healing. Eliot was immersed with the Shamanic work of the Huichol Indians and was a member of the Council of Elders for the Temple of Sacred Fire Healing. Cowan had created a protocol through which we could learn to know plants intimately, not by just looking but by meditating with specific plants he had designated as the focus for our study that day. Eliot Cowan guided us to connect with plant spirits to learn the healing properties of plants from the plants themselves. Eliot gave us simple steps to begin our initiation process:

After a plant is chosen

1. Go to the plant and introduce yourself, much as you would introduce yourself to a person
2. Express some gratitude about the opportunity to meet this plant spirit
3. State your purpose: that you are with the plant in order to become better acquainted
4. Prepare a comfortable place to sit and listen carefully to the messages that may be coming through the air, or the silence if that is all you hear
5. Sprinkle tobacco or some other gift that shows you honor the plant spirit
6. Prepare to draw the plant using your colors and paper that you have brought with you
7. With the plant's permission, touch the plant gently and notice the feeling that comes through your fingers, and also the sensations that you rare left with
8. With the plant's permission, taste the plant to experience the resonance of that plant. Think about how this plant relates to the world.
9. How does this plant relate to other plants, animals and to you
10. Prepare to go inside through your breath and breath the essence of the plant in: In other words, merge with the plant. Become one with the plant. Feel yourself as if you were the plant, blowing in the wind, soaking the sunshine, feeling the elements of rain and snow and cold.

Each day Eliot Cowan gave us a different plant to work with. On one day it was the sugar maple, on another it was the plantain, on another it was the Speedwell, and finally it was the mugwort.

I remember sitting in front of a mugwort plant and absorbing every detail of the plant, the way the back of the leaf was silvery, the way it reminded me of an oak leaf only doubled, with six or eight "fingers" and reminded me of helping hands. We had been told by Eliot that it was fire and air. I remember being in awe of the way in which the stems stretched into the leaf like the skeleton of a body and held it together, how it bent and turned in the wind and then I would listen to what it said. I was never sure whether this was a product of my imagination, but I listened to see if what it said was a surprise, like something I would not have thought to say. Sure enough, it spoke to me about surrender, surrender of the will to the wind. Because it surrendered to the wind it survived as it allowed the wind to carry the leaf wherever it could go.

I felt elated and excited that the mugwort could speak and could convey such sacred wisdom to me. What it conveyed was not just an idea, but a sensation of relaxation, of freedom from worry or anxiety. The plant was transmitting a vibration which was soothing and calming just by being with it in a deep meditative space. I sat with this plant for some time. When the bugs got too annoying, I left and went back to my room to write down what I observed and to finish drawing the rest of the plant.

After lunch, we gathered as a group in the central room where Eliot played the Shamanic drum, and we meditated once again on our plant. More images and even dreams came up for me. I made every attempt to merge with this plant and to some degree I was successful. However, I felt that with repeated sessions with the mugwort I could learn a lot more. The invitations to sit with the mugwort seemed to be ongoing because the information needed to come out in small chunks in order to be assimilated. Not unlike getting to know a person, it seemed that different situations and repeated visits were needed to get to know more deeply the essence of this plant.

I remembered a decision I had made about attending a singing bowl conference in upstate New York. Before me on the highway was a large truck and a hawk was flying above the truck. Suddenly, the bird was caught in a down draft and was struck by the truck. It was flung to the side of the road. The truck continued but I decided to stop by the side of the road. The hawk was still on the road, so I took a shovel I had in the car and lightly moved it to the grassy part of the road. I was so surprised at high light in weight it was. One eye was on me a blinked. By now I was sobbing about this bird and blessing it. I said, "I wish you well on your journey home. I am sorry for what has happened. I love you." Still when I recall this moment it brings tears to my eyes. But this was the moment I remembered as we meditated on our plant. So, I told my story to the group as part of my take-away from the meditation.

At the time, I was not sure why that memory had come as part of my experience with the mugwort leaf. But as I thought of it, the experience in memory taught me that even though there is death, that the essence of what lived, in this case the essence of the hawk and the blink of the hawk's eye, remains with me as a sacred connection, reminding me that we are all one. In memory our vibrations resonate together. Although the physical body has gone, this experience is a reminder that the energy of our souls are bound together throughout time.

After the conference ended, I chanced to read more about plant intelligence and found a book by the same title by Stephen Harrod Buhner[96] who quotes Robert Bly speaking about other senses that are awakened through sitting with nature.

"We move deep into other psyches once we fully enter that kind of immersion. Seeds from some other country attach themselves to our clothes. When we awaken from the dream of our immersion, return to this place, this other state of consciousness, they return with us, hitchhikers from a deeper part of the world. And just as seeds do on the physical level, they detach themselves when we have returned to this familiar country. They drop themselves into the soil of this world, into this part of Earth. And a different kind of life takes root that, over time, spreads."

According to the Buhner, "this immersion, this process of paying attention so closely to what has called you to attend it, naturally

---

[96] Buhner, Stephen Harrod, *Plant Intelligence and the Imaginal Realm: Beyond the Doors of Perception and Dreaming the Earth*, Bear and Company, 2014. 330.

generates synesthesia. You see/feel/hear the organism. A new facility of perceiving develops; synesthetic perceiving begins to become a habituated skill. You possess now not five or six sensory organs but seven or eight or nine, even more, depending on the sensory blendings that are occurring. For all who engage in this process, as Goethe put it…

> *Every new object, clearly seen*
> *Opens up a new organ of perception in us.*[97]

MY ETHERIC TEMPLE

In this life, what remains are the important underpinnings that I have come to know and rely on. These underpinnings form the structure or inner temple where I live and which my soul depends on. My temple is built with etheric "stones" which are huge, not unlike the 1200-ton stones, like the one called "pregnant woman." One can see this stone at Baalbek in Lebanon. These stones cannot be moved by any technology currently in existence and which also cover even larger stones lying underneath.

The first etheric stone is this: holding space for the presence of the Divine. That is the primary function of my temple, to continue to protect and observe this space. I use the prayer, *"May thy will not my will guide me."* I am constantly vigilant that my own will which is strong with Ahrimanic and Luciferian forces still trying to take over and lead me in directions which would serve their purposes. In conjunction with this prayer, I also recite the ho'oponopono prayer with a particular person or situation in mind: *I love you, please forgive me, I forgive you, Thank you.*

What solidifies and reinforces this prayer is daily meditation. Using Steiner's first step in Spiritual Science, I take a natural object like a tree or a flower and concentrate on its life cycle, from the seed which began its life to the decay and ending of its life. I observe and make an effort to remember each stage of development so that all the

---

[97] Buhner, Stephen Harrod, Ibid, 331.

stages are planted in my memory. This helps to sharpen my memory as I take time to add my remembrances day by day as far as I can go back in time. How many can I remember and keep adding to my necklace of memories. At sometime, I must return to the beginning and reconstruct my memories so that I end up with a new necklace. In times when the memories accumulate, I add them to my necklace, where they shift and morph into slightly different shapes and images. This generates questions in my mind as to the reason for these shifts. Often this leads to greater insight and even a prophetic knowing of some change about to happen or that will happen in time. This exercise enriches my observational skills and enhances the understanding of my life experiences and enjoyment of life.

Not the least of these is an acknowledgment and reverence for Sophia as the etheric being: of wisdom of nature and of mother earth. From the Mystery of Sophia,[98] I have included a prayer written in the 16th century by Hildegard of Bingen regarding Sophia:

> Sophia!
> *You of the whirling wings,*
> *Circling and encompassing the energy of God:*
> *You quicken the world in your clasp.*
> *One wing soars in heaven,*
> *One wing sweeps the earth,*
> *And the third flies all around us.*
> *Praise to Sophia!*
> *Let all the earth praise her!*

I spend time listening to Hildegard's Gregorian chant in the CD's,[99] A Feather on the Breath of God. Their tones surround me and create a sonic nest in which my soul rests for a time during the day. I am filled with her passion, infused in the sound of these chants and I rest assured that my soul is safely held in the etheric presence of those

---

[98] Powell, Robert and Isaacson, Estelle, The Mystery of Sophia, Lindisfarne Books, 2014, 2.

[99] A Feather on the Breath of God, Gothic Voices with Emma Kirby, Hyperion or the Canticles of Ecstasy, Sequentia

who are devoted to God. It is through sound that my heart and soul are healed every day, away from the chaos of the world, the demands, both overt and covert, that Ahriman and Lucifer try to make upon my being. At times I play my harp and sing parts of Gregorian chant which I can extract from one recording or another.

Although difficult at times to find a frequency that can carry one to the edge of feeling the Divine within, it is important to continue searching, to continue broadening perspectives, to cross to unknown territories and to continue *to hold the space for God.* As you continue the seeker's path, responses will come if only you have the patience to wait for it. That is what I tell myself. And the responses may not come in the way you expect, in a third dimensional way. It may come from the bird's song, or from the page a book opens to without your looking, or from an voice resonating in the inner chambers of your consciousness. But it will be there because we are all a part of the divine and we can learn to receive the message from the Divine if we will only take time to listen.

Co-partnering with the Stars

This beautiful statement from Valentin Tomberg reminds us that we are part of the universe, the star system and the sun. Our cosmic heritage originates in the stars, and we will return there in time. Tomberg's focus on the heartbeat and breath, consciously taking in the planetary influences is very important as we cultivate connection with the planets that help to shape us and continue to do so.

From Valentin Tomberg

At this moment
I stand within a World constellation
I belong to it with my whole being

My breathing and my heartbeat have as large a share
In the structure of this constellation
As the sun and the planets

The harmony of the stars, the sun, my heart
my breathing and my feeling
produces the constellation of the moment

The tide of the cosmic hour
Flows through my breast
As well as through the heavenly spaces

From a 'stone' that is grounded in the physical body, the ether body, and the astral body, and that rests in itself that is from a 'cube' that is defined by four sides (footnote 5), the human 'I,'must become a living, active 'stone' a totally awakened will, presenting a focal point for the twelve cosmic forces. Footnote 6 (the twelve instreaming forces of the zodiac.) The resting 'cube' should become a shining 'dodecahedron'— this is the spiritually-real formula for the 'how' and the 'what' of the overcoming of numbness of the human 'I'.[100]

Valentin speaks about connection to the sun, stars, to the planets from which our forces originate. He talks about how we must travel through all twelve constellations to remain fluid and organic in our growth, rather than getting caught in a fixed idea of what we think we could or should be, which happens as a result of numbing.

We continue to be influenced by the stars through our lives. The essential forces of the stars which have been present at our birth, or may have even precipitated our birth, continue to inform us about who we are and our purpose in life. If we have access to the akashic records and other occult readings. In order to know who, we are, this becomes essential and is a key to being able to transform not just ourselves but the entire earth environment.

It is no accident that the lion represents the constellation of Leo who visited me when I was a young child. Because I am on the cusp of Leo and Virgo and have been told that the element of fire dominates more than earth in some astrological readings and the lion represents courage, a symbol of my inner self.

Astrology is a way of becoming acquainted with the forces that affect everyone's life. It is not the only way, but it is an ancient science that many persons in positions of power and politics have used through the ages to plan and enact certain decisions.

If one can be opened to the fact that planets have essence and being, then the forces that each planet carries can be seen as a force

---

[100] Tomberg, Valentin, Studies on the Foundation Stone Meditation, LogoSophia Press, California, 2010.

that are a part of me. These interacting beings change and morph through our lifetimes and make themselves known to us as they precipitate challenges in our lives through shifting energies in our personal constellations.

Mind Programs: establishing my mind, ego consciousness, and ancestral healing

Dear Reader,

Whose thoughts is my mind thinking? Thoughts come to me from somewhere, so I continue to monitor the source. At the same time, I have been recovering from the loss of the Lower Ego and replacement with the Higher Self, I have been developing my own ego consciousness, though I did not recognize that at the time. Each decision I made I had to review because if it was not the right decision, a karmic rebound would occur. I would have to pay the price. Here is what happened.

While attending college, I began to study different cultures, spoke with different friends and associates, and learned that many different points of view existed. For example, I learned that many of the friends I regarded as smart and worldly and had not finished college or, in contrast, had graduated and created a life totally divergent from the one they expressed an intention to follow graduation. I changed, matured, grew away from thinking in usual patterns, the agreed upon system of beliefs that we once shared with family members. To that extent, my father did not believe that sharing feelings was important and was appalled when I said we need to tell each other that we love each other. Likewise, my mother did not discuss or encourage speaking about her feelings because she considered the expression of feelings mundane. Instead, she preferred to talk about ideas expressed by her favorite authors.

What continued to shadow my thinking were memories of my many reincarnations as a nun, living in monasteries, praying daily, working in the fields, and living a very simple, even austere life. In the back of my mind, I wondered if I could or should return to the life of the religious. Was my direction in life to continue the monastic life of a previous timeline? Or should I join the so-called conventional world, marry, and have children. I did not see myself as having children or having a conventional lifestyle. At the same time, I was not strong enough to take a profoundly different path, a non-academic path. Yet, I thought I needed to develop my own sense of direction, my own inner voice. Up until that time, my interior voice had been taken over by my mother's desires for me and her overarching force in my life was enormous. She had struggled to make a name for herself and did. She had struggled to achieve a niche in society and did that too. So, I felt I had to find a niche which would allow me to earn money, to facilitate healing and relief from pain to others, and to survive without dependency on my family financially. Even though I still hungered for a life of continual prayer, a former timeline, I put all of that aside and decided I had to return to school, to find a way to be a contributing member to society and to find personal satisfaction as well. But I was uncertain about what the next step in life should be. It seemed that any step was better than returning to my home in Pennsylvania where I would again be under the shadow of my mother's power. To return home seemed like stepping into the jaws of death where I would have had no freedom to find what I thought, how I felt, and I would be confined to follow the protocols of conventional world which were discordant with my own resonance.

While in college and still fraught with difficulty concentrating, I changed my major from English to Art History as a sure-fire way to graduate without an overload of reading requirements. It was also a way of shoring up an imperfections I saw in myself, which was not looking closely enough at details and instead looking for patterns. I thought I needed to be more attentive to seeing and remembering detail. Knowing the aesthetics associated with art and of art history was a natural for me. So, without deep reflection on whether it was wise for me to continue academic study at that time or in that field, I pursued a degree in Art History.

The experience of the Dark Night of the Soul was still with me and

I was still experiencing grief and pain over the loss of love and loss of my old world. Continuing in graduate school was a diversion from the real work that I needed to do on myself, which was to develop my ego consciousness and integrate that with what I felt and knew about myself.

However, still stuck in old patterns, I made a wild and reckless decision—to apply to a Ph.D. program in Art History. I was admitted to the Art History Ph. D. program at Bryn Mawr College but after one semester, realized I had made a huge mistake because I was not interested in pursuing any of the work that was required of me. I could not concentrate, was dragging myself to lectures and was unable to do any justice to the assignments. With the guidance of my mentor, who encouraged me to seek therapy in New York City, I left the Ph.D. program and moved to NYC where I began treatment with an analyst at the Sullivan White Clinic. Attending weekly individual session and twice-a-week group sessions for about two years, I began to learn about expressing feelings and thoughts and that was part of the evolution of my ego consciousness.

DEVELOPMENT OF EGO CONSCIOUSNESS.

In his lectures, Steiner talks about the importance of the development of a strong ego-consciousness. He says:

"Previously, during times of ancient clairvoyance, human beings were able to look into the spiritual world without a strong ego-consciousness so that they saw in a certain sense what will now be seen again—but now they will enter with their new self- awareness." [101]

In the Bible there is a story of the Noblemen who was asked by a father who has a son and who does not feel adequate to claim him as his own son. He convinces a Nobleman to raise this boy as his own, which the Nobleman does. However, in time the son becomes sick. The biological father has heard of Jesus and goes to see him to ask him to heal his son. He stands to the back of the crowd and calls to

---

[101] Ibid, Steiner, 93.

Jesus and says, "Please heal my Nobleman's son." Jesus ignores him. So, the father comes closer to where Jesus is delivering his healing words and again asks Jesus to heal the Nobleman's son. Jesus again ignores him. Finally, the father makes his way to the front of the crowd, and in desperation says to Jesus, "My son is dying, please heal him." Jesus turns to him and says, "Go home and see that your son is already healed." When the father finally claimed the boy as his son, he was taking responsibility for his own and for himself and his protection of his son by call for help using the word MY son.

This story moved me deeply because I recognized that I came from a history of men, my father in particular, who did not stand up for his own ego desires. My paternal grandfather, although educated at Hahnemann University as a Homeopathic doctor, gave up his practice to become a clerk because his wife did not believe he could successfully maintain in business. My father gave up his dream of becoming a conductor because his mother told him they would not fund him if he left the academic course he was on. I too was lost without emotional or economic support from my father or mother, to find my own desires, to make up my mind about what I wanted to do in life. With little or no support, I stumbled into therapy, with the guidance of my art history mentor. I needed to strengthen my ego and engage my feelings. Therapy was the step I needed to take to begin.

ANOTHER COMMUNITY EXPERIENCE

I had been studying Macrobiotics with Michio Kushi in Brookline, Mass. when I met Mark, a crazy but brilliant guy who had come from a university in PA. He had the idea that we should fly to Kennedy Space Center in Florida to see the Apollo 13 shot. With a small group of people from the Titusville area, we sat and watched this phenomenon. The weather in Florida was spring like and I had no desire to return to the snow and cold crunching sidewalks of Brookline. Watching the rocket blast into the air with fire coming from one end was a little like watching the Empire State Building lift into the air and begin to fly into the clouds. That was remarkable enough but the sound, the tremendous sonic boom which echoed in and through each person that watched that day, was unforgettable. Every cell in my body vibrated, every tissue, and every fluid was enlivened by the sound waves that comes through the air. We watched until the ship disappeared in the clouds and the sound slowly faded into the distance. Certainly, this was a part of my life-learning because it led me to discover a way to continue my formal education and training.

I had traveled from Cape Canaveral, Florida after the launch to the Houston area where I befriended two graduating law students from University at Houston with whom I stayed for a time. While in Houston, I decided to investigate the possibility of going to school for further education because it was affordable and because I was still searching for a niche in life. I applied and was accepted at both University of Texas, Houston and University Texas, Austin. With a little financial help from my mother, I enrolled in school, but I was still an out of state resident. As an out-of-state student, coursework and housing were very expensive for me. I struggled with making financial ends meet.

One day, a door-to-door salesman came to my home and offered me a quarter of an acre of land for $100. He stipulated that this land could be in Arizona or Florida or Texas. I thought it would be good to have a piece of land in Texas, so I agreed to purchase this small parcel in El Paso, Texas. On second thought, however, I talked with my law student friend about the advisable of this investment and he did not think I would get anything for my money. Since I was within the decision-making period before the deal was considered final, I call the representative and asked for my money back. He was not happy about returning my check which he flicked to me at my front door, without a word and walked away. However, he never asked for the deed, which I kept.

After two semesters my mother said she could no longer support me financially. What to do? It was up to me to be resourceful. I knew I had to become an in-state resident in order to continue my schooling. According to the university stipulations: I had three options: to marry a Texan, to work for a year paying taxes, or to own property in the state of Texas. I had no desire to do any of these three things. Then I remembered I had the deed for land in El Paso, Texas. After wracking my brain about it for several sleepless nights, I thought finally, why don't I exert my claim as a property owner: after all I had a land deed.

So, I marched into the Administration office and claimed to be a property owner. Interestingly, the administrator did not ask to see the deed which I held in my hand waiting to present it to him. But in a perfunctory way, he awarded me in-state status which allowed me to remain in school with affordable educational fees which I could pay without family help. With scholarships and part time positions, I found I could manage financially to enroll in a graduate program in Counseling and Psychology. This was a path I deeply wanted to pursue but had not been able to afford to do so until that moment.

I was desperate to succeed even though the outcome was daunting at best. Spirit supported my will to overcome obstacles and I decided to pursue it. I felt I had to stay on track to finally be able to achieve my goal, to find my place in the world at this time in life. Perhaps this was influenced in part by Lucifer, not just to survive but to reach beyond the boundaries of what was for me ordinary and modestly inspiring— which would have been to continue a career as an elementary school teacher. I needed something more fulfilling and felt called to a service which was deeply healing on a soul level for myself and others.

Psychological counseling provided a way of studying the mind and healing in the field of counseling and psychology. Armed with a Henson -Hazelwood loan totaling $750 a semester and with the help of work assistant positions on campus, I was able to make ends meet, barely. But with sacrifices, I did. For example, one month I existed on oatmeal and peanut butter sandwiches with little else. Another month, I went without movie-going which was a huge sacrifice for me as I love the video medium. Fortunately, I had obtained part-time work as a R and D (Research and Development) assistant and was in a financially stable position. I even got to see the movie opening of *Star Wars*, 1977 at the local theater in Denton, Texas. This movie reflected a personal victory for me because I had fought my way through the brambles of financial worry and finally secured myself on an academic path which felt right for me.

This was an example of Spirit and perhaps crafty clever Lucifer (who helps people go reach for possibilities beyond themselves) aided me in my conscious decision to stick to my course in life. I was consciously trying to support my education, independent of family financial help, and to find a community of like-minded people where I could sustain myself and serve and help to heal others. I found a way, a bit dodgy in truth, because I had lied about being a landowner, but I was desperate to enter school and find independence in a career which allowed me to be a healer with a clinical degree in counseling and psychology. Ultimately, I did finish my final degree, got licensed and set up a clinical practice as a psychologist, which I maintained successfully for 32 years until I retired.

AHRIMAN AND LUCIFER IN MY LIFE

When C.G. Jung speaks of the shadow, I think he alludes to the part of the self which is not owned or claimed by the self. This part is not seen as integral to the whole self and because it is often a dark or unacceptable part of the self, it is often projected onto someone else. In the eyes of the one who projects, the one who becomes the container for this unacceptable part of the self is the object of negative thoughts and feelings. That person is seen in a negative light and may be ignored or worse castigated for carrying the unacceptable part of the seer's self.

Rudolf Steiner goes even further in anthroposophy when he speaks about the forces of projection of bad or unacceptable parts of the self. According to his spiritual cosmology, each human being has multiple doubles which come into the astral, etheric, or even physical body just before birth. These presences can slip into the unconscious parts of the body even before birth and cling to us just below the level of consciousness, alongside our soul, Rivers[102]. Steiner states that these presences can dwell in whatever sphere of the human astral or etheric plane they chose to. He further states that they have a Mephistophelian Ahrimanic intelligence, no warmth of heart and no qualities of soul. They also have a very strong Ahrimanic will. Rivers[103].

---

[102] Rivers, Karen, Love and the Evolution of Consciousness, Lindisfarne Books, 2016, 54.
[103] Ibid 56-57.

228

Furthermore, these doubles are self- created through the accumulated karma of many reincarnations. (Ibid, Rivers)[104].

Characteristics of the Luciferic Double are pride, self-aggrandizement, being egotistical and prideful, self -righteous, and reckless to name a few characteristics[105]. These forces tend to alienate the soul from the spiritual world, from God, from other human beings, and form a separation between our higher consciousness and subconscious world.

On the other hand, the Ahrimanic Doubles are the claws of fear. The Ahrimanic forces want to blind humans to the presence of the divine spirit, want to promote materialistic scientific thinking and oppose the growth of individual consciousness. The Ahriman presence promotes amoral, atheistic thinking and cleverness to gain whatever is desired at any cost. The Ahriman desire is to take over human thinking, direct thinking to the outer world, perceived by the senses as opposed to the inner world of thought, imagination, and connection with higher selves. The Ahrimanic Will pushes the individual to disregard conscience, to treat people as objects to be manipulated and toyed with for their own ends.[106]

The attributes of both the Luciferic and Ahrimanic double are also seen in those persons who have mental illness to one degree or another. In Medieval times and earlier, people possessing these characteristics who went again societal norms may have been seen as possession in need of an exorcism. Indeed, it is true that some priests connected with the Catholic Church practice exorcism, to rid an individual of the bestial or demonic quality that interferes with their ability to perform in harmony with society. The question of whether these forces are in fact largely present in what is seen as mental illness remains to be seen and needs to be explored as a possible spiritual component which is an important and treatable aspect of a person's mental health issues.

Many examples of Luciferian doubles can be seen in love affairs where one person is obsessed and or addicted to the need for love and attention from another. Many transgressions are committed in the arena of attempting to secure the love and attention from a loved one.

---

[104] Rivers, Karen, personal communication, 7/6/22.
[105] Ibid, 60.
[106] Ibid, Rivers, 113.

The iconic tragedy exists in the example *Romeo and Juliet, Shakespeare,* where these star-crossed lovers meet destruction and death because of the subterfuge they use to try to unite and survive.

Or in the more modern *West Side Story*. Luciferian doubles are at work bringing disaster to both couples in one form or another.

The effects of the Ahrimanic forces on society are ever present in this day. In an Agatha Christie story, *Crooked House*, viewed on Netflix, we see Ahrimanic forces being enacted by a young girl of twelve and her much older aunt to the destruction and demise of both. Over the years, fear has been used by the media and big pharm to control and disarm humanity, through the insistence that everyone be inoculated by a so-called vaccine. This is a ruse for subjugating people to a One World Government through surveillance contract and contact tracing using microchipping and vaccine passports. This *Plandemic* destroyed people's health, their businesses, and maimed those who are unlucky enough to have been tricked into taking the shots. The plan was and is to have ultimate control over who lives and who dies through the control of money, food production, and housing. This is an Ahrimanic plan shaped, orchestrated, and carried out by those who have allowed their own Ahrimanic doubles to guide them in these malevolent acts which are crimes against humanity.

We all have doubles that must be tamed, transformed, and owned as part of our psyche and constitution because they are present in one form or another. So, saying when I think about the Dark Night of the Soul that I experienced, I think that much of what I had to expunge from my being were presences that had been with me for many lifetimes and for which I had made a contract before I was born to claim and transform them in this lifetime.

Just as Jesus the Christ came to me in a sheath of brilliant light and penetrated my physical being as well as my soul, I feel that Ahriman and Lucifer also come as clouds of light. Both Ahriman and Lucifer have at least two sides. When Ahriman comes in to dominate, control, and manipulate, I see this as a dark brown cloud, murky and dense, only moderately penetrable by light. When Ahriman comes to instill discipline, order, and holding focus on a task, I experience Ahriman as an amber or even a light shade of tan. There are variations and mixes of these tones depending on the circumstances. For example, when I received a scam phone call regarding a "blockage on my credit card", this came as a dark brown cloud. But when I received a message, I needed to pay attention to, the symbol of a sunflower facing upward toward the sun came as a light tan color. When I plant my pansies in my railing garden or my hydroponic garden, Ahriman as a Light brown with some darker spots comes in to encourage me to stay grounded with the earth.

Lucifer also has two sides as well. On the one hand Lucifer who encourages me to go beyond the earth, to leave the earth through fantasy and has come in as a bright neon sign yellow, dazzling and so intense I can hardly keep my eyes opened. At the same time, when Lucifer comes in a pale-yellow cloud, I feel encouraged to use my imagination and periodic checking with reality. I like the feeling of expansion and the feeling of connecting with earth. In this way, I think the impulses of both Lucifer and Ahriman are working together and can be helpful, if my heart continues to be the discerning organ with the Christ impulse at its center.

This is the key, to balance both these forces using the Christ impulse (love) centered in the heart. This allows a grounding in nature through the connection with Sophia who resides with Christ impulse in the heart and allows for the expansion of service to others, to the world through the impulse of love, love of self and love of others. Before I was conscious of the Christ impulse within, I was dominated by Ahrimanic and Luciferian forces, and did not know it. Now that I am conscious of these forces, it is possible to work with them rather than having them control me.

What is also true I think is that my mother and father were both wrestling with the Ahrimanic and Luciferian presences within themselves. For instance, why did my mother choose to leave her family behind in her hometown in western Pennsylvania and move to the big city of New York. Lucifer was egging her on, saying she could have an intellectual life in the big apple if she married my father. She could make a place for herself where she could use her intellect, her love of books and literature. Ahriman gave her the staying power to pursue this goal in spite of many obstacles: the war and war economy, her husband being in the Pacific theater for the first three years of their marriage, and the pressure of having to raise a child alone for those years, seeking babysitters, and completing tasks of raising that child, me, alone with no support from family and little from friends and neighbors. But Ahriman was unrelenting and said, "Here is a chance to get your education, free of charge, while your husband is away. If you don't complete this goal, what will you do with yourself, be just a housewife for the rest of your life?" I think my mother could not stand this thought, felt that was no future for her, and pursued her goal even to the point where she put other activities aside so she could excel at school. And excel she did, graduating Cum Laude from Hunter College.

When I think of how much influence both Lucifer and Ahriman had on my mother, to the point where she did not have the space in her heart to think about or digest what I might be feeling, I am sad and even angry because I feel cheated out of the intimate time, I might have shared with her and she with me.

Then my father returned from the war when I was three, and he too was squeezed with the pressures from Ahriman and Lucifer. Ahriman impressed on him the need for a job, to support his family and to stay in the banking industry, which he might have liked, but which was a far cry from learning to be a musical conductor. That is what Lucifer had been encouraging him to do. But this was forgotten as soon as the war came, and my father enlisted in the service as an officer and went away for three years. Did he really want to do this with a new wife and baby? I doubt it. Perhaps he felt it was his duty to his country, or this is what men did. Ahriman must have had a hand in promoting the need for discipline and following authority at all costs, maybe proving himself as a man. If Ahriman had not been so heavy handed, I wonder what my father might have done. Even after the war, perhaps he would have decided to go to music school part time instead of getting a Ph.D. in Economics. What a change in his life and future that would have meant for him. Lucifer would have been so happy for him because he had reached beyond the expectations of his family and supported his developing ego consciousness to galvanize a profession he really loved. When he returned from the war, he might have been a self-contented, self-affirming man, working toward his dream and eventually realizing it.

Would my mother's Ahrimanic forces put obstacles in his way saying music is not a stable career? Would my father's own self-doubts ruled so that he would have complied with the "safer" path of an academic career? Who knows. But with that choice, my father had entered the gerbil wheel of doing what was expected rather than what he loved. He put all his energies into an academic career, sidelined his love of music, his true passion, and pursued an academic goal to bring economic security and stability for himself and his family. Because he was not a deeply satisfied man, because he had not overcome the "nose to the grindstone no matter what" message from his family's indoctrination, he was not able to relax, to have fun and to play, especially with me. He had become the tin soldier who followed commands of his own internal authority, led by Ahriman. He never seemed to take off the soldier uniform, put on some jeans and just play. Because Ahriman had been so overpowering and controlling of him, he did not take time to reflect on what he really wanted or needed to do for himself. Am I angry with him too? Yes, I am. But more sad than angry because we missed so much fun, getting to know each other, and good times playing together.

Nevertheless, as I look back on my life's journey, and its trials and tribulations, I think these were parts of the cleansing process that enabled me to discover my Higher Self with the dissolution of the Lower Ego which was ruling me. My task was to balance the energies of both Ahriman and Lucifer so that in the end they were working for me rather than me working for them. My task was also evolving my" I" consciousness which has led me closer to the Divine and to the Divinity which is the true self of all human beings. In the process I have found a new power in my voice, in the word and in thought. The reward of knowing myself in this deeper way has been worth all the effort I expended in the discovery process.

Another aspect of writing this memoir is that I think it has had an impact ontransmuting the cobwebs of past lives, my parent's and mine.

Strovolos in the *Magus of Strovolos*[107] writes about how Strovolos consciously took on the karma of his son-in-law to preserve a father for his grandchildren and husband for his daughter. This karma was taken into his right foot, which he was told might have to be amputated because it was so diseased. Strovolos disagreed and said it would eventually be fine. After many months that prediction came to pass and Strovolos was able to walk on that foot as if there never had been an injury.

The idea that impressed me here was the idea of taking on someone else's karma. In a way, I think children wittingly or unwittingly take on their parents' karma and see it to the end. The phrase "chip off the old block" speaks to some extent of the transfer of energy, or behavior and of perhaps similar outcomes in life.

As I review the process of gathering memories and incorporating them into incidents and letters throughout this book, I felt a change in my relationship to each parent and a change in their relationship to their heritage. It seemed lighter, more positive, and more acceptable to them in the new light of greater understanding. I felt my mother's pride and her sacrifice because she had made a great leap of faith in leaving her family behind to pursue her education in a different city and state. She was the only one of her five living siblings to pursue a life beyond the boundaries and confines of her home in a small village outside of Pittsburgh. She was the only one who developed her intellect and became recognized as an accomplished educator. She was the only one who followed in her father's footsteps as someone who valued ideas and those who wrote about those ideas. She was in many ways a self-realized person who pursued her dreams even though she sacrificed family ties.

The outcome for my father was tainted by his lack of sufficient development of his ego consciousness which led him to sidetrack his true dream, to become a conductor. Music was his first love. By playing the organ or piano he felt he could speak to many people and could radiate his love of music and the world through sound. I feel his support and admiration of me when I play the harp. His spirit is present nearby and listening with a smile on his face. He is proud that I have

---

[107] Strovolos, Kriakos, Magus of Strovolos, Penguin Books, UK 1985.

carried on the musical thread which he inherited from his mother and passed to me. Although he did not fulfill his true self, and chose a more conventional academic life, he made the best decisions he could make under the circumstances. I feel a deep sadness for him and at the same time am grateful for the fact that he modelled for me the dangers of not developing ego consciousness sufficiently to engage a basic or primary passion in life. His ego strength was lacking, just as had his father's ego strength had been lacking. He had no model to follow, but I did. I had the contrast between what worked for my mother who became self-realized and what inhibited my father who was emotionally crippled by the ancestral elements that were deeply embedded in him.

I have prayed about this and checked with my Higher Self about whether their karmas have been satisfied. The response I received through this book was that their karmic remnants have been satisfied. What is left are my own karmic threads which are ongoing and in need of review which is happening as I write this memoir.

As I look back on my choice of academic career as a psychologist, I discovered that I found great joy and satisfaction in helping people heal, to be relieved of psychic pain and trauma, and to become freer to realize their potential. This choice represents one lifeline. But in another lifeline, I wonder what would have happened if I had simply joined a nunnery so that I could pray eternally. What then? Would this have satisfied my need to help people transmute their pain, to realize their potential, to realize more freedom than they had, or their ancestors had? This question brings me back to the gift I have been given in living long enough to review the threads of my life, to transmute the catacombs of childhood into the rainbow-light of freedom to claim my mind at this time.

(See Appendix C).

Overcoming mind programs

Dear Reader,

THE FORK IN THE ROAD IS THREE PRONGED

As a society and as a human being we have come to a fork in the road. We are invited to choose between two major paths that appear before us. One road leads to the possibility of everlasting life, in consort with the Divine or the Presence of God. The other road promises the possibility of gaining different forms of God-like powers through artificial means, perhaps living for 1,000 years through transhumanism or artificial intelligence. It also promises an artificial means of transferring your consciousness into a box for a future life on another planet. But this life is not everlasting and is totally dependent on the technology that is available now on the good will of the person controlling the artificial intelligence at that moment. From Robert Powell and Estelle Isaacson, we have the following idea:[108]

Even just one individual who is able to overcome the mind programs and will think the thoughts of freedom—freedom inspired thoughts—can effectuate mighty change. It begins without person, and then flows to other souls. Through this can there be a peaceful inner resolution, a wave of mighty force that can prevail over dark forces.

The dark forces gain power through inducing suffering, torture trauma and unimaginable atrocities. They general fear, despondency,

---

[108] Powell, Robert, and Isaacson, Estelle, The Mystery of Sophia, Lindisfarne Books, 2014, 11.

and hopelessness. People will believe that they are feeling their own feelings, when in actuality they are feeling the projected vibrations coming at them. If however, we can refrain from falling into the trap of these generated emotions, then we shall be victorious.[109]

This bifurcation of energies has been present in our lives since the continent of Atlantis, according to Plato and Edgar Cayce, has been on the planet. Through the history of Atlantis, a conflict, even war came to pass between two factions: the *amelias* group, on the one hand, which wanted to use the power of the *tuaoi* stone to shape the affairs of Atlantis through connection with Divine Beings. The *belial* [110]group wanted to capture this power source for its own purposes and use it to dominate and rule over the citizens of their world. In the end, the belial group unwittingly set the stage for destruction of Atlantis by misusing the power of the tuaoi stones. Eventually, the planet exploded and was divided into three islands, and then exploded once again and sank.

Two major forces which have been operating against the ascension of our civilization into the higher dimension of reality are the Ahrimanic and Luciferian forces according to Thomas Meyer[111]. The Ahrimanic forces would like to dominate and control all of life, place it under one central government, and chip everyone so that what they do, how they act, and even what they think are under government control. The Luciferian forces want to engage people in worlds of delusion or illusion, promises of great wealth, or freedom from pain, freedom from death itself.

Each of these have come from our own karmic past as we played out various roles in prior lives and accumulated indiscretions which remained with us through birth in this lifetime. These became our doubles, and these doubles offer the opportunity to transform them in ourselves to reach higher spiritual knowledge and closer affinities with the Divine. Some are very seductive paths, which do not lead to freedom for individuals or for society. Rather they lead to enslavement and dependency on the system that is bound to make serfs out of

---

[109] Powell and Isaacson, Ibid, 15.
[110] Dark Journalist, Daniel Liszt online lectures, 2016-present.
[111] Meyer, Thomas, interview with Catherine Austin Fitts, on Solari Report, 6/24/22.

all humans and to rob humans of the birthright of eternal life. The divergent paths which rely on vaccines and chips to secure health, promise short cuts to becoming all powerful, to perfect health, and to becoming immortal. But in fact, these paths lead to repetitive cycling and slavery without end, much like the gerbil in the cage on its exercise wheel. Someone or something else makes your decisions for you and tries to control your life. You can run and run until you are exhausted and never extract yourself from this control once they have you.

Steiner foreshadows a third evil cosmic force which he calls the Asuras.

The influence of this third force of evil will be distinguished from that of Lucifer or Ahriman, especially in its relationship to the bodily parts of the human being as well as to the changed human I-being itself. When *luciferic* influence, working through the astral body, leads the human I astray and tears it from its union with spiritual hierarchies—when Ahriman through his influence on the etheric body, enslaves the human I—then Asura will completely disintegrate the I thus torn from the spiritual world by Lucifer and enslaved by Ahriman, absorbing it into his own being. Just as Lucifer brings the I out of the waking condition into the dreaming condition, and Ahriman brings it out of the dreaming into the sleeping condition, Asura brings death to the human I. For humanity, the spiritual death of the I-being is the danger of the third stage of evil.[112]

Instead of a duality of energies to contend with in our universe, we now have a tertiary or three -pronged interplay of forces: the Ahrimanic, the Luciferic and the Christ Impulse or love force as described previously. This third impulse came in at the time of the crucifixion when Christ descended to earth in the body of Jesus and sacrificed himself for the good of humanity and for the good of earth itself. He gave his blood to earth which allowed the earth to be etherized, to be filled with divine transmission, and to human

---

[112] Tomberg, Valentin, Christ and Sophia, Steiner Books, 2006, 59.

beings which allowed their blood to receive the divine influence of transmutation and purification through the process of reincarnation.[113]

"But Christ said: grasp the I where you should grasp it now, then the realms of heaven come closer again. They will rise in your I. Even through your eyes close off the spiritual light behind the external sensory light, even if your ears close off the spiritual sound behind the physical one, if you rise to Christ himself you will find the realms of heavens within yourself."

"But now they could become blessed again after the impulse had been given that Christ
Could penetrate right into the human I, Christ the being who was able to give them knowledge of the spirit, of the realms of the heavens."

"Those who take in the Christ impulse will learn to calm what fills their physical body with emotional with regard to possessions of the earth, the astral body, to bring I under control of the spirit, and thereby it will become happy or blessed.[114]

"But if the astral body comes under the power of the spirit, if we develop serenity with regard to earthly things, then we are given the earthly realm as our lot."[115]

As humans, we are faced with sorting out the effects of Lucifer and Ahriman on the "I" or ego-consciousness and know that Christ is in our midst as the third force which mitigates the effects of the forces of pride coming from Lucifer and the forces of doubt and fear coming from Ahriman. This was his gift given to humanity through the Mystery of Golgotha and the subsequent *etherization* of the blood which occurred that time. That *etherization* allows the force of spiritual love to move through human hearts and into our consciousness where it infused us with divine wisdom and even a new clairvoyance, which

---

[113] Steiner, Rudolf, The Christ Impulse, Rudolf Steiner Press, 2014. 52.
[114] Ibid, Steiner 53.
[115] Ibid, Steiner, 54.

was not possible before this occurrence. We now have to continue to cultivate that inner voice as a major protection against the forces that would rob us of our humanity.

DISCOVERING THE ORIGINS OF MY THOUGHTS

The journey to discover the origin of my thoughts has taken a wide and circuitous route, from the struggle to know and define my feelings, to understanding the importance of image in my dreams and in everyday life, to the sorting of analytical thinking as I wrestled with various theories of consciousness as a psychologist, and as a seeker with various philosophies of the meaning of life. To learn that thought origins with the angels was a surprise and a gift. To know that even speech itself is orchestrated by the angelic forces which was shaped by the Christ Mystery was equally a surprise and a gift. Here is Tomberg's analysis of the origin of speech.[116]

Pentecost was the resurrection of the soul in the sense that it brought to life wisdom that had united with the soul. Soul life did not arise out of mere feelings, but from powerful perceptions of the Christ mystery—perceptions that arise from the deepest ground of the heart.

To get a more distinct view of this process, we must begin with the fact that human beings share their outer existence with the mineral world, their organic life with the plant realm, and their movement with the animal world. Nonetheless, human beings are distinguished from those three kingdoms by having speech, the fourth externally manifested attribute. Through this attribute, another member (aside from the Physical, ether, and astral bodies) is revealed to human beings; the "I." This makes it possible for human beings not only to participate in physical existence by living and moving about, but also to speak. Although the human "I" is the actual source of the speech faculty, the existence of language nonetheless depends on the body's threefold makeup. The astral body is needed to combine the predicative with

---

[116] Tomberg, Valentin, Christ and Sophia, Steiner Books, 2006, 308.

the attributive, the verb with the adjective; the ether body is needed to connect the verb with substantive, or noun; and finally, the organs of the physical body are needed to make spoken language sound in the air. The speech impulse of the "I" passes through these three members of the body to reveal itself as spoken language.

This means that the speech impulse of the human "I" can contact the realm of influence governed by the whole circle of spirits of language (the Luciferic archangels) to the extent that it has first acquired the faculty of uniting with the sphere of influence governed by folk spirits (the archangels). It was just this union with the whole circle of archangels (or folk spirits) that the twelve apostles established at Pentecost.[117]

Beyond the gift of thought and speech, is the evolution of ego consciousness, the "I."

As the "I" develops, a complex of other factors enters the mix of decision-making factors: personality, family beliefs and traditions, social and financial pressures, the political climate, and religious or spiritual affiliations. As Steiner points out, it is possible to study spiritual science and to enhance the continued development of ego consciousness so that along with the development of the "I" is an advancement of moral evolution. This means that decisions spring from higher moral evaluation based on connection with the Christ Impulse of love. Or you could say decisions are based on following the Tao which is the flow of life which follows the river of compassion and kindness.

"But Christ said: grasp the I where you should grasp it now, then the realms of heaven come closer again. They will rise in your I. Even through your eyes close off the spiritual light behind the external sensory light, even if your ears close off the spiritual sound behind the physical one, if you rise to Christ himself you will find the realms of heavens within yourself."

---

117 Ibid, Tomberg, 310.

"But now they could become blessed again after the impulse had been given that Christ

Could penetrate right into the human I, Christ the being who was able to give them knowledge of the spirit, of the realms of the heavens."

"Those who take in the Christ impulse will learn to calm what fills their physical body with emotional with regard to possessions of the earth, the astral body, to bring I under control of the spirit, and thereby it will become happy or blessed.[118]

"But if the astral body comes under the power of the spirit, if we develop serenity with regard to earthly things, then we are given the earthly realm as our lot."[119]

WHAT STEPS CAN WE TAKE TO ENSURE OUR OWN SOVEREIGNTY

By listening to my inner voice, by watching what happens to people who get trapped by the need to by-pass the trials and tribulations that they need to experience in order to develop integrity or to strengthen their soul. Yes soul, that part of the human being that is eternal and that lives on forever. The part of the being that lives across many lifetimes in an effort to recover and transmute mistakes and do better the next go round.

Those who lived a monastic life, who lived several hundreds of years ago knew this, but had not yet developed the "I "or ego-consciousness sufficiently. Those who have found connection with their soul, who do not live in religious community, know that I am pointing to a reality that they may have experienced to one degree or another, namely the joy that comes from fulfilling a need or a dream which could only happen with the help of a higher force. Or to put it another way, humans need to remember that they have an indelible relationship to the Divine energy, call it God, or Spirit or Force or Presence. Why is that? Because we are created by that Presence

---

[118] Ibid, Steiner 53.

[119] Ibid, Steiner, 54.

and all of us are connected to that Presence, share the energy of the Presence in our lives, whether we feel it or not. It is there and we as humans all have an opportunity to know ourselves through the eyes of Spirit and to become imbued with the highest attributes that any human can experience genuine love, forgiveness, compassion, and acceptance of others, and harmony. Because of our connections to Spirit, our potentials have no limits, and we have the option to live forever because our consciousness can move through many lifetimes. Each lifetime differs from the previous one; each one presents us with the opportunity to learn the lessons we failed to learn previously and need to learn to endow our souls with greater knowledge of our own divinity.

At this time, we are being bombarded with many forces some of which pretend to lead down a road of quick growth or wealth, or everlasting life based on connection with Artificial Intelligence. This trajectory goes beyond implants which enhance health because they are designed to change and alter the human relationship to self and to the Divine. Many of these products work on changing, re-scripting your DNA, or splicing it. The promise given is that as long as you are connected to machine or nanotechnology you can live a long time, even forever. What you are not told is that as you slowly disconnect from the spiritual world from which you came that you would enter the eighth sphere in which you become a slave, a tool ruled by some other forces. You cannot grow or go beyond certain limits as controlled by the structure. This is a very Ahrimanic world which wants to use humans as products or byproducts for their own energy. And this path leads you to the path of the Asuras which would submerge humans into their web of evil. It is not unlike the image in the first *Matrix* movie where Neo, along with many others, are used as a battery, hooked up to tubing through which human energy is being sucked into machinery and utilized to run hundreds of machines. This is one of many images that depicts the essence of what the eighth sphere's effect on human life would be.

The question of how to protect, avoid, and even transmute this energy remains. The most powerful means I know requires a shift in focus of consciousness from external to internal, or inner world, from

243

being brain centered, to being heart-centered, and from reliance on external authority to internal sovereign authority. Through prayer and meditation, learning to rely on your higher self or higher ego voice, you in concert with the Christ impulse or love impulse which lives in your heart, will be able to cultivate a discerning consciousness, that will be able to foresee and sense deceptive and seductive impulses which want to use and manipulate you in to becoming their slaves, their machines, and their captives in mind, body and spirit. This requires a great deal of sustained consciousness and patience because what is visible may not reveal the underlying impulses and dark forces which may want to dominate or coopt human energy for their own self-centered purposes. When one has seen the path of deception, it is possible to avoid and flourish in a world beyond slavery and in a world where you claim your sovereignty and are able to maintain and honor it as a human being. This value of this journey for me is that I have connected with my voice and continue to honor it as it grows and teaches me the more benevolent paths toward my future self.

One important path according to Rudolf Steiner, is that of Spiritual Science. To meditate, to learn to discipline the mind and control thoughts and to transmute feelings are major steps along the path to entering the supersensible world. That world gives us access to knowledge, understanding, perspective and direction that we need to navigate a world filled with distraction, stress and evil that would separate us from our birthright with the spiritual world. We are spiritual beings, not born to be machines and we have the option to live as spiritual beings eternally with freedom to express and co-create with the Creator. This is our saving grace. Rudolf Steiner offers us a path from which we can manifest being fully realized as human beings. It is our choice and our decision as to which path we will take. We have the right to choose and to choose wisely will make all the difference for us and for future generations. (See Appendix D)

My connection to thought, word and image is enhanced by meditation and by certain exercises. To strengthen my voice, I practice a daily meditation on the throat chakra which is directly connected to speech. Meditation is a crucial and integral part of integrating spiritual science. Rudolf Steiner emphasizes the relationship between the throat, and throat center, and thought and has offered a meditation to open the throat and thought process more fully. The fact that thought is expressed through words which are expressed either through the voice or through the written word ties the importance of the throat to the expression of thought, to communication in sound or words. Also, Steiner speaks about thought being a transmission from the angelic realm.

Through the years I have felt a need to strengthen my throat center or throat chakra because my voice was silenced for so long and because I realized it was an avenue that allowed me to connect with others in a deeper way, to share my thoughts, feelings, my truth about how I perceived my world and to receive the thoughts of others. This is a meditation I find useful as it reaffirms my connection with my spiritual center above my crown, heart, gut and especially my throat.

This meditation involving those four major centers of knowing was developed by Rudolf Steiner in his Outline of Occult Science.[120] The exercise begins with speaking the prayer below:

> In purest outpoured Light
> Shimmers the Godhead of the world.
> In purest Love toward all that lives
> Outpours the god-hood of my soul.
> I rest within the Godhead of the world;
> There shall I find myself,
> Within the Godhead of the World.

This is followed by a pattern of breathing in for six beats, out for twelve and holding for eighteen beats while one concentrates on four centers: I Am, It Thinks, She Feels, He Wills.

First the center above the crown chakra (my spiritual center) while one says internally or thinks quietly *I Am*. After three repetitions of the breathing pattern while concentrating on the crown chakra, one can visualize a two- petal lotus above the crown chakra while one thinks *I Am*.

---

[120] Steiner, Rudolf, An Outline of Occult Science, Chapter V, Knowledge of the Higher Worlds, Andansonia Publishing, 2018.

Second center at the throat resides the phrase *It Thinks*. One does the breathing pattern of six, and twelve breaths and eighteen count hold for three repetitions. At the throat chakra one can visualize a sixteen- petal lotus as one thinks the phrase, *It Thinks* and continues with the breathing pattern.

Third center resides at the heart with the phrase, *She Feels*. Once again one repeats the pattern of six, and twelve breaths and eighteen counts of hold while visualizing a twelve- petal lotus while thinking the phrase *She Feels*.

Fourth center resides in the gut with the phrase, *He Wills*. A person again repeats the pattern of six, and twelve inhale-exhale pattern followed by eighteen count hold while focusing on a ten- petal lotus and thinking the phrase *He Wills*.

After this is done, a period of five minutes or more should be allowed for the integration of these thoughts followed by the breathing. The body should be relaxed and the atmosphere free from distraction so that concentration on the meditation will be uninterrupted.[121]

It is clear from this exercise that the connection between the throat and thinking is unmistakable and not surprisingly is verified in Steiner's work. This means that careful vigilance of what one thinks and says is imperative. Thinking and speaking create energy forms which modulate the environment in which we live, and which have subtle and not so subtle effects on the people in our lives and on ourselves. These effects can be positive or negative depending on intention and the consciousness with which they are delivered.

---

[121] Steiner, Rudolf, Ibid, 2018.

New Portals of Consciousness:
Claiming My Voice

Dear Reader,

As an adult I came to realize that as a child I thought not words, not ideas, but in images. Although my thinking has gone through many stages and has evolved through the development of my own ego consciousness, I realize that my baseline thought process remains as it began, thinking in images. For me, the image holds the kernels of truth which offer many levels of understanding as they are unpacked. Much like a dream in which symbols hold the kernel of truth, not all can be known at once but becomes visible through the evolution of time and consciousness. Symbols and images are organic in that they seem to grow, expand, and deepen into multidimensional layers of meaning as one revisits experience over time. This is certainly true with the image of the Red Crowned Crane, who holds for me the opening of the voice. It has confirmed the use of my voice to express song in image, my definition of poetry through words and image. Through the combination of my mother's love of words and my father's love of music and sound, I have integrated these two expressions into one art form, called the poem. I recognize that I have come full circle to arrive once again at my steppingstone, the poem as a vehicle for my heart's feelings and perspectives.

The Day Before Christmas, 2019, I wrote a poem in response to a film I had seen about the crane in China's Swamp Land. The poem reflects the image and my passion and love for nature. More importantly, I have come to know the form of poetry as a fuller expression of my thoughts and feelings than most other forms of writing. It is my deepest voice as I have come to know it and it infuses my love of image with the use and power of words. I claim it as my true voice and am honored to share it with you.

> Cry
> Cry of the red crowned crane
> weaves the air, threads the grasses.
> Sinewy thin neck pierces the sky.
> Crown thrown back,
> call of surrender, of ultimate knowing,
> a certainty of belonging to the
> fabric of earth's heaving presence.
> Heaven sent, the call skids
> surface of clouds, floats through ether,
> reverberates in each stone, each mountain top.
> Who can deny the sound of voice
> that persists timeless, abandoned within
> rhythmic essence, the fabric of time.
> Glue of the universe in morning light,
> this arching to eternity takes my heart
> beyond the confines of earthly space,
> shatters it to sea, see beyond sensing
> who I am, found in breasted call
> still echoing in dark morning.

This poem reflects the development of my "I" ego consciousness. Part of my identify is my love of nature, of birds, and trees and flowers and all growing plants and is a celebration of the long-awaited renewal of our earth as it morphs into new earth with the help of Sophia, the mother of our planet. Another self-aspect is music, that is the sound of words as they appear in image. In my poem, the sound like a harp plays through my mind. The voice of my higher self speaks to me through sound and image and leads me to the fullness of who I am and who I am intended to be.

Second epilogue: a poem to commemorate all of my unnamed parts that have been shed, left behind, or forgotten. I salute them because they were part of my journey at one time and now have completed their contributions to my life. Letting go is part of moving on. I do not grieve so much as celebrate the future self that has been waiting for me and that I am now stepping into.

Passing (a poem of commemoration)

> Sense eccentric shape of muscle
> > bid you welcome to memory
>
> my last smile skitters across unknown lacunae
> > sinks holes in muscle (tissue and cell)
>
> bloodline serrated
> > feel owl shadow, silent torrents of tree limbs
> leaf slivers shudder
> > strangled feelings sway in windless air
>
> moon's ghostly gash across eyeless face
> > blinded by fate
>
> place ear to ground, moist soft dark
> > in space of unintended thought
>
> soul- scars float to skin surface
> > red throb pulse oozing particulates
>
> > without purpose
>
> oh, ploughed troughs of muddy earth
> > where gaping earthworms wait to receive
>
> > these ashes now on snowy ground
>
> even hungry ghosts have no appetite
> > for what remains

This journey has been remarkable in so many ways as it has given me a perspective on my childhood, allowed me to vent my feelings and explore new images, and offered me a chance to find new depth and meaning in the episodes of my growth spiritually. It has reflected the progress I have been making in the development of my *"I" ego consciousness* which continues to evolve through time and experiences. It has offered me the opportunity to know my parents as individuals growing through their own crises and coping with life circumstances.

And it has given me a chance to know myself more deeply and in very different ways.

A RESPONSE TO THE QUESTION WHOSE THOUGHTS AM I THINKING?

THIS JOURNEY HAS LED TO ME CLAIMING MY OWN VOICE AND MIND

Although you the reader may have discovered your own thoughts and pathway to those thoughts, I want to summarize a response to this question that I have come to at this time.

Thoughts, images, and words come from the Divine. They come through many avenues, through dreams, through daydreams, at *that moment of just waking up*, or in *that moment just before sleep*.[122] They come unexpectedly and without conscious provocation. They come in the silence and space of meditation. They come inconveniently when we are driving a car or between activities that seem important enough to bypass the message and fulfill the expectations of the moment. Often these divine gems are lost or forgotten unless they are written down or recorded somewhere for future attention. What seems most important is my readiness to receive these gifts from the Divine. These are questions I ask myself:

Is my Higher Self in charge rather than my Lower Self?

Am I fully connected with a loving and open heart?

---

[122] Steiner, Rudolf, "The Dead Are With Us," GA 182, 10 February 1918, Nuremburg, RS Archives, on line.

Do I have my own best interest in mind as well as those interests of others?

Am I clear of internal debris and obstacles and are my chakras opened and ready to discern and integrate what Is given?

Am I taking time in silence to allow the image, word or thought to percolate through the layers of consciousness so that they can be distilled in the purest and most potent way possible in whatever form they wish to be expressed?

PROGRESSING INTO NEW PORTALS OF THE EVOLUTION OF CONSCIOUSNESS: A NEW SOVEREIGNTY

Introduction to Marconics and Future Self

A friend, and artist and painter, had taken photos of what she called portals into other dimensions which she later painted and called Interdimensional photos. She also introduced me to Marconics, which was a portal to other dimensions beyond this third dimension that we live in. For the past seven years, those of us in Marconics had experienced numerous protocols which were designed to free us from the etheric lockdowns that had been imposed on us as humans by other forces. The many protocols were designed to open our chakras and other gateways so that we could more easily access messages from other dimensions and so that we could ultimately meet our Future Selves which could access by means of our 12th gate.

Two months prior to our meeting, I had a minor traffic accident in which a jeep had hit the end of my car as I was making a left turn to a two- lane road at a T. The citation was for me to pay a fine or appear in court (even though he had hit me) the day after the Gathering. I knew that I would have to leave the retreat early to fly home in time for the hearing. During the retreat, I received a call that my case had been resolved and I did not have to be home or miss the final half day of the gathering. I checked with my 12th gate and was commanded to stay because the internal voice said, "You must remain for the entire gathering." I felt compelled to change my return flight and extend my stay in the hotel for one more night.

During the final gathering of the Chronos Guild which we came to be called, we were introduced to a protocol known as the Pearl Activation. I confess that I don't know the full picture of what that meant but I will tell you what happened to me during this event. The exercise was related to the opening of the 12th gate which was the overall intent of this gathering.

Alison David Bird, the originator of Marconics, directed us to lie down on the floor of the auditorium and to get comfortable. Then as we became more relaxed and breathed deeply, she directed several questions to us. The last one that I heard was to look to see if there were any hidden or remaining figures in our inner world that needed to come out.

At that point I saw a little girl about four years old, that I knew was a version of myself, a version that had been in hiding for all these past years and was now feeling safe enough to emerge from the shadows. She came out and as she did, I felt something release from my right hip, from the sciatica area. This area had been chronically sore for some years, and I had been taking extra strength doses of Glucosamine, Chondroitin and MSM daily to relieve the pain so that I could walk without obstruction. As the little girl, the shadow of myself came out, I realized she was at last free and that she was loved…. that I loved her. I saw her walk away into a hazy light. Then I felt I was encased in a sphere of mother of pearl shimmering light. It was like a safety net which surrounded me and made me feel contained and protected.

The experience made me weep such tears of gratitude that made it difficult to speak about this healing and to share it with the group. But I felt it was important to relay this experience because it made it more real to me and to others to speak about it publicly. And there was no shame, no shame at all in revealing myself at a deep level, and to a whole group. When I did so, it was with hesitation and pauses because it was so intimate and precious. Lisa, Alison's co-partner asked if I needed to go behind the screen (which she had done earlier when composing herself) to gather myself together. I shook my head no and continued.

We all had the experience of having our 12th gate opened and for me the release of this inner child was the culmination of the work of this weekend. I was so grateful to my 12th gate, my Future Self for directing me to stay for the entire gathering. This pearl activation was the culminating event, the pearl which I will keep forever in my memory as a release and confirmation that my 12th gate was present and directing me to do what was in my most benevolent and appropriate timeline.

It has been three weeks since that event occurred and still, I have no pain or obstruction in my right hip area. The healing has stayed with me and for this I am deeply grateful to my Future Self and to Marconics for preparing the way.

Dear Future Self,

I thank you for directing me to the healing moment was a frequency activation that occurred during the Pearl Activation at the Chronos Gathering. It was in my most benevolent timeline to have this experience and you directed me to stay for it. I can't imagine not having had this experience for it was the culmination not just of this gathering but of the years I have been working with Marconics. This moved me deeply more than any other events. Perhaps I was just ready for it. But it happened in a most perfect way.

I know you are still actively directing me to prepare for ascension into other timelines. This means getting all my paperwork in order, preparing a will and trust, and withdrawing from activities and people which are keeping me tied to this 3d matrix. I have been grieving as I have let go of some activities and people I have come to love and have sustained me for the time being.

During this time, Jenny, my close Marconics friend, died on Feb. 21 after a prolonged bout with the remains of ovarian cancer and kidney disease. Three years prior to her illness, we had travelled by car to Chester Vermont for a Marconics gathering. It was a peaceful and comfortable trip which we both thoroughly enjoyed, probably the highlight of our friendship. And we had met weekly for lunch, studying French together and then just chatting about our lives over a meal. But that ended about nine months ago when she could no longer travel because of pain, had lost her appetite, and did not want to eat. My inner self urged me to see her once at her home just before going to Vermont for the latest gathering. Unfortunately, she was too incapacitated to travel and was no longer able to experience the internal workings of the Chronos Guild. I know she felt disappointed, perhaps let down, that she was not invited to attend and would have been unable to do so in any case.

While I visited her at her home, she offered me a glass of apple cider. When I asked for tea instead, she said she did not feel secure enough in her walk or steady enough with her hands to handle hot water, so she did not feel comfortable doing that. I said it was ok to do nothing and so we just sat in the frequency of our resonance. This frequency filled both of us and nothing more was needed. I knew that her transition was near which Is why I needed to be with her one more time. Three weeks later she died. Her husband Dave called to tell me of her passing. She did not want any commemorative service, just to be cremated and buried. I was glad I had seen her one last time and decided I would play a harp piece for her. I choose the Nightingale by Deborah Henson Conant. "Who will sing for the Nightingale when the day is done, and the light is gone? Who will sing for the Nightingale who sits alone in the sun?" I will with my harp. And I cried as I played this tune because Jenny was a sweet soul and a dear friend. When the phone rings, I still listen for her voice in my mind, but knowing she will speak to me in other ways now.

At this time, I am feeling unmoored, not alone so much as detached and unwilling to disturb or compromise the new frequencies I am nurturing within myself. It is very different to hold frequency as the reality that I am growing and nurturing in consciousness. My Future Self tells me that connecting with frequency is the communication of now and the future. It is taking the place of images and has become a new language that I am learning to consolidate as my new reality.

OTHER QUESTIONS I CONTINUE TO PONDER:

Have I called upon my Future Self to respond to questions regarding the needs and spiritual energies which are required in the world?

Have I been patient and listened for the responses from my Future Self which may or may not have come immediately?

Have I been grateful and thankful for the messages I have received?

Have I asked for help in discerning the messages that are coming from true light?

Am I taking enough time to allow the messages from my Future Self to be fully expressed in whatever form they come in, without compromise or corruption from other influences which dilute its meaning?

Am I deeply and eternally grateful and showing a thankful attitude in the way in which I disperse and share the divine gifts I have distilled through image and now through frequency?

In the end I know this:
I am loveable and loved.
I am worthy (and adequate to the task).
I am enough (to accomplish what is needed).

I feel released and free from so much that blocked my progress into evolving aspects and dimensions of life. In this search I have come to know my true voice as having originated from the Divine and as having come full circle through the exploration of image and evolution of consciousness. My language has evolved from one of image to one of frequency, the frequency of light and sound. This is the language of my higher dimension and my Future Self.

Claiming your mind: establishing your sovereignty

Dear Reader,

I ask the question, "Who chooses the image that preoccupies my mind?"

I want to introduce you to Robert Powell and Estelle Isaacson in The Mystery of Sophia.[123] Robert Powell, a mathematician, studied Rudolf Steiner's Anthroposophy and Blavatsky's work in Theosophy. He integrated the veneration of the Blessed Virgin Mary with the Celebration of the Virgin Sophia, the Holy Spirit of Wisdom as he saw Sophia coming closer to earth along with the Christ. Through his devotion to the Holy Sophia, he discovered the work of Estelle Isaacson, a mystic and seer who had deep connections and visions of Mary Magdalene which she depicted in her books, Through the Eyes of Mary Magdalene. In her visions, she witnessed the details of the lives Mary Magdalene and Jesus experienced together.

Robert Powell and Estelle Isaacson talk about the necessity of understanding the mind programs that are intervening and replacing your own critical thinking.

Even just one individual who is able to overcome the mind programs and will think the thoughts of freedom—freedom inspired thoughts—can effectuate mighty change. It begins with one person, and then flows

---

[123] Powell, Robert and Isaacson, Estelle, The Mystery of Sophia, Lindisfarne Books, 2014, 11.

to other souls. Through this, can there be a peaceful inner resolution, a wave of mighty force that can prevail over dark forces. Ibid,[124]

The dark forces gain power through inducing suffering, torture, trauma, and unimaginable atrocities. They general fear, despondency, and hopelessness. People will believe that they are feeling their own feelings, when in actuality they are feeling the projected vibrations coming at them. If, however, we can refrain from falling into the trap of these generated emotions, then we shall be victorious. Ibid,[125]

I also had a dream about which program to enter for a degree or certificate. If I went back to school, I would study anthroposophy, related to the development of spiritual consciousness. I would develop a thesis topic which would contrast consciousness as seen through the eyes of a psychologist compared with consciousness and though process as developed by Rudolph Steiner. Steiner sees the process as intuitive thinking, which is guided by Spirit, and is directly related to evolving and submitting personal will in lower devachan to higher will in the higher devachan. This is because we are spiritual beings first and foremost, so that if we can release our personal debris and desire, higher thoughts which originate in Spirit can come in. This is orthodox psychology according to Freud, who put a ceiling on consciousness by forfeiting connection to spirit, by separating the science of psychology from religion on the premise that the mind was not connected to Spirit processes. But where does the mind originate, where do thoughts come from? This leads to a broader question; Freud would say this is a question for philosophy or religion. But I say that this represents an artificial break and does not answer the question of why we are here? And what is the purpose of our lives on earth? How can we truly know this world and therefore claim it as our home?

Steiner says the only way to really know the world is to experience it, to immerse yourself in the object at hand, to become one with it. Thus, as the observer sees, the observer changes the world and is changed by what he sees. *Is there* nothing permanent here? But yes,

---

[124] Ibid., p. 15.
[125] Ibid., p. 15.

there is, that is the permanence of Spirit or Life Energy which imbues and saturates everything in life that lives.

Furthering the question of what I chose to see is another opportunity to know myself in the world. I walk in the forest and chose to see a Red Grosbeak feeding on red berries, head stretched upward for the highest berries visible. Why did I choose this rather than a myriad of other possibilities? Is there some connection, some unknown hand guiding me to know something about myself, about the world that I either need to know or that it is important for me to know? This unseen guide, this Force that works within me to choose and collect memories of what I see is Spirit. What I chose to do with these images, whether to explore them or not, whether to use them for good or ill, is my choice based on many factors including my personality and my level of moral development.

The only thing that is constant is Spirit working through us. Freud missed this in his resolve to separate religion from the study of the psyche. Even so, what Freud offered was of value up to a certain point, just as what other psychologists and psychiatrists offered to us a study of consciousness, clarification, and ontology about the nature of thinking, the nature of projective identification, and steppingstones marking the growth of an individual.

With the coming of the technocratic age, which is dominated by artificial intelligence, the technology now exists, that can influence and manipulate the human mind to believe or to follow a line of thinking which may be more in the interests of big business or big pharm than for the individual. This technology is so subtle that it can enter you mind without your permission or without you being aware of its origins. This means that keeping one's focus on the human connection with divine force, the Spirit world, or with Christ is essential to staying alive and human. Otherwise, a human being could become a puppet of the technology which can dominate and take over the human mind and consciousness.

When images and thoughts come into the mind, it becomes imperative to question where they may be coming from, their meaning, impact on your thinking activity, and its resonance with your moral and ethical constructs which underly you moral fiber as a human being. We as humans must be ever vigilant that we are not the victim of computer or algo rhythmic programs which might have us act in ways which run counter to the ethics that we humans depend on to keep us connected with God and with each other. If there is doubt, or concern, taking time to breathe, to meditate, and to sleep on decisions which would allow the subconscious to provide further information and perspective on whether action is required or not and if so, what kind of action. The process is not instantaneous and requires patience and an open mind so that whatever comes to the conscious mind is useful information can be extracted and digested. It is not a one step process nor is it a process which is uniform between individuals. On the contrary, each individual must discover the process that works for each self, but each decision made will define that person and become the foundation for a future self and future life. Ultimately, the building blocks of this life are built on the choices each person makes. It is therefore critical to have an open, clear, and questioning mind in which options are entertained in the most neutral internal space possible. Once decisions are made and a path becomes apparent, it is then important to gaze at this path in a critical manner to determine if this is path resonance is the one that connects with who you are, or who you want to be.

Choice: chose your image, chose your action or non-action, and chose your path. And be conscious of the choices you are making. This is your right and obligation as a human undergoing an initiation on earth and moving into higher dimensions. The only failure is in refusing to choose, refusing to take responsibility, and losing the opportunity to develop yourself as a sovereign, independent human being.

SEED MEDITATION

One of Steiner's exercises to enhance your control over your own thinking is a seed meditation: to gaze on the image of a flower over time[126]. Watch as it blossoms, as it radiates its energy through its petals, then slowly as it begins to fade and finally turn brown and

---

[126] Steiner, Rudolf, *How to know Higher Worlds*, Anthroposophic Press, 1994, 59.

limp as it does. Keeping all these stages from birth to growth and maturing to death without distraction, is a beginning exercise Steiner has suggested for those on the path of Spiritual Science.

What I discovered is that thought originates in the Divine, in the Supersensible universe.

Here is a synopsis of Rudolf Steiner's ideas on the divine origins of thought. When I began to investigate the origins of thought, I was surprised to learn the degree to which thought could be initiated and brought into consciousness from another realm, another dimension. Rudolf Steiner indicates that this is not only possible but is the source of our thought from the beginning. This means that the origins of our consciousness come from a divine source and are fed by the divine through our lives.

According to Rudolf Steiner, every person is assisted by beings from the Third Hierarchy called Archai which endow certain capacities to children. The Archai endow the child with the ability to walk, the Archangels with the ability to speak and the Angels with the ability to think[127].

Rudolf Steiner goes on to spell out the history which occurred during the Lemurian Age of the seven Sun Elohim which led the Spirits of Form which endowed man from the energy of the Sun with ego and implanted the spark of the logos, the true ego. RS goes on to say that the mediating link between the true ego and the actual or Higher Ego was established through the Elohim. And that during the post Atlantean age, the task of awakening man's faculty of thinking was undertaken by the Angels.[128]

At our present time, it is up to each individual human to take hold of the destiny of his ego through the new relationship with the Christ Impulse or the Love impulse, which Rudolf Steiner claims is the ultimate purpose of man's evolution on earth.[129]

---

[127] Prokofieff, Sergei, Riddle of the Human I, An Anthroposophical Study, Temple Lodge, 2017, 32.

[128] Ibid, 33.

[129] Ibid, 37.

This path connects with the path of intuition which man develops within himself and which is the path of true (not romantic) love.[130]

Rudolf Steiner goes on to say that moral intuition is in steeped in love which can be strengthened through development of the ego (consciousness) which brings itself forth in true selflessness and leads to having its roots in the ego which is increasingly able to maintain a view of the world in a loving way.[131]

The roots of our thinking, our speech and even our ability to walk come from the world of heaven which has given us the chance to explore and evolve our ego consciousness so that we can experience the origins of our divinity and ultimately to connect with the higher worlds from which we came and to which we owe our very existence.

As our ego consciousness evolves, we have a chance to strengthen and connect with higher moral values and enlarge our perspective in such a way that we can become conduits for spiritual influence and thought in the world of third dimensional earth. Eventually, this influence can spread into the astral and the etheric as our ego development continues to expand and mature into the spiritual worlds that in a sense are waiting for our arrival as we merge into higher and higher levels of knowledge and participation with levels of expansion which are possible for each human being.

Tomberg spells out the language process in detail according to Steiner's thinking on origins of thinking.

"To get a more distinct view of this process, we must begin with the fact that human beings share their outer existence with the mineral world, their organic life with the plant realm, and their movement with the animal world. Nonetheless, human beings are distinguished from those three kingdoms by having speech, the fourth externally manifested attribute. Through this attribute, another member (aside from the Physical, ether, and astral bodies) is revealed to human beings; the "I." This makes it possible for human beings not only to participate in physical existence by living and moving about, but also to speak. Although the human "I" is the actual source of the speech faculty, the

---

[130] Ibid, 43.
[131] Ibid, 43.

existence of language nonetheless depends on the body's threefold makeup. The astral body is needed to combine the predicative with the attributive, the verb with the adjective; the ether body is needed to connect the verb with substantive, or noun; and finally, the organs of the physical body are needed to make spoken language sound in the air. The speech impulse of the "I" passes through these three members of the body to reveal itself as spoken language."[132]

"This means that the speech impulse of the human "I" can contact the realm of influence governed by the whole circle of spirits of language (the Luciferic archangels) to the extent that it has first acquired the faculty of uniting with the sphere of influence governed by folk spirits (the normal archangels). It was just this union with the whole circle of archangels (or folk spirits) that the twelve apostles established at Pentecost.[133]"

Our connection with thought and the mind is brought about by the influence of the Divine. What we do with these gifts depends on many factors: our personality, our family beliefs, the culture and pressures from society, and changes in the outer world of finance, politics, and the environment. Because we can speak and to think, we can learn to make decisions which are for our own benefit and the benefit of others. This depends on whether we have sufficient connection to our spiritual roots so that our connection to our higher mind which incorporates a higher code of moral thinking becomes part of our decision-making process in the world. With a strong connection to our higher self, the influence that Ahriman and Lucifer can have on our decision-making process is greatly reduced. We become freer and more sovereign the more we develop the higher self which comes through the development of our ego-consciousness. Anthroposophy offers us the science of spirituality, a guideline for evolution of our ego-consciousness, and a path which can lead us to greater depths of personhood, and potentiality across higher dimensions of existence. Through reincarnation, we can evolve our souls to endless existence in which growth and connection to Source can grow and mature. On

[132] Tomberg Valentin, Christ and Sophia, Steiner Books, 2006, 309.
[133] Ibid, Tomberg, 310.

this path, the soul does not die but can live on to experience greater evolution and have transcendent experiences as it merges more and more with the Source from which it came. The good, great news is that the path to the eternal exists and is available to us if we only dare to take it. (See Appendix C).

Coming full circle: We Live to Become the Oneness

Dear Reader,

We live to become the oneness. That is the alpha and is the omega of my journey into the Sea of Consciousness. Although we humans have personified Light Beings as God or as Jesus his son, or as Mary, or as the Holy Spirit, in fact that are light energies, archetypes of frequency which emerge as light bodies or even as sound. To see light beings as energy rather than as gods to be worshipped means we have entered a new universe. This can happen through opening to the 13th gate or Mother Arc. It is the aqua light of the Mother Arc that is initiated through the Andromeda *Aqualine* Sun which becomes a passage or portal to the world of light beings beyond the third dimension. In this sense it is possible to hold the frequencies which are connected with the rainbow tribe of light, the Force which surrounds us.

Because we live in the third dimension, it is difficult to recognize that we are light beings. Using Kirlian photography (which captures electronal coronoal discharges on film), it is possible to see auras of the human body as they change and morph and change with the human energy shifts. In fact, these light rays are a more authentic representation of who we are. But our eyes are trained to perceive within the limits of the third dimension. However, it is possible to open the third eye, the conduit into the pineal gland and pituitary gland, which when released can reveal other dimensions of reality that were closed off.

My explorations into the sea of mind and consciousness have led me to the beginning which is the sea of oneness, that is experienced through frequency, light and sound, through energy holograms and through sacred geometry fractals. Opening these gates allows us to know telepathy, and to know and live out our moral codes: to love one another, to honor each person in their uniqueness, to respect and include each energy as different and essential to the plasma of the world of which we are all an integral part. Yes, we are part of the plasma that surrounds us and unites us with the stars, with our sun and in fact with our galaxy, the Milky Way. When we open to these light presences, we open ourselves to universal healing, love, and eternal life.

This beautiful statement from Valentin Tomberg reminds us that we are part of the universe, the star system and the sun. Our cosmic heritage originates in the stars and we will return there in time. Tomberg's focus on the heartbeat and breath, consciously taking in the planetary influences is very important as we cultivate connection with the planetary influences that helped to shape us and continue to do so.

A confirmation statement from Valentin Tomberg.

At this moment
I Stand within a World constellation
I belong to it with by whole being

My breathing and my heartbeat have as large a share
In the structure of this constellation
as the sun and the planets

The harmony of the stares, the sun, my heart,
    my breathing and my feeling
produces the constellation of the moment

The tide of the cosmic hour
    flows through my breast
As well as through the heavenly spaces

From a 'stone' that is grounded in the physical body, the ether body, and the astral body, and that rests in itself that is from a 'cube' that is defined by four sides) footnote 5, the human 'I' must become a living, active 'stone' a totally awakened will, presenting a focal point for the twelve cosmic forces. Footnote 6 (the twelve instreaming forces of the zodiac.) The resting 'cube' should become a shining 'dodecahedron'—this is the spiritually-real formula for the 'how' and the 'what' of the overcoming of numbness inf the human 'I'. [134]

Valentin speaks about our connection to the sun, stars, to the planets from which we originate. He talks about how we must travel through all twelve constellations to remain fluid and organic in our growth, rather than getting caught in a fixed idea of what we think could or should be happening with the resulting numbing effect.

We continue to be influenced by the frequency of the stars through our lives. The essential forces of the stars which have been present at our birth, or may have even precipitated our birth, continue to inform us about who we are and our purpose in life, if we have access to the akashic records and other occult readings. In order to know who we are, this becomes essential and is a key to being able to transform not just ourselves but the entire earth environment.

If one can be opened to the fact that planets have essence and being, then the forces that each planet carries can be seen as a constellation. These interacting beings change and morph through lifetimes and make themselves known to you as they precipitate changes in your life through the shifting frequencies of light and sound in your personal constellation and the universe, and through the Oneness of all that is.

I have benefitted greatly from the journeys through religions, through spirituality, through anthroposophy and Buddhist philosophy and through the exercises of the Tao. My spiritual pilgrimages have helped to seed and deepen my sovereignty and propelled me into territory which is beyond the matrix and connected with my future self through the ascension protocols of Marconics. With gratitude and appreciation for all I have experienced, I move beyond those parameters to embrace my Future Self through Marconics and prepare

---

[134] Tomberg, Valentin, Studies on the Foundation Stone Meditation, LogoSophia Press, California, 2010.

myself for ascension beyond the confines of this matrix, to the most appropriate and benevolent timeline connected *with enduring* grace.

In the end TS. Eliot affirms my journey when he says:

We shall not cease from exploration and in the end
Of all our exploring will be to arrive where we started
And know the place for the first time.[135]

Thank you, reader, for sharing this journey with me. Many blessings to you on your journey wherever you may be.

---

[135] T.S. Eliot, Little Gidding, quote.

Appendix A

Steiner on Intuitive Thinking and Consciousness

NOTES ON THOUGHT PROCESS AS DEFINED BY STEINER

On Intuitive Thinking and Consciousness: comparing different types of thinking

Defining intuitive thinking: from a neutral stance, noticing patterns, symbols, and images and taking time to extract the possible underlying meanings and resonances that connect these observations.

Developing inner processes of the mind which include imagination, inspiration and intuition

Nature of Spiritual Science and Freedom (development of sovereignty or autonomy)

Anthroposophy," anthropo" means man, and "sophy" is from the Greek term for wisdom, Sophia

Anthroposophy is not a religion, but a way of knowing the higher spiritual world through an amalgamation of scientific observation, moral development, and the development of a higher ego.

Why is this important? Man has eternal life through conception by and connection to Source. Therefore, man's birthright is to evolve freely through reincarnations into higher states of evolution with the help of the Christ impulse (love). This Christ impulse as a love impulse is available to all regardless or religion or belief. [136]

The Christ impulse is a necessary impulse for all mankind because it helps man to discern the difference between impulses that compromise the freedom and sovereignty of man. Man's birthright is to be free, to be an individual's own authority, and not to have to look to someone outside the self for direction. Two forces vie for ownership of man's soul: one is the Luciferian force which on the one hand plays with human pride and offers a delusion of power and even "divinity". On the other hand, the Luciferian force also inspires creativity and spirituality. These two impulses must be discerned in order to make choices which would promote well- being and freedom. Ahriman is the other force, a dark force, which temps man to live on the material plane. It too promotes the temptation to be 'god'. At the same time, it also promotes technology and intellectuality. It is incumbent on everyone to be able to choose wisely which path to be taken. In both the Luciferian and the Ahriman case, the wrong decision leads to slavery and profound loss of freedom for the soul. [137]

Steiner (Anthroposophy) suggests that man can achieve contact with the higher spiritual world through discipline and a combination of spiritual exercises which develop moral knowledge, control the lower instincts, thoughts, feelings, and the lower ego. These exercises develop an openness, (of mind), tolerance, and flexibility. They help an individual to cultivate the following attributes: control over one's own thinking, control over one's will, composure, positivity, and impartiality. This prepares an individual to experience and to access energy and healing from the higher spiritual world and further to join with the higher world beings to co-create new worlds.

---

[136] Steiner, Rudolf, Intuitive Thinking as a Spiritual Path, Anthroposophic Press, 1995
[137] Steiner, Rudolf, The Christ Impulse, Rudolf Steiner Press, 2014.

In his book, *How to Contact Higher Worlds*,[138] Steiner spells out steps to be taken toward honing and honoring one's creative imagination.

1. Meditation, to learn to concentrate and enhance the power of thought, and I would add memory
2. Focus on symbolic patterns, images, and poetic mantras, consciously allowing directed imaginations to allow sensory phenomena to appear as the expression of underlying beings of soul-spiritual nature
3. Become aware of the observing self, conscious of meditative activity and how individual thinking process information
4. Intensify will forces (through memory) by review of the previous days 'life events

   Or other means which can lead to direct or even union with spiritual beings through intuition without loss of individual awareness

   All of this enhances moral development as well as the expression of love and acceptance of self and fellow human beings.

Steiner's statement on the nature of the human being and evolution

> According to Steiner, human beings are basically spiritual in nature don a physical body of substance and return to the inorganic world. Each living being including plants has a life body or etheric body. In common with all animals, humans have a level of sentience or consciousness. They have an ego which anchors their self-awareness in their body.
>
> When humans began their evolution, they had a natural clairvoyant perception of spiritual reality which gradually was eroded as humans became more reliant on intellectual faculties. As they did so, they lost their

---

138 Steiner, Ibid, 1994.

access to their clairvoyance. This over-reliance on the intellect has led to an over reliance on abstraction and a loss of contact with natural and spiritual realities. In order to resurrect human's capacity for clairvoyance and this is possible to do), humans must work on the capacity to have clarity of intellectual thought with imagination along with inspired and intuitive insights. To my way of thinking, humans must learn to experience and believe in their inner voice, the higher self which is connected to the higher worlds.

On Reincarnation: man's birthright

After the death of the physical body, the human spirit recapitulates the past life, and perceives events as they were experienced. The human uses these reflections to prepare for the next life. An individual's karma leads that one to a choice of parents, a physical body, a disposition, and capacities that provide challenges and opportunities that help further development in the future life.[139]

---

[139] Steiner, Rudolf, Reincarnation and Immortality, Rudolf Steiner Publications, New York, 1970.

Appendix B

Notes on the Ego, Consciousness Soul and Three-Fold Spiritual Constitution according to Steiner

The ego dwells in consciousness according to Steiner.

This is a synopsis of Rudolf Steiner's views on the ego and consciousness soul.[140]

The ego dwells in the Consciousness Soul and radiates outward filling the soul and exerting influence on the body through the soul. Within the ego, the spirit is alive and streaming into the ego, taking it as its garment. The spirit shapes the ego from the inside out and the mineral world shapes it from the outside in. We call that part of our spirit, the Spirit Self that shapes the ego.

The Consciousness Soul teaches the autonomous truth that is independent of all sympathy and antipathy, but the Spirit Self carries this truth inside itself by taking it up, enclosing it and individualizing it by means of the ego, thereby incorporating itself into the individual's independent being. Through becoming independent and uniting with the truth, the ego itself achieves immortality.

The Spirit Self is a revelation of the spiritual world within the ego, just as a sense perception, coming from the other side, is a revelation of the physical world within the ego. We call the revelation of physical things, sensation, and we call the revelation of spiritual things intuition.

---

[140] Steiner, Rudolf, The Essential Rudolf Steiner, Wilder Publications, 2008.

As we grow on the path of spiritual development, we learn to create intuition-filled thinking.

The intuition announces itself on the lowest manifestation to the Spirit Self. This is sense-free thinking or supersensible thinking.

Through intuitions, the ego awakening in our soul receives messages from the spiritual world.

The spiritual world has built the organ of intuition into the Consciousness Soul.

Over the course of spiritual self-development, Spirit Self transforms the astral body, the Life

Spirit Buddhi into the etheric body, and the Spirit Human (Atman) transforms the physical body.

Thus, the body is subject to the laws of heredity; the soul is subject to self-created destiny or karma; and the spirit is subject to the laws of reincarnation or repeated earthly lives.

We are surrounded and accompanied by thought beings. Those who have learned to use their spiritual eyes perceive their surroundings as filled with a whole new world of living thoughts or spirit beings.

Sense-perceptible things are nothing other than condensed spirit beings.

Sense-perceptible things originate in the spirit world and are another manifestation of spirit beings. We must imagine this sense-perceptible thing as a condensed thought being.

If we want the path of higher knowledge, we must be able to obliterate ourselves and all our prejudices at any moment so that something else can flow in. Truth must become sovereign in us, filling our whole being and transforming us into a replica of spirit country's eternal laws.

The earthly ego comes to birth in the soul realm and merges with the Spirit Self, creating the reincarnating soul/spirit of the individual. On the other hand, the higher ego, that contains the Christ and is intimately connected to the Life Spirit part of the *three-fold spiritual constitution* of the human being (Spirit Self, Life Spirit, Spirit Human) may be found in the realm of the Life Spirit that is the home of the higher ego or Christened self.

When the soul is purified and the astral body is tamed, the eternal thoughts gleaned from life by the Consciousness Soul are offered as the Virgin Sophia to the Spirit Self as a sister of wisdom, ready for the spiritual wedding of the earthly ego to the higher ego, or Spirit Self to Life Spirit.

Most traditions are clear about the lower ego (self) and higher ego (self). Where does the third ego, the Cosmic Ego of Christ come from? The more the soul develops supersensible cognitive powers, the near it comes to the Christ being. The third ego is the ego of the world, the group soul.

The intuition announces itself on the lowest manifestation to the Spirit Self. This is sense-free thinking or supersensible thinking. Through intuitions, the ego awakening in our soul receives messages from the spiritual world.

The spiritual world has built the organ of intuition into the Consciousness Soul.

Over the course of spiritual self-development, Spirit Self transforms the astral body, the Life Spirit Buddhi into the etheric body, and the Spirit Human (Atman) transforms the physical body.

The more the soul develops supersensible cognitive powers, the nearer it comes to the Christ being.

To live in the realm of Spirit Human or Atman, the initiate would know Sophia as an ever-present companion on the spiritual path that leads to direct union with Christ, our highest ego. Each individual takes on a part of the etheric Christ to exist in this realm that will only come to full fruition in the far future.

Appendix C

On the divine origins of thought according to Steiner

Prokofieff has written a synopsis about the divine origins of thought and moral intuition according to Rudolf Steiner. According to Steiner, every person is assisted by beings from the Third Hierarchy called Archai which endow certain capacities to children. The Archai endow the child with the ability to walk, the Archangels with the ability to speak and the Angels with the ability to think[141].

Rudolf Steiner goes on to spell out the history which occurred during the Lemurian Age of the seven Sun Elohim which led the Spirits of Form which endowed man from the energy of the Sun with ego and implanted the spark of the logos, the true ego. RS goes on to say that the mediating link between the true ego and the actual or higher ego was established through the Elohim. And that during the post Atlantean age, the task of awakening man's faculty of thinking was undertaken by the Angels.[142]

At our present time, it is up to each individual human to take hold of the destiny of his ego through the new relationship with the Christ Impulse or the Love impulse, which Rudolf Steiner claims is the ultimate purpose of man's evolution on earth.[143]

---

[141] Prokofieff, Sergei, Riddle of the Human I, An Anthroposophical Study, Temple Lodge, 2017, 32.
[142] Ibid, 33.
[143] Ibid, 37.

This path connects with the path of intuition which man develops within himself and which is the path of true (not romantic) love.[144]

Rudolf Steiner goes on to say that moral intuition is in steeped in love which can be strengthened through development of the ego (consciousness) which brings itself forth in true selflessness and leads to a having its roots in the ego which is increasingly able to maintain a view of the world in a loving way.[145]

The roots of our thinking, our speech and even our walking come from the world of heaven which has given us the chance to explore and evolve our ego consciousness so that we can experience the origins of our divinity and ultimately to connect with the higher worlds from which we came and to which we owe our very existence.

As our ego consciousness evolves, we have a chance to strengthen and connect with higher moral values, and enlarge our perspective in such a way that we can become conduits for spiritual influence and thought in the world of third dimensional earth. Eventually, this influence can spread into the astral and the etheric as our ego development continues to expand and mature into the spiritual worlds that in a sense are waiting for our arrival as we merge into higher and higher levels of knowledge and participation with levels of expansion which are possible for each human being.

The roots of our language and our thinking come from the heavens, from the etheric world and are filtered through us across a variety of levels of evolution until we can finally realize our true nature as it originated in the Divine and as it grows steadily toward its own divinity once again.

---

[144] Ibid, 43.
[145] Ibid, 43.

Appendix D

Lion as Primordial Image:
A Psychoanalytic Search

Dr. Jung, a psychiatrist and expert of analytic psychology explains that an animal image, Jung, Memories, Dreams and Reflections, 1957,[146] as the lion is, comes to an individual as an extraction from the collective unconscious. Images from the collective unconscious can emerge through dreams or waking states as they did with me. Images from the collective unconscious are a resource which is accessible to all humans at different moments in life. The image is a distillation of information which has been compressed and molded into a form which carries many layers of meaning and which often requires time and attention to uncover the layers of meaning. These meanings are often not immediately apparent but are hidden plain sight.

However, the resonance of the image continues to transmit an energy to the viewer as it did to me, a frequency and a feeling which continues to live in the psyche of the person and to compel attention. Sometimes the image can be forgotten for a time or overlooked. But generally, the image continues to return at unexpected moments again, almost a haunting of the soul, which Invites further investigation. The image carries a thread of something mysterious and curious which continues to weigh on the psyche. Its presence is not easily dismissed. Inner life, dream life, can become uneasy, unsettling, and even distressed that something foreign has entered the Interior world

---

[146] Jung, Dreams and Reflections, 1957, 42.

and is waiting for inclusion into the consciousness of an individual. So, it was with the lion who visited me.

Jung, 1997[147] talks about the shadow, which is the unconscious part of the self, the denied aspects of the self which are waiting to be incorporated into the Self. The lion, therefore, can represent some unknown and unacknowledged part of who I am. I was too young to know or to understand how to think in those terms. But the image was so strong that it has stayed with me through my life. To a large extent, parts of this image and their meanings are yet to be digested and integrated into my life. To uncover more of the layers, I decided to do more research.

The Archetype of the Self according to CG Jung

"The lion is the symbol of concupiscentia effrenata or frenzied desire. My soul roars with the voice of a hungry lion says Mechthild of Magdeburg."* CGJung,.[148]

"It is no accident that for many years Metro Goldwyn Mayer used the image of a roaring lion to announce its new film production. The roar of the lion is an unmistakable sound which announces the presence of the King of the Jungle. Of all animal voices possible, the lion's voice is huge, mighty and connotes the majesty and power of an enormous beast which resonates through the jungle. It is an undeniable symbol of the power of the voice."

According to Jung, the lion used as a Theriomorphic symbol is also an archetypal symbol of self.

Theriomorphic symbol means this is a transcendent symbol, a symbol of God but in an animal form. The lion is my first connection with God or Spirit which begins my journey into the exploration of the self and into the mystery of transcendence through religion and spirituality over time. The image of Self contains the unified unconsciousness and consciousness of each individual. Jung represented this as a circle within a square with a center point suggesting the ego with the other archetypal symbols surrounding it. The goal for each individual is to work toward achieving a cohesive sense of self in which has been described as an individuation process.

---

[147] Jung, 1997, 3
[148] CGJung, 1956.

"In The Archetype of the Collective Unconscious, 1959,[149] CG Jung describes the self as symbolized by the circle with a dot in the center framed by a square. "The basis motif is the premonition of a centre of personality, a kind of central point within the psyche, to which everything is related by which everything is arranged, and which itself is a source of energy. The energy of the central point is manifested in the almost irresistible compulsion and urge to become what one is, just as every organism is driven to assume the form that is characteristic."

"Of its nature, no matter what the circumstances. The center is not felt or thought of as ego, but, if one may say so, represents it, as the Self. Although the center represented by an inner most point, it is surrounded by a periphery containing everything that belongs to the Self—the paired opposites that make up the total personality. The totality comprises consciousness firstly the personal unconscious, and finally an indefinitely large segment of the collective unconscious whose archetypes are common to all mankind. A certain number of these, are permanently or temporarily included within the scope of the personality and through this contact, acquire an individual stamp as the shadow, anima, animus, to mention the best-known figures. The self, on the one hand simple, is on the other hand, an extremely composite thing, a "conglomerate soul", to use an Indian expression. "CG Jung, 1956.

Being confronted with the lion was being confronted with a symbol of self as it was connected to and coming from the depth of my unconscious self. It was a reminder of what I needed to remember about who I am even though I could not embrace it the time. But as I review that symbol now, the power of the voice, of the spoken word, resonates as a tool for interaction in the exterior world as well as in the interior world when addressing the existence of the higher self. By extension, the use of words in the context of writing dreams, journaling, and any other form of communication exercises the power of the voice to communicate individual and universal needs and perspectives.

The lion drawing (see Part V) showed the huge mane orange and the light from the kitchen where my mother was cooking is also

---

[149] C.G.Jung, 1956, 357.

280

orange. So, the presence of this beast could also represent my mother who is cooking in the kitchen and who overwhelms me with her presence. My mother had a mouth that could communicate what she wanted and could dominate my unexpressed thoughts. I know that I felt envious of her ability to use words. My ability to speak my thoughts and feelings was overshadowed by the ways in which you could command language.

Although being invisible was an option, it had many undesirable consequences. The other option, disappearing completely was more frightening than being invisible. At least with being invisible I had the chance to return, that was not necessarily the case if I disappeared. Nevertheless, I was immobilized by being silent, by not using my voice to articulate what I needed. At that time, it was a way to avoid and sidestep painful consequences. During my childhood, I practiced being invisible often and got good at it, even though I paid a heavy price...sacrificing my voice.

In this moment, I imagine that my mother may have felt inadequate, even criticized by me or felt not good enough as a mother. This may have led to a sense of anger and self-hatred at me (inadvertently) for pointing out her inadequacy. Over time my mother's feelings may have culminated in rage and violence which erupted in a physical attack against me, years later.

According to Rudolf Steiner, he spoke about the astral dimension: in Rudolf Steiner's book, Steiner says the astral dimension is more open to us as children than as adults, and can appear to us as an animal, which represents an extraction from the karmic world. In another of Steiner's Writings, he indicates that animals that appear to young children can represent divinity, God, or a sacred aspect of the self. In this case, the lion was not attacking, but was a huge presence in my life. Because he had a wide opened mouth, it seemed to me that the lion was suggesting that I use my voice, that I have courage and that I speak out. The lion was terrifying, but also in another way, it felt protective. The lion was a companion that let me know I was not alone even though I felt very alone. The lion symbolized many things. [150]

---

[150] Steiner, Rudolf, Rudolf Steiner Library on line, Berlin lecture, November 2, 1910, 2000.

FURTHER RESEARCH: LION BEINGS

Through my life I have added information and understanding of what this image meant to me. For example, from Gigi Young's online lecture, 2019, Gigi has gone into considerable detail about what she has gleaned from her meditations. Gigi is a spiritual guide and psychic intuitive who has taught many spiritual courses online and who has had encounters with interdimensional beings. She speaks about the lion as being closely related astrologically with the fiery quality of Leo.

Born on the cusp of Leo, I was intrigued about what she might have to elucidate which would help me deepen my understanding of the lion image. She said people who are shadowed by the lion or have Leonine energy are strong people who have confidence, fearlessness, and conviction. Since I don't feel confident or fearless most of the time, I did not think this was on target for me. But then she said that Leonine people have courage because they know they are connected to the Divine. Oh, this clearly resonated with me. Gigi went on to say Leonine people are great protectors of others. This too fit with what the view of myself. She added that their convictions of connection to Source are an integral part of who they are. Leonine people are natural leaders. They battle with pride and ego but once they have overcome that conflict they rise to a higher purpose beyond ego and pride. They are committed to serving the whole, helping others. They practice leadership through love., helping others gives them supreme joy.

Further research into the analysis of the image in a Jungian context according to Theodor Abt, 2019.[151]

Summary of questions to ask about the picture drawn according to Abt.

1. What is constellated: where does picture come from?
2. What is relationship to the feminine principle (instinctual bases) relationship of earth and water?
3. What is the relationship to masculine principle (fire and air)?

---

[151] Abt, Theodor, Introduction to Picture Interpretation, according to CG Jung, Living Human Heritage Publication, Switzerland, 2019.

4. In which direction might the development go?
5. What is the quintessence of the picture for our work: What is the conclusion or consequence?

The picture was drawn June 22, 2020, in response to and at the suggestion of a friend who is a retired art teacher. It is admittedly a drawing done many years after the actual experience which happened when I was 4 years old. Also, the use of color along with the rendering of the lion head was a product of my imagination as even at the time of the event, it was dark in the bedroom. The lion was positioned behind me so I could not have seen it if it had a physical presence and certainly would not have been able to notice the color of the hair or eyes or face.

Sensation function: I feel the immense size of the lion, the sense of the huge mouth. I felt the sense of hair which made the skin on the back of my neck stand up. I felt my legs crumble and my hand slid toward the bedpost for support. I tried to open my mouth to scream but nothing came out. I was paralyzed physically and mentally.

Feeling Function: I was terrified and in shock. I felt frozen in place. Not able to move or to scream or talk. I was in a state of terror.

Thinking Function: I was thinking I should be quiet because I did not want to let the lion know I was not dead. I wanted to pretend I was dead to avoid more confrontation. I did not want to further arouse the lion.

Intuition Function: I thought I was on my own. My mother would not understand my fear even if I could scream. I did not want to disturb her as she might feel impinged upon. I wanted to find a way out of this situation myself, not depend on anyone but myself. I thought I could do that if I just waited for a bit.

Analysis of the drawing:

Colors and Shapes

The blue of my head, throat, and arms indicates coldness or rigidness. I could not move or speak. My facial expression appears terrified and distressed to the extreme. One had held the bedpost in brown. Perhaps the brown represents a grounding which radiates to my legs and to my chest. Even so I am not on the ground but seem suspended and held on earth by holding the bedpost. This experience does not seem to be of this world but of some other world and yet terrifying as if it were real.

The lion's mouth is huge and dark. The black color represents a black hole or cave like opening, something I could be swallowed up in. There are no teeth which is surprising. So, it is more like a hole which I could be sucked into. The lion's eye watches and is underlined red. It stands out but does not look menacing. Rather it seems more watchful and neutral, neither welcoming nor menacing. The red of the lion's hair reminds me of soft fur, something fluffy, something I would like to rub my nose in. The dots on the face seem to be more decorative and artistic rather than anything ugly or scary.

The rest of the lion's body does not appear and is not remembered. Only the head which represents a kind of portal or doorway into another universe. I am too terrified to turn around and face it. Yet it seems to be offering a new opening, a way out of the isolation and despair that I felt living with my mother who was too busy trying to survive to notice me and my condition.

Where does the picture come from? It seems a constellation of hope for a new life, a new future, if I can turn around to face it. It seems to be a challenge to creating or acknowledging my independence. It is up to me as to where I go. I cannot go to an outside authority for help. It seems to be offering a kind of safety or protection (because it has no teeth) even though it is terrifying because it is so large. [152]

Relationship to the feminine: I think the hair being soft like fur that I want to bury my nose in is like the fur collar on my mother's coat which I loved to bury my nose in. In that sense, the lion could be a mother who protects and who offers a haven. This is the opposite of what I felt with my earth mother. I needed warmth and protection of the soft mother and instead felt that I got the cold mother. She taught me to be independent and to raise myself. It was up to me. In fact, when I was an adult, my earth mother said to me ruefully, "you raised

---

[152] Ibid, 2019.

yourself." It was not an apology so much as an admission of a reality which she found hard to face but did face in that moment.

I still had a hard time facing the fact that she was right. I was caught between the recognition of my struggle and pride that I had survived in an almost heroic way, and the devastation of my soul which hungered for the love and support I missed all those years. All I said was, "You did the best you could," and I meant it. What could have been an opening to a more vulnerable and intimate interchange was left hanging in the air, waiting for resolution which never came.

Relationship to the masculine: my father was missing from this picture and from my life in reality. Even when he returned from the war, he was a stranger to me. My own masculine side felt silenced, subdued even crippled by this experience. (Perhaps this is the way my father also felt in our household after the war). It was only after some minutes that I found I could slowly, ever so slowly move my legs, crawl. Each movement was very painful and required an extreme effort. It was through an exercise of will that I was able to finally crawl to the doorway of the bedroom and with hands on the door frame pull myself upright. Then walk to the living room and enter my home-made cave under the dining room table. The lion's open mouth does represent a protection, but it is more feminine than masculine. There is no tool, no weapon that I see that can be used to protect myself. It could have been my voice, but I felt I could not use it for fear of disturbing the lion.

In what direction might the development go?

Much to my surprise, I realize that the voice was what I suppressed and what I needed to use as my protection. The opening of the Lion's mouth is a gift promising the possibility of haven. I had suppressed my voice thinking that would protect me when if I had opened my mouth, I might have experienced a very different outcome. The power of the voice, the power of speech. The power of communication is about relationship to another. It is about sharing a need or a feeling or a request. As an introvert, I had more relationship with the interior of my being and less experience with getting what I needed through the power of my voice. In fact, I often felt penalized or repressed when I used my voice. Silence was the golden rule that I was taught to adhere to. The adage that children should be seen and not heard was a moto that I was raised with in my family.

What is the quintessence of this picture for our work?

For me the lion image is about the power of the voice. It was about breaking rank and using my voice to speak my truth. It was about opening mouth and using language and words to convey what I needed or wanted or my thinking on various matters. My voice had been suppressed both by myself and my family. It was overlooked during my growing up years, and was now being invited, encouraged to come forth, to express thoughts, feelings, and desires, all in the service of healing for myself and for others. The lion's open mouth is a portal for a new world and for healing and expression in that new world.

REFERENCES

Jung, C.G, Symbols of Transformation, trans, R.F.C Hull, Bollingen Series XX, Princeton, N.J., 1956, 388.

Ibid., 419.

Jung, C.G. Memories, Dreams, Reflections, New York, Vintage Books, 1961. 170-99.

Ibid., 419.

Jung, CG, Transcendent Function, Structure and Dynamics of the Psyche, Trans RFC Hull,

In, Collected Works of CG Jung, (vol.8), Princeton, NJ, Princeton University Press, 1957. (Original work, 1916), 48.

Jung, CG, Jung on Active Imagination, (ed. and trans, Joan Chodorow,) Princeton, NJ, Princeton University Press, 1997, 3.

Young, Gigi, Lecture "Lion Beings", gigiyoung.com, August 2019.

Appendix E

Further Reflections on the Origins of Thought

I discovered the work of Wilfred Bion, schooled in the British Psychoanalytical theories, who spoke at length about thinking which originates in what he called linking. He was an original thinker in the school of psychoanalysis and contributed to theories of projective identification, splitting, unconscious phantasy and countertransference.

PROJECTIVE IDENTIFICATION

Melanie Klein initiated the use of the term projective identification in 1946 in the school of British Psychoanalytic Theory. This theory relates to a complex and unconscious projection of unaccepted or unknown parts of the self or ego being processed on the mind of one and unconsciously projected into the psyche or person of another. This is not an uncommon occurrence and happens frequently. Problems arise when a person unconsciously projects his or her own unacceptable part of self to another person or character of the other and sees that person as bad or negative. That person then fails to own his own negative parts and may either avoid contact with the other person, or worse punishes or even tries to persecute the other. Because what is projected is not tolerated in the mind and psyche of the original thinker or perceiver, it is placed outside the self into another who contains it until or unless the originator of this projection can learn to accept the perceived negative aspect of the him or herself and transform it from within into a form that is acceptable or even beneficial.

According to Grotstein[153], Kleinian theory involves "external and internal objects which included (a) the infant's image representation, of the external object, (b) affects, impulses, and all the infant has projected (with his mind) into the world."

Bion worked with Melanie Klein's theories of infant phantasy and developed his own theory of thinking. He was deeply influenced by the psychoanalytic work of his teacher and analyst Melanie Klein. However, his theories extended beyond Klein's projective identification.

He states that projective identification is an intra-psychic unconscious phantasy by proffering the notion that it was also a realistic intersubjective communication between infant and mother. The mother in this scheme become the container of her infant's projections. Grotstein[154]

Theories on thinking concerned the destruction of linking which Wilfred Bion explored to great extent. He felt that thinking was linked to the infants' capacity to tolerate frustration, the frustration of not being able to contain a thought, to know how to express or communicate that thought or to the sense that even though the attempt had been made to communicate feelings of fear, anger, or dread that the mother or caretaker had not been able to receive or understand those feelings or contain them within herself.

Bion said, "A capacity for tolerative frustration thus enables the psyche to develop thought as a means by which the frustration is tolerated, is itself made more tolerable." Bion[155] 1967, 112.

He continued exploring the relationship of anxiety related to frustration where the process of projective identification proceeds from infant to the mother who may either deny, dismiss these feelings or where the infant may feel attacked by the mother or want to attack the mother for her lack of acceptance of the communication. The nature of the attack can be a person's mental thoughts or images, feelings, or sensations. Bion was interested in what allowed people

---

[153] Grotstein, 2009A, 155.
[154] Grotsstein, 2009A, 336.
[155] Bion, Second Thoughts, 112.

to think, even to think unthought thoughts, what he called the Alpha function, Grotstein.[156] He called the things that cannot be thought, raw sensory impressions which have no organization and do not seem to have meaning attached to them. He claims that what is important is that the infant have enough tolerance to hold a sense of a thought or an unthought until language or a concept is used which adequately mirrors that thought. Bion[157], second thoughts.

These elements are the ingredients that are used to develop thinking in the mind. A young baby having these raw elements can tolerate this deluge of sensations from the world at large by having another mind which can think for him, like the mind of his mother or caregiver. The child's experience is metabolized by the mother whose thinking becomes the container for the child's experiences. The child relies on the mother's ability to assimilate these raw elements and place them in an organization and context until the child can learn to assimilate these elements into himself. Bion[158]. The mother is important in her ability to transform these elements, and thus to begin the thinking process for the child. She holds them until the child can learn to create and build his own alpha functioning. Thus, the mother models for the child the capacity to think and to take in raw sensory experiences, add meaning to these raw elements and project them back to the child who can begin to incorporate them as new thoughts. The child is contained within the mother, rests in the container (the mother) until the child learns to think for himself. Bion calls this mother child interaction the thinking couple, container--contained. Grotstein[159].

As I review the interaction or the lack of interaction between my mother and I at the time I experienced the lion, I remember thinking my fear and anxiety would not be received. (See the Lion Part 3). I saw my mother as being preoccupied, unavailable, and busy with other activities or people. By default, I was learning to be independent, to suck it up, and find a way inside myself to metabolize my own fears

---

156 Grotstein, 2009B, 26-28.
157 Bion, Second Thoughts, 115.
158 Bion, Attention and Interpretation, 12.
159 Grotstein, 2009B, 186-7.

and anxieties. So, for the time being many of my unspoken or even unthought feelings would remain dormant and hidden away perhaps lost forever. Understandably, I did not see any alternative at the time.

Bion, Second Thoughts, Selected Papers on Psycho-Analysis, William Heinemann, Medical Books, London, 1967, 112.

Grotstein, James, S. Who is the Dreamer Who Dreams the Dream? A Study of Psychic Presences, Routledge, New York, 2009b, 26-28.

Bion W.R., Second Thoughts, Selected Papers on Psycho-Analysis, William Heinemann, Medical Books, London, 1967, 115.

Bion, W.R., Attention and Interpretation, Jason Aronson, New Jersey, 1983, 12.

Grotstein, Ibid, 2009b, 186-87.

Printed in the United States
by Baker & Taylor Publisher Services